TONYA R[...] al speaker, seminar [...] en featured in the *N*[...] *ime, Cosmo-politan,* [...] thor of *The Power of* [...] k.

"Tonya [...] nunicating effective[...] for anyone who see[...] as well as nonverb[...] *Than Words*

"A big 'Y[...]
[...] *ime Signals,*
[...] ictionary"

"Tonya Reiman's approach to communication is approachable and methodical. *The Yes Factor* delivers a packaged approach to selling yourself."
—Greg Hartley, author of *How to Spot a Liar, Get People to Do What You Want*, and *The Body Language Handbook*

"*The Yes Factor* is a life-changing book. Tonya Reiman's techniques—powerful verbal and nonverbal skills—allow you to be successful in any relationship. This book guarantees that you will improve your communication and make excellent first impressions."
—Mark McClish, former U.S. Marshals Academy lead interviewing techniques instructor and author of *I Know You Are Lying*

THE YES FACTOR

Get What You Want. Say What You Mean.

TONYA REIMAN

A PLUME BOOK

PLUME
Published by the Penguin Group
Penguin Group (USA) Inc., 375 Hudson Street, New York, New York 10014, U.S.A. • Penguin Group (Canada), 90 Eglinton Avenue East, Suite 700, Toronto, Ontario, Canada M4P 2Y3 (a division of Pearson Penguin Canada Inc.) • Penguin Books Ltd., 80 Strand, London WC2R 0RL, England • Penguin Ireland, 25 St. Stephen's Green, Dublin 2, Ireland (a division of Penguin Books Ltd.) • Penguin Group (Australia), 250 Camberwell Road, Camberwell, Victoria 3124, Australia (a division of Pearson Australia Group Pty. Ltd.) • Penguin Books India Pvt. Ltd., 11 Community Centre, Panchsheel Park, New Delhi – 110 017, India • Penguin Group (NZ), 67 Apollo Drive, Rosedale, Auckland 0632, New Zealand (a division of Pearson New Zealand Ltd.) • Penguin Books (South Africa) (Pty.) Ltd., 24 Sturdee Avenue, Rosebank, Johannesburg 2196, South Africa

Penguin Books Ltd., Registered Offices: 80 Strand, London WC2R 0RL, England

Published by Plume, a member of Penguin Group (USA) Inc.
Previously published in a Hudson Street Press edition.

First Plume Printing, July 2011
10 9 8 7 6 5 4 3 2 1

Photo credits: p. xiii courtesy of AP Photo/Tammie Arroyo, Getty Images; pp. xvi, 6, 20 (top; bottom center and right), 22 (top right, bottom), 23 (top), 24, 25 (left, center), 26 (left), 67, 88, 99 (top), 100, 104, 122, 124, 125, 126, 127, 128, 129, 130, 131, 135, 136, 137, 142, 143, 144, 145, 146, 147, 148, 150, 151 (bottom), 152, 153, 156, 160, 161, 164, 167, 168, 189, 199, 200, 201, 202, 206, 208, 209, 210, 240 courtesy of Shutterstock; pp. 20 (bottom left), 22 (left), 26 (center, right), 99 (bottom), 110, 259 courtesy of Getty Images; pp. 23 (bottom), 25 (right), 86, 133, 151 (top), 158 courtesy of Tonya Reiman.

The Library of Congress has catalogued the Hudson Street Press edition as follows:

Reiman, Tonya.
The yes factor : get what you want, say what you mean, the power of persuasive communication / by Tonya Reiman.
p. cm.
ISBN 978-1-59463-068-2 (hc.)
ISBN 978-0-452-29721-0 (pbk.)
1. Persuasion (Psychology) 2. Interpersonal communication. 3. Nonverbal communication. 1. Title.
BF637.P4R355 2010
153.6—dc22 2009051853

Printed in the United States of America
Original hardcover design by Catherine Leonardo

To Kenny, my best friend, soul mate, and the love of my life.

To my three hunnybunns, Stephanie, Christian, and Jaidan.
There is nothing more precious than each moment I share
with you—every minute away from you proves that.

CONTENTS

INTRODUCTION

ONE-TENTH OF A SECOND; THE FIRST STEP TO *YES*

With a loud and long display of pants, groans, gasps, hair ruffling, caresses, table pounding, and ecstatic release, she yells: "Yes, Yes, YES! YES! YES!"

—*Tim Dirks reviewing* When Harry Met Sally *for Filmsite.org*

"And will you succeed? Yes indeed, yes indeed! Ninety-eight and three-quarters percent guaranteed!"

—*Dr. Seuss*

"Yes, I see your point."

"Yes, let's talk."

"Yes, you're hired."

"Yes, I'll buy it."

Three simple letters with so much power. *Yes* opens doors; *yes* gets you a job; *yes* seals the deal for a first (and second, and third!) date. The *yes* factor is what allows us to move forward with our goals, to accomplish what we aim for. As an expert specializing in communication, I can tell you that getting where you want to go is the equivalent of getting a series of *yes*es. Spending my professional life thinking about how we as human beings relate to each other through verbal and nonverbal communication has made me realize that achieving my goals means focusing on the *yes* factor—communicating my best side to those around me, and ensuring that they say yes every time.

Every day, many times a day, you are selling *you*—your ideas, beliefs, products, services, desires. No matter what you do for a living or what you hope to achieve in your personal or professional life, you can change the impressions you make on others by changing the way you communicate. Getting those *yes*es will ensure that you become your best *you,* your Alpha You.

You're more transparent than you think. Every time you gesture or open your mouth to speak, people read you. Your gestures and the words you do (or don't) say impact how those around you *perceive* you. Studies from Princeton University have shown that our initial judgments of another person are formed within one-tenth of one second.[1] One-tenth of one second! That's all you have. According to Princeton psychologist Alex Todorov, we decide how likable and competent someone is before we so much as exchange a single word.

That means it isn't simply enough just to be your Alpha You. And it isn't enough just to know what you want in life. Getting a *yes* involves knowing exactly how to *instantaneously convey* your Alpha You to everyone you encounter, each and every time.

Now back to that first one-tenth of a second. In my career I've been asked to analyze what celebrities' and public figures' body language and verbal communication say about them. Let's go from the ridiculous to the sublime. Conjure up Brangelina. Can you picture them? There is no denying the appeal of Brad Pitt and Angelina Jolie. Separately, they are hot. Together they sell millions of tabloid newspapers.

Back in 2005, the two were photographed at the press conference for their film, *Mr. & Mrs. Smith.* At the time, Brad was married to Jennifer Aniston. Soon he was separated. Rumors flew. And you know what? Even though this is a one-sided communication (your average *People* magazine reader won't ever meet these two), it took only a few seconds for the world to realize *exactly* what was going on.

In the photograph, Angelina has her back turned to Brad with her hands behind her. Usually, hands behind the back is a way of telling others that we are not intimidated by them. Instead of curling up into a fetal position, we put those hands behind us as if to say, "Poised, coy, and confident." That's what Angelina conveys in her pose.

Angelina Jolie and Brad Pitt arrive onstage at ShoWest's Fox Luncheon at the Paris Hotel in Las Vegas on Thursday, March 17, 2005, to promote *Mr. & Mrs. Smith*. Although their goal was to promote their new film, their body language was saying something else.

Brad has his right hand in his pocket. He's unsmiling, with lips pinched in. The lip roll is a gesture frequently used by some people in an almost unconscious attempt to keep themselves from speaking, as if the person has a secret he's trying not to reveal. Combine the lips with his hand in his pocket, and again, you have the image of someone hiding something.

Now, how does this all add up? Typically when actors take pictures together, they take pictures *together*. In this picture it looks as if they are purposefully trying to demonstrate a "disconnect." In doing so, they unconsciously reveal what many had already guessed. Although it was several years later that Angelina told a reporter that she and Brad had fallen in love while making the film, the photo announced it to the world.

Okay, let's look at something with a little more bearing on the world stage. Do you remember the 1984 presidential debates, when many were concerned about Ronald Reagan's age? One of the most memorable lines on the topic came from Reagan himself.

"I will not make age an issue of this campaign," he said. "I am not going to exploit, for political purposes, my opponent's youth and inexperience."

Notice how Reagan was able to reframe his situation. He turned the age issue on its head—his age was an asset, his opponent's youth a detriment. This is a tool that is simple to utilize and important to learn. When you reframe a situation, you change the outcome to one that favors you. We will discuss it at length later on.

So maybe you are thinking, *This is important for celebs and politicos, but not for me.* Nope—how you communicate to the world is relevant in every single setting. Here's an example that's a little closer to home: a grocery store in the middle of the afternoon in my hometown, on Long Island. Two female clerks were gossiping off to the side. I smiled at them as I pushed my shopping cart. They didn't appear to notice me.

"So do you know where the mayo is?" It was a male voice, confident and booming. Alpha all the way. It was coming from a cocky guy wearing sunglasses and a baseball cap. His confidence was like gold, his posture powerful. Now, I've been shopping at that store a long time, and let me tell you, the clerks are stiff as boards—but not around this guy. The two women snapped to attention, directing all their energies at this Robert Pattinson (the mysterious *Twilight* dude) type looking for mayo. In that moment, he owned the room.

Then, he took off his glasses. Something changed. The intense, mysterious aura was gone. With his windows to the soul bared, he was an ordinary guy looking for a jar of mayonnaise. Nothing about his appearance matched the promise in his voice or the mystery behind the glasses. If the clerks had seen him before they heard him, it was unlikely they would have been falling all over themselves to try to help him find the mayonnaise. But they had heard him first, and what do you know, despite his ordinary appearance, the two almost broke into a fight over who would get to show him where the mayonnaise was. In other words, they still related to him as they had imagined him.

Once we truly have someone under our spell, it takes a lot for that spell to be broken. This guy had engaged the clerks by using a subtle form of sub-communication—his body language and his voice. He may simply have been looking for a jar of mayo, yet he commanded that room with merely his naturally confident voice and his assured body language. And it worked. In a place where the norm was to ignore customers, he was getting a *yes.*

You may be thinking that this was only a grocery store, and the prize was only a jar of mayonnaise. Still, every day, on any number of playing fields, other people are doing the same thing for far greater rewards. For some, it is natural—they are born charming and charismatic. For others, it is because they have learned how to present their best possible selves.

It is also because they have learned how to read people and gauge when it's important to step into someone else's world or to bring others into theirs. In other words, they have learned how to be the alpha, and thus influence other people's perceptions, thinking, and actions.

For me, this concept of unconscious influence snapped into focus when, as a college student, I sat in the front row of a psychology class at Pace University. On that particular day, Professor Mitchell was discussing the zones of personal space. Unbeknownst to me, as he lectured, he moved closer and closer to me. I continued taking notes, but I remember becoming increasingly uncomfortable. I didn't know it at the time, but he was using his body to convey messages of power and control over me.

Finally, he leaned over my desk, his face close to mine. Then, all of a sudden, he stopped the lecture and directed the class to look at me. "Look at her posture," he told them. As the professor had moved into my personal space, my body had stretched as far back as possible in an attempt to get away from him and his steady invasion. I hadn't known what was happening, yet on some level, I had recognized the signals he was sending. And I had reacted to them.

Having experienced such a powerful introduction to this unconscious communication, I was eager to learn more. One of my first "real" jobs was as an analyst and staffing specialist for a Fortune 500 financial firm. Part of my job was to make quick decisions about people. I soon realized how much is conveyed in those first few moments of meeting someone. For instance, job applicants want to hear yes in an interview, yet all too often they demonstrate their lack of *yes* skills. If you cross your arms, avoid eye contact, and mumble your way through the interview, what is going to convince the interviewer that you can handle the hectic day-to-day duties of the job? Unfortunately, this may be an unfair assessment. And, yes, *job stress* is sometimes different from *interview stress.* Just try getting that through the interviewer's primary competence filter, though. And although much of the weight is carried by the nonverbal impression, studies show that interviewers make their decisions about applicants very early in the meeting. Decisions tend to be based more on how much the interviewer likes the applicant than on the applicant's professional background and likelihood of fulfilling the requirements of the position. It doesn't end there, either.

Good eye contact and other positive body language will make a strong first impression at a job interview.

One major placement firm coached job applicants to answer questions with, "Yes, and . . ." and "No, but . . ."

"Have you ever supervised others in a print shop?"

"Yes, and I was able to improve production by almost 20 percent."

"No, but I supervised the product we were producing. I had to see the in-house magazine from conception to design, all the way through printing."

Yes is a power word, and following it with reasons and explanations only prolongs the positive response. *No,* on the other hand, that most hated of all words, jerks us right back to childhood. Following it with *but* softens the negative and still provides an honest answer to the interviewer's question.

My professional experience lent itself to understanding the messages our subconscious conveys and how we can intentionally alter these messages *and* their reception. After graduating from school, I decided to study hypnosis and went on to become a certified hypnotist. Hypnosis is a rigorous and complex body of work that offers unbelievable insight into how the mind operates.

I've put that education to use working as a corporate trainer both in the U.S. and internationally. I help people improve their lives and careers by teaching them subtle verbal and nonverbal cues. Whether it be sales, persuasion, marketing, or just basic social skills, learning to read others and frame circumstances can help improve any situation. And what's important to remember is that we are pretty much born with the ability to naturally read nuances. Sometimes we just need a bit of practice to tune in to that native ability that we've lost somewhere along the way. Keep in mind, these subtle little cues are the way we communicated before there was language, so they are primal to us. We read movements and grunts.

In addition to making many national television appearances, I'm a contracted Fox News staff contributor. I analyze body language and verbal communication across the board: Were Alex Rodriguez and Roger Clemens lying in denying steroids use? Did Sarah Palin feel nervous when she announced that she was stepping down as Governor of Alaska? Was Brooke Shields sincere in her comments at Michael Jackson's memorial? And how genuine were Michelle Obama's tears at the girls' school concert? (My impressions: yes, yes, absolutely, most certainly.) I get to have a little fun, too: On Greg Gutfeld's *Red Eye,* I had the dubious honor of analyzing cartoon characters such as Wile E. Coyote, Scooby Doo, and Yogi Bear as if they were presidential hopefuls.

BONDING, NOT MANIPULATING

Now, some people think that certain aspects of my job (bonding, in particular; more on that later) are manipulative. My first experience with that negative attitude happened to coincide with one of my first big speaking engagements. It was for a major corporation, and I was proud, even giddy, that I had landed it. I mean, I had been paid a real speaking fee for this event, and I had to deliver.

I did deliver and delivered B-I-G. I could feel the support of everyone in the room, see their smiles, their nodding heads, and their applause. Then, a very important woman in the company rose to confront me.

"I find these tactics you describe to be offensive," she said.

"Why?" I asked. "When it comes to putting your best self first, we're all influencing others. For instance, you're wearing makeup to enhance the image you convey."

She glared at me and said, "So?"

"So did you shower this morning? Style your hair? You use all that to enhance your image. I use words and movement."

She and I had both prepared for this event. I had put on my "appearance" makeup, not the beach makeup or the family makeup. I had made sure my notes were perfected.

If anything, her protest helped make my point to the group. Let's be honest. We all try to primp and pamper, make small talk, and laugh at unfunny jokes. I could have the worst day of all days from hell, but I'm not going to announce that to a client. Neither are you. At the end of the day, when the speech is over and I'm exhausted, I'm still in the room answering questions, signing books, and posing for pictures with the participants.

When I talk about the Alpha You, I'm talking about manipulating yourself—in a good way—to be the best possible you, and getting others to see you in your best possible light. What the woman in my seminar didn't understand was that I was offering her another tool, a valuable one, to help her put her best foot forward and be her Alpha Self in a completely different way than wearing makeup.

We all either live by the communication sword or die by it. The gestures, tones, expressions, and words that I analyze on television and for companies reveal not only what the person we're viewing is trying to convey, but what he or she may really be feeling. Imagine getting inside people's heads and being able to understand their true intentions and emotions. And more than that, imagine being able to command their interest and demand their attention. Imagine getting a *yes* time after time.

After the publication of my first book, I heard again and again from readers that learning how to understand body language in both others and themselves helped in every single aspect of their lives—business, romantic relationships, family and friends. Those readers learned to recognize the subtle, and sometimes not so subtle, signals of muscle movements that indicate emotion, behavior, and deception.

What I told those who reached out to me is to just wait until they had the full scoop on combining their body language skills with verbal communication. This book does just that. It will teach you a set of extremely effective nonverbal *and* verbal skills that you can seamlessly incorporate into your daily communications. These skills will allow you to put your best foot forward and, better yet, covertly influence those around you, create positive feelings, and influence outcomes on a daily basis. In short, you'll get your *yes*!

My personal journey has allowed me to interact with people from all walks of life, in all aspects of their lives. I love it. Whether helping to increase their sales, attract their soul mate, or raise their own personal value, I have learned that getting to that magic *yes* begins with that first one-tenth of a second. It's about getting into another person's world, and you'll learn exactly how to do it in the pages of this book. At the end of the book, you'll have a twenty-one-day plan to help you take all you've learned and make it part of you.

15 Reasons You Should Read This Book Right Now *So That You Can:*

- Make an excellent first impression immediately by winning trust and credibility before you even open your mouth.
- Learn to pick up on the subtle cues that let you know what others are really thinking. Observing word choices and body language will enable you to respond to the motivations behind what everyone else in your world is saying.
- Persuade others to see you as a *yes* for job interviews. That decision to interview you (or show you the door) will be made in seconds, not minutes. You have no time to waste.
- Develop phone confidence. Perfect your pitch so that you can avoid both the anxiety-driven shrill voice and the too-low monotone.
- Feel comfortable in your own skin and make others feel comfortable around you. In other words, connect.

- Relate easily to the opposite sex. Learn how to send the message you intend.
- Make others feel special—and not because you want something from them.
- Be an inspiration by example.
- Control situations without being Machiavellian.
- Communicate your ideas with subtle authority.
- Gain long-term trust.
- Build relationships—for life.
- Exude confidence through authenticity.
- Be the Alpha You!
- Get anyone to say yes to you.

You can do it, and this book will show you how.

PART I

The Alpha You

ONE

BODY LANGUAGE BASICS

"A man is not good or bad for one action."

—*Thomas Fuller*

My friends love it when we walk into a room of strangers and I check out anyone within sight. When I look at a person for the first time, I silently take it all in: how she moves, how she stands, the tone of her voice, all the micro (as well as macro) expressions and gestures that she doesn't even realize she makes but that speak so loudly to me. I know that is the fastest way to see what someone is all about. Of course, that usually works until the group finds out what I do for a living, and then everyone pretty much freezes.

Before we dive into verbal communication, I'd like to give you a quick overview of some important body language tools.

Studies have found that in certain settings as much as 93 percent of our communication is nonverbal. Paul Ekman and his colleagues have determined that forty-three finely tuned muscles in the human face can be combined and reorganized into ten thousand possible combinations of expressions. In a single interaction, approximately one thousand nonverbal factors help convey your message.[2]

Your brain's communication system changes with every nonverbal interaction, providing the information you need to know about another person before he so much as speaks.

Body language is the core of who we demonstrate ourselves to be. You can typically tell the mail-room clerk from the CEO, even if both wear suits. When they are at work, regardless of their attire, they each present differently.

No matter what, there are times when everyone is intimidated. Frequently that intimidation is based on your perception of who you are in a given situation. Years ago while doing a show, I met a gentleman who was well known within his circle of peers. I asked if we could take a picture together, which is something I rarely do. I heard my own apprehension as soon as the words started, and he either consciously or unconsciously picked up on those cues of insecurity, and—*wham!*—what a shift in his interaction with me. I automatically gave away my power and with that my alpha position. We went from equals—two individuals who were guests on a TV show—to superior and inferior. (Guess which one I was?) I actually watched the entire scene unfold and was helpless to regain my status in the brief time that I had. What a lesson that was.

I had a speaking engagement at a large hotel recently. As is my habit, I got up early that morning to go into the area I would be speaking in and "own the room." As I walked to the meeting area, I noticed one of the hotel staff members just ahead of me.

"Good morning," I said.

"Good morning," he replied with a big smile. Then he looked down.

That one movement told me so much about him and his position in that hotel. Maybe in a bar he would have acted in an entirely different manner. But in situational body language context, he knew that I was the paying customer and he was the paid staff.

When I walk down the corridors of Fox News, I'm loving it—confidence all the way. If I were to encounter someone I really admired and was intimidated by—gulp—I'd probably instinctively look down too.

BASELINE FIRST

In order to understand someone's nonverbal signals, you need to **baseline** that person. This is also called **norming.** Everything from the handshake to the way someone stands reveals who he is. A handshake can tell you if someone is dominant or submissive. Baselining will also tell you if someone is right-brained or left-brained, extroverted or introverted—great information to have. You'll also be able to tell if this is the type of person who wants just the facts and only the facts, or a person who deals with information based on instinct. In later chapters, you'll learn how to read stance, gestures, and facial expressions. You'll understand the language of the eyes.

Note the person's normal eye position when he is speaking and remembering. Watch where the eyes go while the person is speaking, and then during a nonthreatening conversation casually ask a question that will make the subject try to remember something visual and factual. Watch his face as he answers. Does he look up left or right, side left or right, or down left or right?

"Do you remember that crazy HR file clerk who worked here a couple of years ago? You know, the one who was caught on camera going through everybody's files. What was his name?" Continue asking similar questions until you see a pattern of eye movements from your subject. "What year did he work here, anyway?" That incorporates a name and a number. Where is the person looking to retrieve this information? "Didn't he date someone from corporate finance?"

Soon you'll be aware of how this person recalls facts. Then when you want the truth about something ("Did you call Jane Brown when I asked you to last week?"), just ask. If he has been consistently looking up to the left when recalling facts, he will probably look up to the right when fabricating a false story, because he must access a different part of the brain to construct a lie than he would to recall actual details.

Although body language is often context driven, it can tell a lot about a person and how he feels about himself. What comes first, charisma or confidence? Whether it's the CEO walking into a meeting, the teacher entering the classroom, the girl entering the bar, or the sales rep stepping into the doctor's office, everyone is unconsciously (or consciously) telegraphing a message to everyone else. That message says, "This is who I am." This is true both in the crucial first seconds of meeting and throughout the entire relationship.

Using and understanding body language benefits the person who has mastered the movements of dominance and confidence. Confidence breeds charisma, which leads to the perception that you are a success. A lack of confidence can lead to a negative aura, which can cost jobs, money, and social influence.

Closed body language literally closes you off. If you are having a bad day or feeling off, change your physiology. When you change position, you can literally change your outlook. Your brain chemistry gets shifted, and you might find that you feel better. Pick your head up, put your shoulders back, smile, open up your arms and legs, and *stretch*. Our emotional state is usually reflected in our position. Allow your state to be transformed as you stretch and change your physical self. Go ahead, right now, take a second and stretch your neck, your shoulders, and your torso. Do a big morning stretch. No matter how good (or bad) you are currently feeling, I bet you'll feel better.

Change your body and you'll change your brain chemistry for the better.

This can be done with others, as well. In fact, two news anchors at a local station share an on-air morning stretch every day around seven-thirty. She stands, yawns, and stretches. He stands, yawns, and stretches. The camera sweeps through the studio, and all of the staff members in view are doing the same thing.

When you find you are confronted with an individual who just won't budge on his position, change his physiology. Since we now know that a person who is emotionally closed off to an idea will usually close off physically as well, if we get him to unlock his body, we have an opportunity to unlock his mind. The phrase "Try to see it from my side" is a visual of this and means a lot. Get your target to physically move to a different angle or into a different position so that he can see a new perspective.

One of the physical signs of anxiety is breathing. If a person is feeling anxious and trying to hide it by masking his facial expressions, watch his breathing. Typically, someone who is upset or highly frustrated will take shallow breaths. Look for an occasional deep breath, which signals the person's need to pull in a large amount of oxygen in an effort to calm the nerves.

Body language also benefits those who have mastered the verbal aspect of persuasion. By simply changing position, moving closer, smiling, and nodding at key moments (and a few other techniques you'll learn about later), you are able to influence situations, get the girl or guy, make the sale, close the deal, or win over the discussion.

At all times, you need to be demonstrating confidence via good posture, subtle touch, open, smiling expressions, appropriate spatial awareness, cooperation via open arms and forward stance, and reassurance by way of smiles and pats on the back. And, of course, the golden nugget is to make sure that you are always listening to what others say as well as what they don't say.

Often, people will use seemingly innocuous movements that they do not realize are perceived as negative by others. In general, any display of insecurity, anger, hostility, contempt, or boredom is considerably dangerous to social dynamics and business.

Poor body language is the nonverbal equivalent of throwing in the towel, and it signals defeat. Unfortunately, it does not take long before these nonverbal cues begin to dictate your moods, leading to a self-perpetuating cycle of frequent bouts of low energy, gloom, and diminished confidence.

HIS SIGNALS/HER SIGNALS

Revealed with a Kiss

Just because you're kissing doesn't mean all is right in your world. Body language is just as revealing in your personal life as it is in the office. For one of my *Life & Style* magazine pieces, I analyzed the body language of several Hollywood couples while they were kissing.

Uma Thurman and André Balazs. First, I noticed that he is looking at her and gripping her arms. She is looking off to her left, a sign of distraction. Eyes, unless they're gazing longingly, should be closed during a kiss. Shortly after the photo was taken, the couple broke up.

Ben Affleck and Jennifer Lopez. Her eyes are closed. His are open. His arms are down, and she is leaning in to kiss him. His forehead is scrunched because he's looking up. My opinion was that she was into the kiss and he wasn't. Shortly after the photo was taken, they called off their wedding.

Scarlett Johansson and Jared Leto. Her head is tilted and her eyes are closed. He is barely acknowledging her, eyes open, looking at his phone, apparently checking messages. This one didn't last either.

As you can see, understanding body language is more than just figuring out facial expressions. Although the face is often what we notice first, a major source of outflow comes from the lower half of the body. The legs and feet can tell you a great deal about someone. For example, when speaking to another person, look to his feet to see the direction in which they are pointed. Are they pointed toward you? Then you are probably holding his interest. Are they pointed toward the door? If so, this person you are trying to impress is probably not that impressed and wants to be elsewhere.

Most of the judgments you make about another person take place within seconds. If what you see and hear makes a positive impression in your subconscious, the person is going to have to do something pretty awful to change your thinking. If you doubt me, remember the first time you fell in love, bought something on impulse, or voted for someone based on appearance alone.

THE HARDING EFFECT

Many people did vote based on appearance back in the early 1920s. Warren Harding was our twenty-ninth president. With his chiseled features, booming voice, and piercing eyes, he appeared to have everything going for him. He was the first sitting senator to be elected president, and one of three to do so. (The other two are John F. Kennedy and Barack Obama.)

Some, most notably Malcolm Gladwell, author of *Blink,* have suggested that Harding's political success was based on his appearance. That is, that he *looked* like a president. Gladwell calls that process by which we judge people by their appearance the Warren Harding Error.[3] We judge by appearance, and we judge quickly. A part of our brain called the ventromedial prefrontal cortex is in charge of these snap decisions, and it can *sometimes* be wrong. Large stature: strong. Small stature: weak. Deep voice: in control. High voice: untrustworthy. Is it fair? Absolutely not. Is it true? Absolutely.

By his sheer commanding presence, Harding bypassed everyone's good judgment. After his sudden death two years into the presidency, his corruption and marital affairs came to light, and he didn't look like such the perfect leader after all.

The Harding Effect says basically that just because your brain is capable of processing rapidly doesn't mean it is always right. Most of us have met people who looked perfect on the outside and failed to live up to expectations once we got to know them.

On the other hand, you might want to borrow a little of the Harding magic for yourself. You can't make yourself taller, but you can square your shoulders and stand straighter. You can refrain from conveying insecurity by not touching your face, biting your lips, or picking your nails.

You can develop a persona that radiates power, charisma, and magnetism. Just stay away from the corruption and the extramarital affairs and you'll be able to live up to that magic you create for yourself.

THE FIRST FOUR MINUTES

Have you thought about what you convey in those first seconds? Do you project warmth and confidence, which in turn is spread to the other person? Do you walk with a purpose? Do you smile and initiate the handshake?

After that initial handshake, monitor the space your target needs. Is she leaning in closer to hear you? Allow it to happen. Are you standing too close? If so, you should subtly step back a little from the other person's zone. Maintain excellent posture (no slouching), regardless of whether you are sitting or standing, and keep your feet pointed at the person and not the door. Your hands should be at your sides, not crossed in front of you like a barrier. After the first few seconds, that person has an impression of you. After the first three or four minutes, she has her **baseline** of you. And if you did all of the above, you are now ready for some verbal magic.

ASK TONYA

Q: What happens when body language confirms or conflicts with oral communication? This happens frequently with my business partner.

A: We automatically believe the body language over the oral communication. If there is an incongruity—if the two do not match—believe the body. How many times have you heard through gritted teeth and crossed arms, "No, of course I'm not angry." The signs are always there; however, we sometimes doubt our instincts because the words contradict what our instincts tell us. Body language is primal to us; it's instinctive. Nonverbal messages are what we relied on before we had words. Start listening to those instincts and paying attention to what sets the alarm bell off. You will begin to notice those sometimes subtle nuances that contradict verbal communication.

TWO

YOUR THREE-POUND ENIGMA

How Your Brain Rules Your Life

"I believe in an open mind, but not so open that your brains fall out."

—*Arthur Hays Sulzberger*

Thanks to the use of modern brain-scanning equipment, we are constantly learning more about how we are wired by studying living brains.

Getting to *yes* begins in the brain, and understanding the general lay of the land, as it were, will help you understand how we humans operate. Here you will find a basic overview that will give you an idea of what aspects of communication happen where. Keep in mind, the brain is way too complex to localize specific functions, so that means each element of

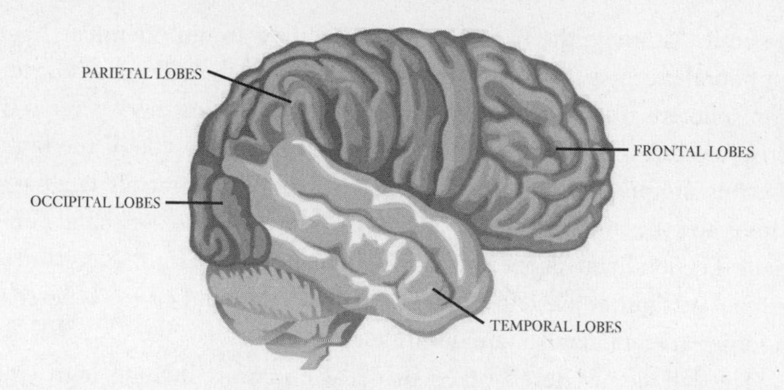

The Neocortex

verbal and nonverbal communication is activated in multiple parts of the brain at the same time.

The top of the brain, the **neocortex,** is the part that makes us the creatures we are. It takes the sensory information that enters into the brain and transmits it to specific areas, where it is translated into thought and perception. The evolution of the neocortex has allowed us to enjoy awareness and consciousness.

The neocortex is divided into four lobes. The **frontal lobe** is associated with reasoning, speech, movement, and emotions—it helps us organize our lives, choose right from wrong, and solve puzzles. The **parietal lobe** is related to orientation, sensory information, recognition, and perception. In other words, it helps us with math, reading maps, understanding language, and evolving thoughts and emotions. The **occipital lobe** is the part of the brain associated with vision. This lobe directs the eye and focuses it on the line of vision. It contains association areas that help with the visual recognition of shapes and colors. That is, it allows us to see and remember what we saw. The **temporal lobe** allows us to distinguish between different smells as well as different sounds. They also help with visual and verbal short-term memory.

In addition to the four lobes, the neocortex is divided into two halves, a right hemisphere and a left one. The right hemisphere controls the muscles on the left side of the body; the left hemisphere controls the right side. Damage one side of the brain and you'll affect the opposite side of the body. Although the two sides are alike, they are not identical. Each has neural mechanisms that control certain functions. In humans, the left hemisphere is usually responsible for language. In fact, in 95 percent of those who are right-hand dominant (meaning the left side of the brain controls motor function), the left side of the brain controls language. This is also the case with 60 to 70 percent of those who are left-hand dominant: The left hemisphere is used for language. That's right. Ninety-five percent of righties are left-hemisphere dominant, and 60 to 70 percent of lefties are left-hemisphere dominant.

The left hemisphere's other primary functions include logic and math. The right side of your brain is typically responsible for spatial abilities, music, visual imagery, and facial recognition.

Your two hemispheres communicate with each other by way of thick bands made up of nerve fibers. This bundle of nerves is referred to as the **corpus callosum.** You can think of the corpus callosum as a giant cable that connects two very powerful computers, the left hemisphere and the right hemisphere. When you communicate with another person, you engage both sides of your brain. The left brain deciphers words in their most basic form—it's the court reporter, simply getting down what was said. The right brain is the translator. As your emotional brain, it recognizes tone, innuendo, and deeper meanings. When the right and left brain work together, you understand not just the words spoken, but what the speaker means.

For instance, a friend you find attractive has just taken your side in a debate at a group outing. As you walk out of the party together, you say, "I love you. Thanks for covering my back."

If only the left brain were at work here, you could be in trouble, especially if you and your friend are both single. Instead, although your friend's left brain hears the words *I love you,* the right brain senses the emotion and meaning with which you spoke those words.

None of us is totally left-brain or totally right-brain dominant. But just as you have a dominant hand, eye, foot, and ear, you probably use one side of the brain more than your use the other.

This can lead to overdependence on a certain side. When you rely more on the left side of the brain, information is not transferred to the emotional, right side. Studies demonstrate that occasionally the left brain refuses to give up control over behavior and overlooks the perceptions of the right brain. The bad news is you lose the strengths of understanding tone and nuance. Every word you process is reduced to cold, hard logic. The good news is that in first meetings, you can probably size up another person in short order. When you line up your right eye with the new acquaintance, your left brain will analyze what is going on.

Although it may help in an unbiased, unemotional first meeting, ignoring the right brain can mean that you ignore your intuition and potentially important red flags. The right brain is in charge of your gut feelings, and if you rely too much on the left side, you deny yourself the benefit of intuition.

FOUR WAYS TO TELL IF YOU ARE RIGHT-BRAIN DOMINANT

- You are shopping with a colleague at an office-supply store. On your way to the department that sells easels and other presentation equipment, you spot a sale on computer monitors. It's too good to pass up. You stop and grab one, then continue with your friend to buy that easel. Yes? Score 1 for right brain.
- A coworker you like is getting married. You can go to the Web site where he or she is registered or come up with a gift on your own. You decide to do both. The site will show you what the coworker wants, and your shared experiences will help you figure out the right gifts. Score 2 for right brain.
- You have three major projects that must be completed by the end of the month. Do you analyze the number of hours and assign a time limit to each project? Or do you choose the one you love

most and finish it first? If you go for love, score 3 for right brain.

- Your best friend's mother is visiting from another town. You are the lucky one assigned to show her around the city while your friend is at work. Do you show her the sights from a guidebook? Or do you take her to places you love? If you choose the latter, score 4 for right brain.

Now that you have a basic overview, let's look at how emotions originate.

The neocortex, with its ingenious ability to deliberate intricate information, is also capable of deception. We are capable of lying because our very smart neocortex knows how to bend the truth verbally (which is why people like me advise people to believe the body over words).

Fortunately, there is the equivalent of checks and balances in the brain: The neocortex can fib, but right beneath it, the mammalian brain, the limbic system, will leak the truth.

The **midbrain,** or limbic system, is the second-oldest part of the brain to have evolved. It is the emotional brain, the place where you process images and music, and where your pain and pleasure sensors are located. If you want to test how it works, listen to a song that reminds you of a

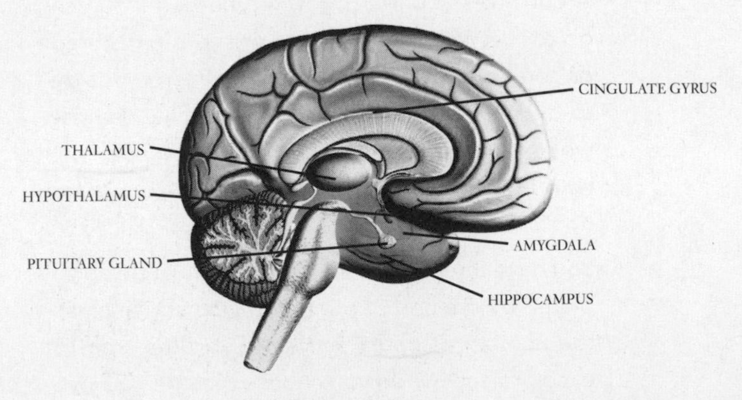

The Limbic System

time you fell in (or out of) love; play something upbeat when you're depressed, and experience the way you can alter your neurophysiological chemistry without "thinking." You might end up in a better mood than you started, just by listening to a favorite tune.

The limbic brain is primarily concerned with preservation, and tends to be the seat of emotions and moods ranging from happiness to anger, surprise, fear, motivation, pain, and pleasure. It is also where we find the freeze, flight, or fight response that is hardwired in the reptilian system (more on that in a moment). The limbic system interacts with both the reptilian system and the neocortex. The moment you become aware of an emotion is the moment that emotion is transferred from the reptilian system to the neocortex.

Once information is processed in the midbrain, it reveals itself through movements in your head, neck, torso, and limbs. These movements are primal, nonverbal reactions, and they reveal the truth about you, regardless of what you might do or say or how much you try to control it.

REPTILIAN BRAIN

The reptilian system, which is the oldest part of your brain in an evolutionary sense, is located at the base of your brain stem. It controls all of your bodily functions and regulates your survival needs: heart rate, blood pressure, circulation, respiration, digestion, and reproduction. It is in the

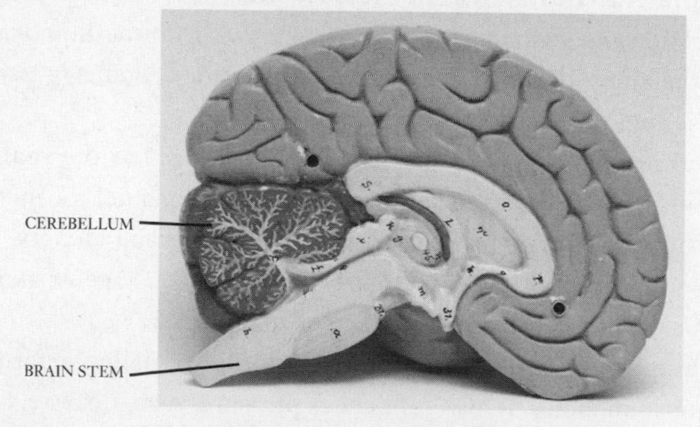

The Reptilian Brain

reptilian brain that we find the drive to establish and defend our territory and compete for dominance. It is the part that makes you instinctively jump when a car backfires or when someone suddenly shouts from behind you. The purposes of the reptilian system are simple: survival and maintenance. Note that there is no thinking here. It is automatic, and it serves us just as it served Fred Flintstone and his cohorts. Its job is merely continued existence. The reptilian brain communicates with the limbic system, and the limbic system takes the instinctive behavior and modifies it based on more complex emotions.

WHERE YOUR EMOTIONS ORIGINATE

Sadness, surprise, fear, anger, disgust, happiness, contempt. The numerous emotions you experience every day are reflected *truthfully* in your gestures and expressions, and they originate in the brain.

As we already discussed, the limbic system—which houses the pituitary gland, amygdala, thalamus, hypothalamus, cingulate gyrus, and hippocampus—is located beneath the cerebral cortex and is involved in the control of emotions, motivation, and memory. This has been referred to as a fifth lobe. The functions of the limbic system include seeking food, drink, and sex, as well as emotional responses such as anger and fear.

The structures in this part of the brain interconnect, and the **amygdala** is one of the main areas involved in emotions. Located deep within the temporal lobe, the amygdala assigns emotional significance to everything we do. It interacts with areas of the neocortex in order to process and then experience a given emotion. In connecting with the hippocampus and the thalamus, the amygdala influences fear, rage, and aggression, as well as feelings of friendship and love.

Neural responses from a fear stimulus are carried to the **thalamus.** This brain structure, near the amygdala, acts as a channel for incoming sensory signals. When triggered, it gives rise to fear and anxiety, which lead the animal (including the human animal) into a stage of alertness, freezing, and then getting ready to flee or to fight.

The **hippocampus** is involved with memory, especially the formation of long-term memory. It also influences pleasure, rage, distaste, annoyance, and a tendency toward uncontrollable, loud laughter.

Next is the **hypothalamus,** which works with the **pituitary gland** to instruct your **adrenal glands** to release stress hormones in response to dangerous situations. These stress hormones flood your body so you have the energy to fight or flee. The hypothalamus and pituitary gland release other hormones in response to stress, some of which can contribute to feelings of anger or depression. The pituitary also controls good hormones, such as endorphins, that make you feel happy.

As mentioned earlier, Paul Ekman and his colleagues found that the facial expressions of seven emotions were universal. Of course, just because the appearance of specific emotions is shared globally, it doesn't mean everyone wants them out on display. When we express our emotions on our faces, those emotions are unmistakable, even if they are fleeting. They might appear on the face for only one-twenty-fifth of a second to four seconds, but our brains can gather quite a bit of information from that brief glimpse. The more information we have, the easier it is for us to determine what someone is telling us facially. Although the face is the primary medium for communicating emotion, it is also the most easily veiled when we are looking to deceive; often people use their "block face" to hide their true emotions.

Let's take a look at each of these emotions and their most distinctive characteristics.

SADNESS

You lose your big client or your job. Your lips may tremble. Sadness brings with it a depletion of energy and enthusiasm as well as a slowing of the metabolism. You might fight tears as well. Crying is most likely produced by several different brain regions located in the reptilian brain. It appears to start at birth and has a very definite set of facial expressions as well as specific breathing patterns.

A one-hundred-year-old California department-store chain went bankrupt and closed all of its stores in 2009. The faces of longtime employees and customers in the daily newspaper all expressed the same emotion as they said good-bye. As different as they looked, they all wore the same faces.

How it looks: Raised inner eyelids in the form of an inverted V, ac-

Firefighter grieving after hours of attempting to save lives.

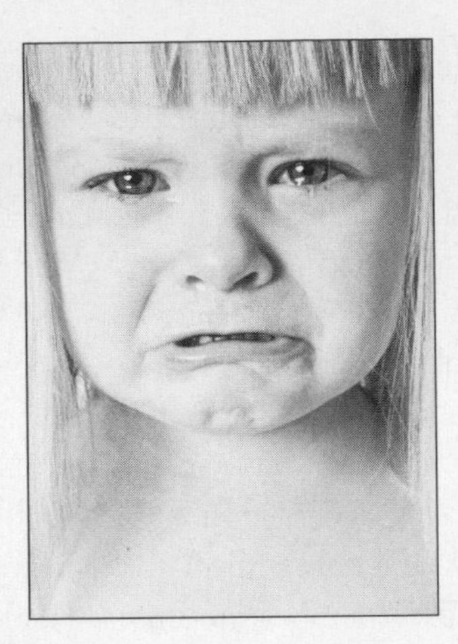

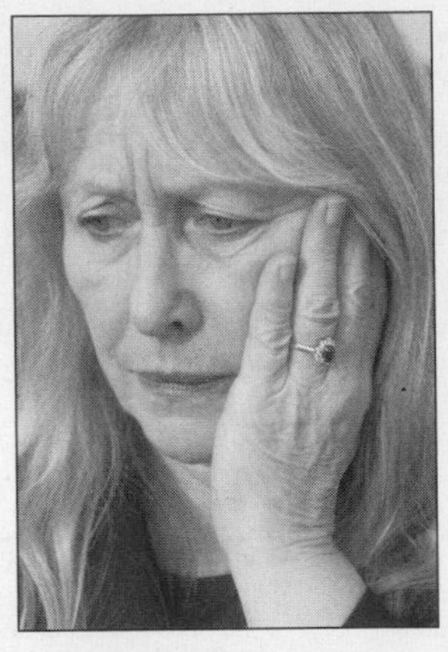

Sadness brings with it a depletion of energy and enthusiasm as well as a slowing of the metabolism.

companied by lifting of the lower eyelids. You might see lines across the forehead. The mouth is pulled downward, and the eyelids droop.

SURPRISE

You learn that your nemesis at work will be your new boss. You feel a flash of amazement, shock, and surprise. Then the emotions blend

An American scientist shares the Nobel Prize in Medicine.

to something else—fear, anger, or happiness. Everything that goes on in the body happens for a reason, and with the added lift of the eyebrows, the retina absorbs more light, making it easier to take things in visually.

How it looks: Eyebrows curve and rise up. Whites of the eyes can be seen above and sometimes below the iris. Upper eyelids go up. Lower eyelids stay round. Wrinkles appear across the forehead. Mouth opens—lips part.

When my husband turned twenty-five, I threw a massive surprise party for him. A bunch of people were standing on the steps leading to the second floor of our town house—all of them getting ready to shout, "Surprise!" as we entered.

As we approached the front door, we could hear the unmistakable sounds of someone inside. My husband thought it was a burglar and threw open the door. When he realized it was a surprise party, the look of shocked astonishment on his face announced those mixed feelings of his.

FEAR

You are rushing to work, and as you hurry toward the entrance, you slip on the ice. Or you're working late and hear something or someone outside your office. Your brain sends the information to the thalamus, which sends it to the amygdala as neural impulses. The amygdala tells the hypothalamus to initiate the fight-or-flight response. The hypothalamus activates the sympathetic nervous system and the adrenal-cortical system. This neural activity combines with hormones in your bloodstream to prepare you either to fight or to escape the impending danger. Blood moves into your muscles and limbs to help provide energy and fuel for fleeing and is moved away from your digestive tract. Your pupils dilate. Your awareness intensifies. Your perception of pain diminishes. All these reactions work together to help you unconsciously make the right decision for your survival.

How it looks: Eyebrows are raised and drawn together. Upper eyelids rise up. The whites of the eyes can be seen above the iris. Lower eyelids are tensed. Lips are parted, pulled down, and tensed.

Bareback rider expresses fear.

Sebastian Ryall falls down after being tripped by Cassio on February 14, 2009, in Melbourne, during the A-league Major Semifinal between Melbourne and Adelaide.

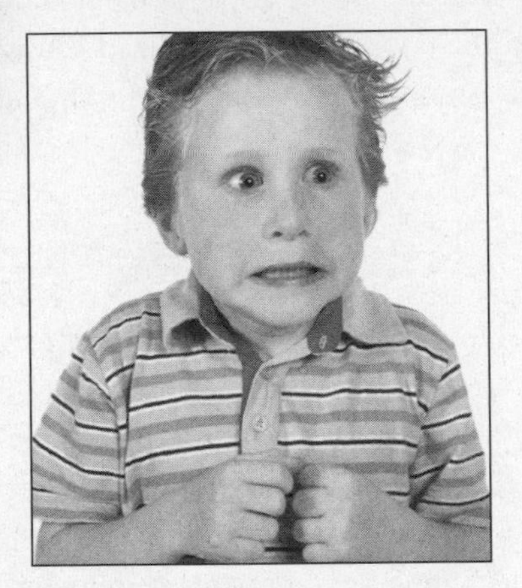

ANGER

You get a bad review, and even though you were kind of expecting it, you are furious. How dare they? You've worked at this stupid company for fifteen miserable years. Or a driver tries to pass you on a mountain road and almost causes a wreck. The time between an event and the anger response from the amygdala can be a quarter of a second. You begin to feel the blood flowing into your hands, perhaps in preparation for battle, your heart rate speeds up, and your blood pressure may even rise. You feel the sweat as you clench your fists. You're just about ready to tell the

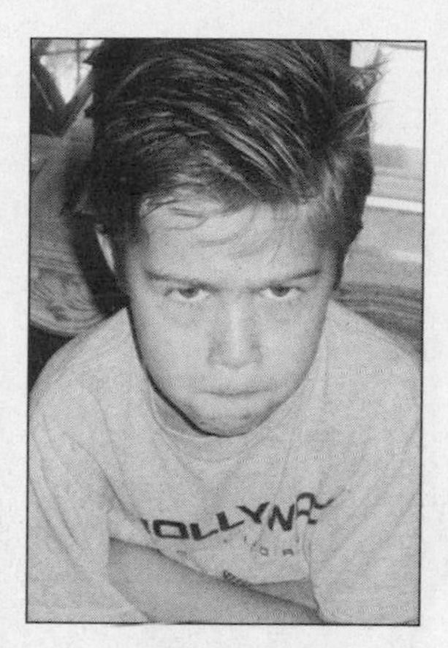

boss what to do with the job, or blast your horn at the offending car, and luckily your blood flow increases to the frontal lobe, above the left eye, where reason is controlled, and hopefully you calm down.

How it looks: Brows are furrowed and lowered. Upper eyelids lower. Gaze becomes intense. Lower eyelids tense. Nostrils flare. Mouth is sometimes open and square, with lip tension and your lower lip bulging.

In my first job, I worked as an analyst, and our office was arranged in cubicles with a secretary in front. One day, I was chatting with a male employee over the cubicles. As we were usually treated like children at this job, this conversation earned me the scolding from one of the vice presidents of our department. She rushed out, put her finger to her lips, and announced to all within range, "Shhhhh. Tonya, cool your jets." It was the first time I had heard that expression, and I still remember the moment detail by detail. Not only did she humiliate me, but she treated me like a child. Can you guess which direction my brows, eyelids, and lips went?

Tonya angry

DISGUST

Everyone has worked with someone who doesn't practice good hygiene. While employed at one company, I had to interact daily with someone

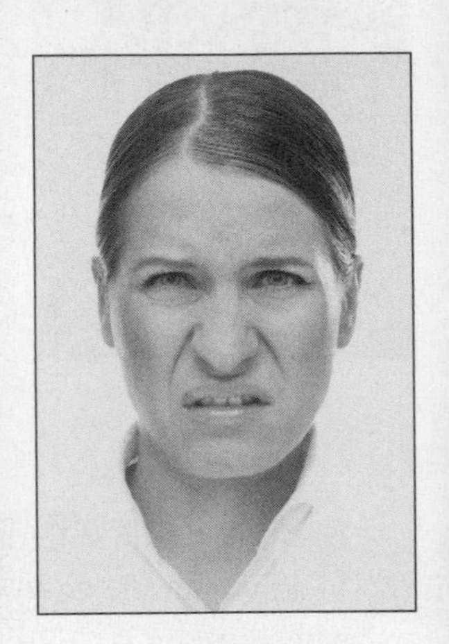

Three expressions of disgust.

who must not have known the definition of showering. One whiff of someone like this and you feel sick to your stomach. Your amygdala is activated, creating feelings of disgust. Seeing something repulsive, smelling a foul odor, or tasting or even thinking of tasting something unpleasant can trigger disgust. It basically communicates contaminants, toxins, or poisons. This emotion can be close to contempt, except in this case your revulsion is almost physical, as if you've just taken a drink of sour milk.

How it looks: Forehead is usually relaxed. Eyebrows are lowered. Upper nose area wrinkles. Lower lid tenses. Lips are pursed. Upper lip is raised, leaving mouth slightly open.

HAPPINESS

You get the new account you were working so hard to land. It's a woo-hoo moment. In your brain, endorphins flood the opioid receptors of the emotional limbic system. You experience a rush of pleasure and satisfaction. The wonderful thing about happiness is that it is strengthening.

Danny Glover's turned-up lips and scrunched brows are signs of a genuine, happy smile.

Actress Kate Beckinsale attends the red-carpet premiere of *Harry Potter and the Goblet of Fire* on December 6, 2005, in London, England.

When you experience happiness, you are also spreading the virus of positive emotions.

Have you ever noticed that it can be difficult to be sullen when around a ray of light? I have a friend who, no matter how down you are, just seems always to see the brighter side, and when I'm around her, it might take a few minutes, but I start seeing the brighter side as well.

How it looks: Forehead is relaxed. Outer ends of eyebrows are slightly pulled down. Eyes are narrowed. Crow's-feet appear, with lines under the eyes. Cheeks are raised, and lines can be seen in the nasolabial folds. Mouth corners are turned up. Lips are slightly parted, with top teeth showing.

CONTEMPT

Somebody disapproves of your behavior or feels superior to you. Faces are programmed to let you know that you are less than worthy of consideration. Out comes the contempt.

How it looks: Wrinkles appear on the nose. One lip is often raised in a sneer. Lips are sometimes pushed forward. Mouth is tight with slightly raised corners.

This sneering expression is a clear message that somebody feels superior.

Former New York mayor Rudy Giuliani speaking at "Washington Briefing 2007: Values Voter Summit" on October 20, 2007, at the Hilton Hotel in downtown Washington, D.C.

Protesters rally at the State House on June 4, 2009, in Columbus, Ohio, to protest proposed state-budget changes.

Now you know where emotions originate, and you know how they look when expressed. It's important to keep in mind that although we constantly need to monitor the face, we must also monitor the movements of the body *in conjunction with* spoken word; combined, these three elements—face, body, and language—confirm behavior and intentions. When we experience contentment and well-being, our body movements are harmonious and align with our words. When we are in a state of discomfort, the distress escapes through subtle flaws in our nonverbal fluency. Understanding the source of your emotions and the emotions of those around you brings you one step closer to learning how to get a *yes.*

THREE

THE CRITICAL FACTOR

Bypassing the No *Barrier*

"The newest computer can merely compound, at speed, the oldest problem in the relations between human beings, and in the end the communicator will be confronted with the old problem, of what to say and how to say it."

—*Edward R. Murrow*

The sky is blue.

All things are possible.

You need what I have to offer.

What happens when you consider these statements? They go through a filter. That is the part of the mind that tosses out what you feel is untrue or believe is unethical. If the statement were "The sky is green," you wouldn't even bother to look up. You already know the color of the sky—that statement automatically gets tossed. However, deciding which information to accept and which to reject isn't always that easy.

Known as both the **critical faculty** and the **critical factor**, this barrier between the conscious and unconscious parts of the mind is formed early in life. It protects you from deception but is also limited by what you believe is true or false, which is not necessarily what *is* true or false. For example, some people have a critical factor that believes smoking is good. Why? Because to their subconscious, smoking makes them *feel* good, and therefore it must *be* good, which makes the statement "Smoking is good" true. Getting past the critical factor is key in influencing those with whom you communicate.

Bypassing the conscious mind's critical factor requires you to tap into the subconscious. It's only in the subconscious that you can change beliefs and behavior. As master hypnotherapist Dave Elman said, "Hypnosis is a state of mind in which the critical faculty of the human is bypassed, and selective thinking established."[4] By combining nonverbal techniques with spoken-language patterns, you will zip past the critical factor and covertly influence specific mind strings in much the same way a hypnotherapist does.

And how is that helpful? Well, by bypassing critical factors you can influence not only potential clients, supervisors, and friends, but yourself too. Huh? Seems dubious. Believe me, by pulling on your own mind strings, you'll also be able to improve your own outlook and bypass the critical factors that limit what you believe about who you are and what you can or cannot do. Translation: You can access your own *yes* factor, entering your own mind and improving your own take on life.

I was introduced to the concept of mind strings by my friend Kevin Hogan, Psy.D., author of numerous books on persuasion. So what is a **mind string**? Well, think of the brain as a piano. When you press a key, it pulls at a different string, and that creates a predictable response programmed into the other person, often since childhood. Take the word *because,* for instance. As a child, you asked why or why not, and your parent replied, "Because." Despite the fact that it doesn't provide a reason, the word became an answer. And when you say it to someone, it tugs on a mind string. So what accessing mind strings really does is influence the individual's autopilot and level the communication playing field, because you're tapping into something that exists deep in the other person's subconscious—you just have to give it a little tug!

In a frequently referenced experiment, Harvard-based behavioral scientist Dr. Ellen Langer had an associate approach a line of people who were waiting to use a Xerox machine and ask if she could cut ahead of the line. "Excuse me, I have five pages," she said. "May I use the Xerox machine?" Sixty percent agreed to let her cut in. When the assistant added the word *because* ("May I use the Xerox machine *because* I am in a rush?"), 94 percent agreed to let her do so.[5]

Because made all the difference. Notice here that there is an actual reason behind the request: "I am in a rush." Here is the really phenomenal piece of that study, though. When the associate went in and simply said, "May I use the Xerox machine *because* I want to make copies," a fascinating thing happened: 93 percent of the people still let her go. What, you say? She offered a non-reason and still had 93 percent compliance. Of course I want to make copies. Why else would I be standing at the copy machine? *Because.* We are wired to respond to it.

Each one of us is walking around in our own world, and that world is the key to how we filter and process information. Think about it. Our world is filtered through the people we know, the movies we have seen, celebrities we respect, books we have read, lessons we have learned in school, as well as our daily living. Overall, our life experiences dictate our frames. That's why the best salespeople are good listeners. They don't try to blather you into submission. They just ask questions and let you take it from there. *Because* isn't the only mind string; in fact, there are an infinite number, and they exist as single words, phrases, or abstract ideas.

Let's think about the sales situation. You walk into a car dealership and eventually reveal that you have three kids. Salesperson says: "This minivan will be awesome when you go camping."

You reveal that you are single and work as a caterer. Salesperson says: "This minivan will be awesome for transporting food to your events."

You reveal that you are a doting grandparent. You guessed it. "This minivan will be awesome for hauling around the grandkids."

Think about every time you were sold anything by a great salesperson. Didn't it happen because this person got inside your world and matched up your need to the product or service? Too many people don't bother to listen to what their prospects say or give much thought to who their potential buyer really is. In your own life, instead of planning your next great response, you will learn so much more by shutting up and paying attention to what the other person says.

New studies are suggesting the power of language may be even greater than imagined. One of Langer's recent studies focused a group of eighty-four hotel maids and their perceptions of exercise. The work of a maid is far from sedentary, yet Langer found that more than one third of the group reported that they didn't get any exercise at all. Further, even though they all exceeded the U.S. surgeon general's recommendation for daily exercise, when Langer's team measured and weighed them, the results matched the perceived and not the actual amount of exercise.

The eighty-four maids were divided into two groups. Researchers explained to one group about how many calories were burned by their daily tasks. The maids were also told that they met the surgeon general's description of a healthy lifestyle. The other group continued as usual and didn't receive any information.

One month later, the groups were weighed and measured again. The educated group had reduced weight and waist-to-hip ratio, and there was a 10 percent drop in blood pressure. Other recent studies also suggest that there is more to the placebo effect than previously believed and that we really may be what we perceive ourselves to be.

It appears the group of maids who received the information about the exercise they were getting perceived themselves differently and then acted differently. When you are told that you are exceeding national exercise guidelines, perhaps you're more likely to expend extra effort as you go through your daily tasks. Maybe you're even more willing to pass on that extra slice of chocolate cake.[6]

Regardless, what we think affects who we are, and not in some magical woo-woo way.

The manipulation of mind strings happens all the time in relationships. I think a lot of us have seen how both sexes can present themselves as attractive sexual partners, even when they're not. I recently watched a former client—a confident, attractive, and successful woman—allow a less-than-average man to walk into her life, say and do all the right things, engage her in a whirlwind relationship, and leave her brokenhearted and wondering how she could have been so foolish.

Let's examine this situation for a moment. How was this vice president of a bank, this strong, savvy woman, swept away so instantly? Here's how: He played on her weaknesses. He met every one of her hardwired needs; he piqued her curiosity by being fun and playful, he toyed with her self-esteem by *not* falling all over her, and he played on her underlying biological need for a strong alpha male by presenting himself with an air of vigor, power, and protection. In other words, he made her invest in him. The guy knew what he was doing, and he did it well. He bypassed her critical factor and preyed on every one of her genetic requirements. He tapped into her subconscious. Smart as she was, my client's mind strings were manipulated, and she took one right in the solar plexus, so to speak.

We'll examine the techniques this guy used in greater detail later, and you'll learn how to recognize and protect yourself from those who try to pull your strings without your awareness. For now, it's enough to know that we all have filters that process the information we receive, and that there are ways you can learn to bypass those filters. We're all individuals, but we're hardwired the same way. Let me show you something about your own mind strings right now.

LEMONS

Let's try something, just to demonstrate my point. I want you to relax for a moment. Take a nice, deep breath in and then exhale. Imagine that I have just handed you a lemon. Look at how bright and beautiful and yellow it is. Picture it in your mind. Mentally rub your fingers over its bumpy surface. Draw your fingernail down its flesh. Breathe in the fragrance of the oil. Now I want you to imagine you are holding a knife. Hear it begin to slice through the lemon, and as you do, allow yourself to see how pulpy and juicy it is. Squeeze it and watch the juice flow from it. Perhaps you notice your lips begin to pucker. Bring it up to your nose and take another deep breath as you allow yourself to see your tongue running along the pulp of the lemon.

Are you salivating yet?

You have just experienced the *yes* factor. Even though we have never met, my words triggered a physiological response in you. And while you didn't grant me a formal *yes,* what I did do was influence your thinking, persuading you to imagine exactly what I wanted you to. What actually happened? The thoughts in your brain were translated into nerve impulses. Your brain went on autopilot, and you believed you were touching, smelling, and tasting an actual lemon.

The power of the unconscious isn't limited to our ability to respond to those powerful citrus images. Researchers at University College London found that when we imagine a future purchase, the brain responds in much the same way as when we actually make that purchase. Those in the study experienced the pleasure of buying simply by imagining it, just as you imagined and experienced the lemon. No wonder fantasizing about our vacations, our successes, and our futures is so satisfying.

As I mentioned earlier, you can't tug on those mind strings until you've bypassed someone's critical factor. You can't influence anyone to do anything until you get past that.

When I was working as a hypnotherapist, one of my clients was a man in his mid-sixties who smoked three packs of cigarettes a day. A man in his mid-sixties is usually pretty set in his ways, and I wondered how long it would take to get past his critical factor.

A man so set in his ways might possess all the willpower in the world, but willpower, which comes from the conscious mind and brings about the desire to change, is seldom enough. In order to help this client, I needed to bypass his critical factor and change what he believed.

"Do you enjoy smoking?" I asked.

"Yes," he replied. "I love smoking."

This was a red flag. Often people try to quit only because their doctors or their loved ones tell them to. I wondered if the desire to quit smoking was really there.

"Are you ready to quit?" I asked my new client. "Do you want to quit?"

"I absolutely want to," he told me.

The session took longer than usual because he was clearly agitated. His conscious mind was holding him back. After forty minutes of my deep and low and sometimes monotonous hypnotic voice, and some feedback and assurances, he seemed to calm down.

I went for a covert suggestion. "It's amazing that in just these few minutes, you have made so many changes."

When he came out of the hypnotic trance and after we had discussed how he felt about the session, I asked, "How long do you think you were sitting there?"

"Probably eight to ten minutes," he said.

"Forty," I told him.

"How the hell is that possible?" he demanded.

Because of my covert suggestion, time had been distorted for him. That was a good sign. I only hoped that he had accepted the other suggestions.

After our first meeting, I called and e-mailed, and to my continual frustration, received no response. What had happened to him? Had he continued smoking and decided to avoid me altogether?

While I was worrying about him, he was on a lengthy vacation, one he had forgotten to mention to me. Six weeks after our first and only session, I received a voice mail from him with thanks from his entire family. Next I received a note from him, counting down the number of cigarettes per day that I had saved him from smoking. Sixty cigarettes a day, 420 cigarettes a week, 1,800 cigarettes a month. Both the call and the letter once again demonstrated to me the power of accessing the subconscious mind.

Okay, so what happened here? By using a few covert suggestions while he was in a hypnotic state I was able to bypass my client's critical factor and access and manipulate his unconscious mind. Does it always work this effortlessly? No. But trust me, you don't have to hypnotize someone deeply to get results—the skills you learn here will help you put your *yes* target (the person you're trying to convince) into a state of simple waking hypnosis so that you are perceived in the best light.

Okay, let's not put the cart before the horse. Before you jump right into pulling mind strings indiscriminately, let's work on identifying and improving your own communication style. The first step is understanding and *branding* the most important product you will ever sell. And that product is you.

FOUR

"SO TELL ME ABOUT YOURSELF."

The Hidden Meaning and How to Address It

"Enough about me. What about you? What do you think about me?"

—*Anonymous*

The techniques of persuasion are not new. Aristotle, way back in the day, described them in *On Rhetoric* as Ethos, Pathos, and Logos.

Ethos addresses the persuasive appeal of a person's character and what qualities make him appear credible. **Pathos,** the second mode of persuasion, addresses the appeal to emotion. And **Logos,** from which the word *logic* is derived, addresses the facts, or so-called facts, that support a given argument. Those techniques are just as relevant today as they were in ancient Greece. We do have a slight leg up on Aristotle, though: Modern research has allowed us to delve deeper and learn how to capitalize on Ethos, Pathos, and Logos in order to get a *yes*. Now research has confirmed how we can appear credible from the first meeting, how to appeal to emotion, and how best to present our facts to get a positive response.

You're interviewing for a job, or maybe having coffee with a date, someone you like. "So tell me about yourself." The request is innocent enough, isn't it? Then why does it make you squirm in your seat? Because you sense the unspoken question. What the other person really means is "What makes you special?"

Certainly few would dare to ask you that. Not in a job interview. Not on a first date. Still, it's what he wants to know, and the sooner, the better. In business, it is called your USP, your **Unique Selling Point** (sometimes called Unique Selling Position). For example, the USP of this book is that it is the only prescriptive nonfiction book on the market that combines the science of verbal and nonverbal communication to help you get others to do what you want them to do.

What candy melts in your mouth, not in your hand? Which hamburger lets you have it your way? Whether it's M&M's or Burger King, from the largest to the smallest company, everyone in the business of persuasion is searching for a phrase that is reflective of its product and its message.

Think of your personal USP as your brand. What makes you stand out from the crowd? What "branded" aspect of your personality shines when others see you? Knowing what brand you are not only makes it easier for you to "sell" yourself in a business exchange or on a date; it also increases your awareness of all your positive attributes. And that will send your confidence through the roof.

It might sound blatantly commercial, but it truly is essential to know who you are before you go out engaging other people. If you don't, poor preparation can potentially lead you down the path of low self-esteem, and that will overpower any message you hope to convey.

Years ago, the study of hypnosis helped me understand the human psyche and the skillful art of manipulation in order to help individuals overcome fears and bad habits. I gained confidence in who I was and what I could accomplish with my clients.

When you can influence your own mind the way a hypnotherapist does, you can and will influence your behavior.

Caveat: I am not talking about the use of generic positive affirmations. I'm sure you've read that by using positive thoughts about yourself, and by writing or repeating them daily, you can change your life. It's not a new concept, but with the success of books such as *The Secret,* among others, positive thinking would seem to be the new shortcut to success. However, what I'm talking about goes a step further: putting your goals together by formulating realistic, attainable objectives.

For instance, when I trained for the New York City Marathon in 2004, I dealt with some very tough mental challenges. I knew it was going to be difficult, but I decided I was going to do it and not let anything stop me. In training, I was told to run no more than eighteen miles, yet the marathon was 26.2 miles. Hmmm.

You could say my goal was to prove to myself that I could do something insurmountable, to prove that I could do anything that I set my mind and body to. But in order to get there I needed a real, tangible goal. The marathon was that goal. And to get myself there, I needed to convince myself—my subconscious self—that I was a marathon runner. Each day as I ran, I repeated to myself: *I am a marathoner. I am a marathoner.*

This forced my unconscious mind to acknowledge that I was indeed a marathoner. I knew that once my unconscious believed it, I would indeed *be* a marathoner (which was a good thing, because my body certainly felt the aches like a marathoner).

The day of the race, I wore a shirt with the names of everyone who had made a difference in my getting that far. They included my husband, Ken; my three kids, Stephanie, Christian, and Jaidan; my running partner, Steve; and my chiropractor, Dr. Valle, who adjusted me constantly while I trained.

The day of the marathon comes, and as I anxiously await the cannon going off, I feel the adrenaline pumping inside me. I am ready. *Boom!* goes the cannon, and with a burst of excitement, I start running. Then after what seems like just minutes, I feel run-down and shaky. Everything drains out of me, and I quickly learn that the NYC Marathon is *looong.*

I am a marathoner. I am a marathoner. Yeah, right. Try as I might, I can't get past my own barrier, which is telling me to up and stop right here.

Finally I reach what most marathoners call the halfway point: mile twenty. Granted, there are only six more miles to go, but those six miles can be even more challenging than the previous twenty.

I am a marathoner. . . .

I am ready to drop. I feel as if I have been hit in the knees with a sledgehammer.

At that moment, a man yells out to me, "Go, Tonya. Remember you are part of the elite. Only 2 percent of the population will ever run a marathon."

That, I think, *is because the other 98 percent are so much smarter than I am. What was I thinking? Back on track . . .*

I am a marathoner. I am a marathoner. I am a marathoner.

At mile twenty-one, my cell phone rings. It is my baby girl, Stephanie.

"Hi, Mommy," she says. "I'm watching the marathon on TV, and I don't see you."

"That's because Mommy is at the back of the pack, baby."

"Well, that's okay. Mommy, are you going to win?"

"No, sweetie. Mommy is so tired that all she wants to do is stop."

"Oh, no, Mommy," she says. "You can do it. Are you trying your hardest?"

"Yes, baby, but Mommy is very tired."

"Mommy, I'm so proud of you, and I know you can do it."

At that moment, my perspective changes. My eight-year-old is proud of me, and I know I can do it. I have prepared myself mentally as well as physically.

Everything becomes crystal clear. With that comes the realization that this is my goal, my mountain to climb. After that, I dedicate each mile to someone who is important in my life. And each mile becomes a triumphant victory.

Twenty-two.

Twenty-three.

Twenty-four.

Twenty-five.

Twenty-six.

I am a marathoner.

When I cross over the finish line, I am smiling from ear to ear—not just because I have finished, but because I know that I have broken through a wall that only an hour earlier seemed impenetrable. My daughter's words reminded me of the message I had drummed into my mind during all of those hours of practice.

Too often affirmations are based on unrealistic goals or goals that require numerous steps to achieve. *I'm going to wake up tomorrow and be ten pounds lighter* isn't going to happen. *I am going to be stronger and run faster. I am going to achieve something great* can happen if you're willing to take the steps. Repeating empty affirmations will make you nothing more than a day older tomorrow. You'll achieve much more, perhaps more than you've ever imagined, by mastering the techniques I am going to share with you in the following chapters.

So let's work out your USP so you can change your perception of yourself.

EXERCISE: USP BUILDING

Let's take a moment to see how you are going to sell you. Start by writing down the answers to these questions.

- What are the three things you love best about yourself? What other qualities stand out? Don't stop until you have seven or more.
- What do your best friends and clients tell you they like or admire about you?
- Why would the employer of your dreams be lucky to have you? Minimum five reasons.
- What would a romantic partner most value about you? Again, at least five things.

- What are four of your greatest professional accomplishments? What qualities helped you achieve them?
- What are four of your greatest personal accomplishments? What qualities helped you achieve them?

This is where you start the groundwork for your USP. You assess your strengths and your skills. Focus only on the positive. Write them down and then find that combination of qualities that makes you who you are.

Next, take those first three thoughts you wrote down. Sit with them awhile. Live with them. Eventually, once you're comfortable with them, put those words into a nice little catchphrase that tells others and yourself what makes you special.

Those involved in the business of persuasion understand the importance of an "elevator pitch" when they try to interest someone else in their product, project, or service. They are prepared when the *yes* target says, "So tell me what you have in mind." The idea is to pretend that you are on an elevator and have only the ninety or so seconds between floors to answer the question with a focused, catchy, and (you hope) memorable statement.

Try to develop your own elevator pitch, that quick phrase that says the most and best about you. Imagine that you have two résumés, one for the business world and one for the relationship or dating world. You need a USP one-liner for each one.

You can't take the first step toward building rapport with and persuading others until you feel good about yourself. You will then have the confidence to make eye contact, lean forward, smile, and speak with self-assurance.

That's the whole idea behind creating the USP. Knowledge leads to confidence. Confidence leads to changing your posture, which then changes your body chemistry. Suddenly you can be in a better place than you were ten minutes ago. Just as eating a piece of chocolate changes your brain chemistry and makes you feel better, USP has you moving, acting, and engaging differently. It's the first and perhaps most pivotal step in building your Alpha You. When someone says to you, "Tell me about yourself," you won't have to stammer and struggle for an answer. You will know.

ASK TONYA

Q: I work with someone who makes me extremely uncomfortable. During meetings, she crosses her arms when I speak. Frequently, she rolls her eyes if I ask a question. When we interact at the office, she invades my personal space. I have been trying to develop my alpha side, but it's pretty difficult to present myself to others as a strong leader when I am constantly being undermined by this colleague.

A: You are only as stuck as you allow yourself to be. Remember the high-school bully? Well, this one never grew up. The next time your colleague moves into your personal space, stand your ground and even move forward, into hers. Woo! There's nothing that gets a bully's attention faster than someone who refuses to be a victim.

Make eye contact, even when she's rolling her eyes. Think about the language you use in meetings. Are you using power words and avoiding being pulled into someone else's way of describing a situation? (See the next chapter on Framing.)

At this point, you aren't looking for your colleague's approval; you're just showing, by what you say and what you do, that you are not intimidated by her. Remember, we are constantly sending out signals that affect how others perceive and thus react to us. Perfect those outgoing signals and you will see a change in the incoming signals.

PART II

THE POWER OF WORDS

FIVE

THE RIGHT FRAME IS WORTH A THOUSAND WORDS

"All great ideas look like bad ideas to people who are losers. It's always good to test a new idea with known losers to make sure they don't like it."

—*Scott Adams, creator of* Dilbert

Previously Owned versus Used.

Inexpensive versus Cheap.

Half-full versus Half-empty.

Rudolph's nose: Guiding Light versus Blinding Nuisance.

Go-getter versus Too Pushy.

Later we'll learn about the danger of dwelling on the negative. **Framing** is a way of spinning something or, to reframe *spinning*, a way to redefine a situation or put it in a more positive light.

Suppose we're in the lunchroom at work, and I mention to you that I have a priceless painting in my office.

"This masterpiece is so amazing," I say. "I can't wait for you to see it."

"Wow," you reply. "Let's take a look."

Down the hall we go. As we enter my office, you are full of anticipation.

"Just look at that." I point at the wall, and there, right over my desk, is a colorful painting, all right.

But it isn't the painting you notice. It's the frame.

"It is wonderful, isn't it?" I demand. "You do see that, don't you?"

But all you can see is that this painting I have been bragging about is placed in a big, cheap, tasteless-looking plastic frame.

How impressed are you right about now, and how convinced are you that I have anything of value? The same is true of the message you are trying to convey to yourself or someone else. If it isn't properly framed, it is not going to be taken seriously.

Before we get into framing situations in conversation, let's look at how you can use framing to run that marathon, get that new job, lose the weight, or achieve just about any goal you'd like. My dictionary defines "frame of mind" as: a mental attitude or outlook; a mood. Reframing is changing your or someone else's perception of something that happened to you. It transforms beliefs, and it transforms the context of an experience. A good example: a rainstorm. Rainstorms can mean two different things to a bride on her wedding day and a farmer who is losing crops because of a dry spell. It's all in the frame or situation.

When I was working on this book, I caught a nasty flu bug that really did me in. I felt terrible, and for several days I could barely get out of bed.

As I began to recover, my friend and literary agent called to check in.

"How are you feeling?" she asked.

I spared her the symptoms but did admit to feeling pretty lousy.

"So how would you reframe that experience, Tonya?" she asked.

Hmmm.

I thought for a moment and replied, "Well, I lost five pounds."

Now, I could have bemoaned all the lost days of tapping keys to write this book. But I used a reframing technique on myself. I construed the situation as positive by establishing a new frame. Any statement I could have selected to describe my flu experience would have been true, and they all would have had equal weight—but the frame I chose was key in convincing myself that it would all turn out for the best. You have that same kind of power over your experiences. Change the frame and you change the meaning and the value. OK, here are a few more examples: "I have too much work to do" becomes "I'm lucky to have such a good job in this economy." "I'm afraid of getting fired" becomes "Regardless of what happens, this is a good time to look at the job market and possible career training."

There are two basic types of reframing:

CONTEXT REFRAMING

Context reframing means changing the context to increase the value of the behavior or experience.

Useless frame: My boss doesn't have a clue. That means more work for me.

New frame: My boss needs me to explain what's going on, which makes me even more valuable.

Useless frame: You'd have to be a math wizard to get ahead in this company.

New frame: Taking an online math class will help me move up faster in this firm.

CONTENT REFRAMING

Content reframing means searching for other meanings for an experience.

Useless frame: Three people in my department failed to connect with our new client.

New frame: I'm going to figure out how to be the first in our department to connect with our new client.

Useless frame: My boss is a slave driver.

New frame: I'm learning by fire, and it's going to make me a better worker wherever I go after this place.

Now, I didn't invent the concept of framing. Virginia Satir[7] and Milton H. Erickson[8] used it in their work in family therapy. Framing and reframing are components of neuro-linguistic programming. NLP cofounder John Grinder developed a six-step reframe for changing habits and behaviors.[9] But framing is a key step in implementing the *yes* factor. By combining the right words with the right nonverbal signals, you can bypass people's conscious minds and manipulate their mind strings. You can get them to *yes.*

It can start with the power of a single word. Words evoke emotions and ideas. Just by setting up a phrase, you can gain leverage and plant subconscious seeds. A perfect example of this is the way George Lakoff, a linguist at the University of California–Berkeley, discusses how George Bush used the phrase *tax relief* as opposed to *tax cut.*[10] Substituting the word *relief* for *cut* when talking about Bush's tax policies, Lakoff explains, allowed the Republicans to associate a sense of morality with their agenda.

"If you have relief, there has to be affliction, an afflicted party." According to Lakoff, activating the idea of affliction plants subconscious seeds, and each political party is given a distinct role to play. The party that relieves the affliction is a hero, while the party that attempts to thwart the relief is a villain. Why is that? Because we, the listeners, have preexisting ideas about heroes, villains, and the afflicted. Using that one word changed the way a reduction in taxes was perceived by the public. Instead of a loss of revenue, it was a way to provide relief for the underprivileged. One word—*relief* versus *cut*—got Republicans closer to *yes.* Surprise, surprise; the bill passed.

IN YOUR OWN WORDS

Let's use some framing exercises to identify how you can impact your own outlook by adjusting the frame in which you view the events in your life.

- What is the most negative aspect of your job? Write it down. How can you put a new frame around it? Do it visually first. Now ask yourself how you can turn that negative into a positive. What is a possible benefit to that negative that you never before considered?

- Write down the name of a client or a colleague who is a challenge for you. What do you think is the problem? Write it down. Now reframe the answer, and write that down as well.
- Think of the last time you wanted something—a sale, a promotion—and someone else got it. How did it happen? Did this person have more credentials than you? A louder voice? A more aggressive presence? Or even a victim mentality? What made you lose yourself and your focus?
- What is the next goal you want to accomplish in your career? Write down the name of the person who can get you there. Frame and, if necessary, reframe why this person can and will want to help you.

REFRAMED INTERACTIONS

Lucky for you, framing can not only help you adjust your own thinking on a topic; it can also alter others' perceptions about something that might be, at first blush, construed as negative, but that after you've framed it appears as a positive.

First things first: Bring your *yes* target into the frames you've created. How can we use this in business? Well, in order to establish a powerful frame, you must recognize what your *yes* target values. For example, if you are a top-notch employee and you are looking for a raise, the first thing you need is for your boss to recognize your worth, especially during these hard economic times.

Your boss might ask you what you have done to deserve a raise. Of course, you should be prepared to demonstrate your past and current value. But what's really on your boss's mind is the question he won't ask but will unconsciously wonder: *What will you do for me in the future?*

This is where a powerful frame such as *imagine* really becomes persuasive.

"Well, that deal that I closed for Mahoney was tough," you say. "Ralph said he couldn't imagine closing it without me."

Look what you have just done. You have allowed your penny-pinching boss to see a clear vision of your wonderful self being gone, not to mention the possible loss of revenue resulting from your artfully crafted and vaguely spoken potential departure. You threatened to quit with one word. *Imagine.*

Your own daily frames need to be consistently positive. The professional and personal rewards of this are manifold and obvious. A simple personal example would be your friend complaining that her son is lazy. Your reframe could be as straightforward as telling her she must be grateful he is relaxed and easygoing.

Your spouse complains about your high taxes. "I can't believe how much we owe," she says.

You reply, "Babe, do you realize that means we earned megabucks this year? I'd rather have to pay lots in taxes and earn what we did last year than get a check back from the IRS because we made squat."

FRAME-OFF

But be careful. Most of the time, you want to bring others into your frame instead of being devoured by theirs. In a way, it's verbal warfare: your frame versus their frame.

I learned this lesson the painful way very early in my career, when I was giving a lecture to some extremely heavy hitters. There probably wasn't a person in the room who earned less than seven figures, and the secretary and I were the only women there. Anxiety, anybody? I didn't think so, at least not consciously. They were great people, and this was my second time speaking to them, so I knew that they found value in what I had to say.

That day, though, right in the middle of my description of the most effective way to set up proper spatial relations in a specific business context, the alpha male running the show jumped to his feet.

"I disagree with that," he boomed. "And I want my guys to know that in our field, you need to stick to the way I have taught you."

Gulp.

I backpedaled.

"Well, you know this area better than I do." The minute the statement came out of my mouth, I wished I could reel it back in.

He had pulled his credentials on me, and I had allowed myself to be devoured into his frame.

If I had it to do over, I would have been quicker on my feet and responded with the right answer, which is: "I understand how you feel, and in certain circumstances I might have felt the same way, but in the situation we are discussing, I've found the most effective way to do it is . . ." Even that situation can be reframed, though: I learned a priceless lesson versus making a monstrous mistake.

Okay, here's another example: A major health-insurance company was deluged by customers who could no longer afford the hefty rate increases for policies and had decided to cancel. One of those customers was a colleague of mine. The day he received his price-increase notice, he called the company's 800 number. Once he got a real person on the line (and that happened really fast), he expressed his intent and his frustration.

"I want to cancel my policy," he said. "I can't afford your latest increase."

"You want to restructure?" No, he wanted to cancel, but he listened to her pitch anyway. "Are you aware of our new options?" she asked. "For almost two hundred dollars a month less, you can have a more comprehensive policy than you have now. And with no co-pay."

"If you have a plan that much better than mine," my friend said, "why wasn't it offered to me when I enrolled in the first place?"

"It wasn't available then, sir."

Of course not. The resourceful company had instituted the new "option" only after the economy tanked and customers could no longer afford the policies of the past. Furthermore, every cancellation call was being routed directly to telephone salespeople like this one, who reframed those cancellation calls into reenrollments.

The tactic worked. My friend faxed back the new form the company rep had e-mailed him. When he did not receive a reply right away, he called again.

"Your new policy is in effect," the representative told him. "We've just been so busy with this new program of ours that the paperwork is backed up."

Backed up by insurance policies that had been restructured instead of lost—because the company had reframed its approach to cancellations. A less resourceful organization could not have dealt successfully with those calls. Instead, this forward-thinking firm turned them into new policies instead of lost ones.

You can do the same, in every aspect of your job, once you learn the power of reframed interactions.

Words help us digest information. Some words are easier to swallow than others. Learn to use words that diminish pain or elicit excitement. When you change the frame of the words, you change your delivery and others' receipt of the information.

As a ten-year-old living in Brooklyn, I invited a few friends over one summer for a block party. While we were doing gymnastics, I flipped Susie, one of the girls, over my back, and she landed flat on hers. Her parents came running over to pick her up. I was totally distraught at what I might have done to this poor girl and immediately dispatched Sarah, another friend, to check her status.

When Sarah came back, she said the news was not good. Susie had to go to the hospital and might have fractured her skull. I almost fainted right there and immediately went into hysterics.

After a few seconds of watching my breakdown, she said, "Tonya, Susie really only has a small cut on the back of her shoulder where she landed. It's nothing."

"What?" I demanded, puzzled. "I don't understand. A cut—that's nothing. Who cares about a cut? What about her head?"

Sarah very seriously explained to me that had she told me the truth initially, I would have been upset and made a big deal about making Susie bleed. "Don't you feel better now that you know she only has a small cut?" Now, after learning what could have been, wasn't I relieved to learn it was only a cut? At nine, Sarah was already a master manipulator. Suddenly, I felt like I was lucky; meanwhile I had still caused someone to bleed.

THE PYGMALION EFFECT

The **Pygmalion Effect** is a form of self-fulfilling prophecy that states that people with low expectations will do poorly and people with high expectations will do better. In addition, we tend to live up to the expectations of others, both positive and negative. We tend to internalize our labels, and fail or succeed accordingly.

According to the story by Ovid, Pygmalion, prince of Cyprus, was a sculptor who carved an ivory statue of Galatea, his dream woman. He instantly fell in love with his creation and begged Aphrodite, goddess of love, to bring the statue to life. The goddess granted his wish, and Pygmalion married Galatea. The statue became the dream woman he had been seeking. He got what he expected.

We all have expectations regarding others. They are clever or dimwitted, powerful or weak. We communicate these expectations with various verbal and nonverbal cues, and others adjust their behavior to match them.

Let's look at a work example. Imagine you are an individual with a normal level of self-esteem who has a manager who doesn't like you. You perceive signals and signs that validate your beliefs. What happens is that ultimately you give off signals that spark an unconscious reaction from her. Your manager winds up treating you the way that you have anticipated because you have unwittingly set the stage for that exact relationship to develop. We perceive that an individual behaves consistently with our beliefs, and those expectations may even cause that individual to behave in that way. In other words, belief and anticipation play a major role in how our relationships develop, because people behave toward you the way you expect they will.

On a personal level, I have a dear friend who, perhaps because of the way she was raised, always put up with poor treatment from men. She is a wonderful person, but a date consisted of pizza and chips at her place with a guy who would yell at her to get him another beer. Then she started dating a new man, and everything changed.

He sent flowers. He took her to dinner. In short, he treated her with the respect she had never had. One night she called me in tears, overcome with emotions, explaining that he had opened the car door for her the way, ". . . Kenny does for you." What was normal to me was extraordinary to her. She was beside herself. No one had ever treated her with so much respect and dignity. It changed her and it totally changed what she expected in a relationship. That relationship made her a better person.

Don't allow your frame to be immersed in someone else's world. If an individual takes something out on you, rather than jumping through her hoop (sometimes people just want someone to fight with), help her melt away her anger by changing her frame, or force her to hold on to her anger and keep it to herself. Years ago, when I worked for a financial firm, I remember one manager who whenever something was brewing would immediately burst out in anger and lash at anyone within twenty feet who had their eyes in her direction. We had a new supervisor in our department, who didn't know the "rule" of keeping your head down when Miss Thing went off the deep end, and the new supervisor became the target for the brunt of the manager's contempt. Instead of yelling back, breaking down, or walking out the door (which is what I might have done), she looked the manager right in the face and so empathetically said, "Wow, that meeting really upset you," and then she walked away. By not getting self-protective and putting out fighting words, she defused the situation, utterly confusing the manager and keeping her own frame intact. She didn't absorb the manager's negative energy; instead, it bounced right off of her.

THE FRAMING OF POLITICS

Framing and reframing are done constantly on both ends of the political spectrum. Although several books on the use of words to frame situations are available,[11] I found that the creative abilities of both Frank Luntz, author of *Words That Work,* and George Lakoff, author of *Don't Think of an Elephant,* illustrate the ideas of framing a situation to perfection.

Luntz believes that effective language transcends politics and business, and he offers tools and insights into political and commercial "wordsmithing." He speaks the undeniable reality: No matter how powerful your message, people will filter it through their own reality, and in doing so they will input it through the lens that they perceive as their world. What does this mean? Everyone interprets messages in their own unique way. And, of course, how each individual perceives what you say is more real than how you even perceive it yourself.

Luntz is exceptional at using language and words to ensure damage control for specific policies and ideas that might not be popular in society. He is able to change the impression of ideas—and therefore redefine them—by manipulating the definition, using softer and kinder word choices. He has a potent ability to package information, finding better words and phrases to sell the same ideology. For example, tax cuts are now tax relief. Privatization is now school choice. Global warming is now climate change. Drilling for oil is now exploring for energy. On the flip side, he can use the Democrats' frames to his advantage. For example, the estate tax now becomes the death tax. In other words, Luntz puts the best or worst spin on each and every situation, depending on what that situation calls for.

Both Lakoff and Luntz offer tools to reframe old or unpopular ideas into breakthrough, trendy, accepted initiatives. Luntz comes at it from an angle of specific spin on word choices, whereas Lakoff frames an issue by spinning toward an individual's values.

Lakoff reframes entire issues, changing *taxes* to *membership fees.* He feels that Republicans surpass Democrats in weaving better stories and offering effective slogans and catchphrases. He deems Republicans the "strict father model," in which they believe that children are born bad and need discipline in order to be made good. Democrats, he believes, are more about the nurturing parent; their views are based on empathy and responsibility coupled with progressive values.

Lakoff believes we are better off framing issues in terms of values, not merely words. He discusses how, time and time again, Republicans pull

Democrats into their frame by constantly repeating Republican frames. For example, a Democrat being absorbed into the Republican frame will then use the phrase *tax relief* (as opposed to *tax cut*), thus strengthening the Republican frame and making it the more powerful and accepted one.

Each party might feel like the other is merely, if I may, putting lipstick on a pig.

IN YOUR OWN WORDS

Reframed Interactions

Reframing is powerful in any context, but the most successful settings are your interactions with others and your own frame of mind. This exercise will help you focus on the issues you need to reframe.

- Imagine, for a moment, all you can accomplish once you are able to reframe every canceled appointment, and the plain lack of interest from clients and coworkers. Write down at least four negative interactions you have recently had to deal with. How can you reframe them into positives?
- Think about the last conversation or sales pitch that didn't work out the way you had intended. What was your frame going into that conversation? Did it change? Did you make the mistake of letting your frame be devoured by someone else's?

Now that you know how to work on your message, it is time to take a closer look at the person who is receiving it. And it is time to move beyond by-the-book communication styles.

ASK TONYA

Q: My husband and I get into these really horrific arguments sometimes and then don't speak for hours. Later, after I calm down, I look back and think how ridiculous they were. How can we love each other so much one minute and then hate each other the next?

A: When we feel strongly about an issue, our ability to focus goes out the window. We become engulfed with emotion, and we lose our capability to communicate rationally. Start recognizing the signs earlier on. Stop yourself from losing control and take a moment to regroup. If you begin to make some changes, he will follow.

SIX

GETTING INTO SOMEONE ELSE'S WORLD

"I like to listen. I have learned a great deal from listening carefully. Most people never listen."

—*Ernest Hemingway*

As a hypnotist, I know that connecting with a client is all about getting into that person's trance. In order to be heard and appreciated by your target listener, you must get into that person's world—you must move past her critical factor and into her subconscious.

REPRESENTATIONAL SYSTEMS

"Can you hear what I'm saying, George?"

"Do you see what I mean, Tina?"

HIS SIGNALS/HER SIGNALS

More Connections Equals More Information Exchanged

As we've already discussed, the two hemispheres of the brain are connected by the corpus callosum, a group of fibers. Research has shown that the more connections we have between the two sides of the brain, the more articulate we are. Recent tests have led scientists to believe that not only is the corpus callosum thicker in women's brains, but that there are also more connections between the two sides. This doesn't mean that men are less capable; it means only that we are wired differently, and that some tasks are easier based on our gender.[12]

"Understand what I'm feeling, Doctor Murphy?"

Each of the above speakers wants a one-word answer from George, Tina, and Dr. Murphy. That answer is yes. If the speaker is a master communicator, she has probably crafted her statement in response to unconscious signals she has been given by the *yes* target. One of the first steps in influencing, however, is recognizing *how* the person you're speaking to communicates.

If you go back to our lemon visualization and think about what we did there, you'll see what I mean by **representational systems.** You'll notice that I hit on the five major senses. First I had you *imagine* that I handed you a lemon (visual). Next, I asked you to *feel* the bumpy surface (kinesthetic). I then prompted you to *breathe in* the aroma of the lemon oil (olfactory) and *hear* the knife slice through it (auditory). Finally, I asked you to *run your tongue along* the pulp (gustatory). It created a total impression, didn't it? Most people don't communicate that way.

We are all more comfortable with people who speak our language. That's why the use of jargon is so prevalent. Still, when you understand the way in which an individual communicates and how he or she processes language, it is far easier to build rapport.

John Grinder, one of the original neuro-linguistic programming developers, stumbled upon five representational systems, each of which treats language as if it is processed through one of the senses. Grinder and a colleague, Richard Bandler, were leading a therapy group. On their way there, Bandler mentioned a client who had said, "I see what you are saying." Well, that really got Grinder thinking. "Let's take it literally. Suppose it means that people are making images of the meaning of the words that you use?" When they got to the group, they tried an entirely new procedure on the spur of the moment. They took green, yellow, and red cards and asked people in the group to state their purpose for being there. Those who used words and phrases relating to feelings got a yellow card. Those who used words and phrases related to hearing and sounds got green cards. Those who used words and phrases related to seeing got red cards.

They then asked those with the same-color cards to sit down and talk together for five minutes. In the next exercise they asked participants to sit and talk with someone who held a different-color card.

The differences were apparent in a way Grinder and Bandler couldn't have imagined. People whose cards were the same color hit it off extremely well—they had better rapport than with those whose cards were of a different color. The three primary representational systems were born.

Now, the participants had the advantage of two smart communication gurus and a handful of color-coded cards. Imagine what speed dating would look like if you could navigate the room based on whose color matched your own. Out there in the world, though, we're not so lucky. We need to listen and interpret the representational systems that our *yes* targets are using. The tricky part is that representational systems are unconscious. Your *yes* target doesn't say, "Hey, Tonya. Nice to meet you. I'm a Visual (or Auditory or Kinesthetic). Why don't you make my life easier and increase your chances of impressing me by using my style of communication, okay?" Unconsciously, however, that's exactly what needs to transpire in order to build rapport.

IDENTIFY YOUR SYSTEM; EXPERIMENT WITH STYLE

Any number of tests and quizzes promise to reveal to you which representational system you use. I have yet to find one that provides a clear pattern. Instead of answering somebody else's questions, you might have better results if you just talk to yourself about who you are.

Sit in a comfortable chair, alone and out of earshot of anyone else. Next, speak into a recorder about an experience in your past or perhaps a future goal. Maybe it is an incident that occurred when you were in elementary school. Maybe it is a memory of your first day at a job. Maybe it's what you would like to be doing next week, month, or year. Pick two and then make the recording. This is just for you, so don't worry about how you relive or imagine the experiences or how anyone else might judge you. Remember, no one's listening.

Now, play back the recording. Each time you hear a visual word, make a *V* in your notebook. For auditory words, mark an *A*, and for kinesthetic, a *K*. You might want to play back the recording two or three times. Once you have covered the plate with enough *V*'s, *A*'s, and/or *K*'s, do the math. What letter dominates? Are you using primarily visual terms, auditory terms, or kinesthetic terms?

Do you *see* the people and the building? Do you *hear* what they are saying? Or are you focused on your *feelings* in those situations?

Now repeat the story using one of the remaining two styles, and then the other one. If your first recording was visual, repeat it using as many sound words as possible and then using as many feeling words as possible.

How easily could you access the lesser-used systems? Can you understand the value of increasing your comfort level with all three? Consider repeating this exercise weekly, drawing on other memories. Experimenting in such a way will help you define your own system. Furthermore, it will teach you how to shift gears, almost effortlessly, to someone else's. It becomes imperative to use your own senses to pick up on the representational system of each particular *yes* target. In addition, it is even more crucial that you arm yourself with a list of words to help you enter into and become comfortable in their representational world.

Visual Communicator: I see

Style: This person sees pictures in his head. He speaks rapidly, with a high level of energy.

If communication styles were mapped out in a pie shape, most of that pie would belong to the Visuals. Some suggest that the highly visual nature of our society is the reason we have so many of these types. I'm not sure if they dominate to the degree they are said to—up to 60 percent. Some people are more comfortable claiming a visual style over, say, an emotional one. Regardless of the percentages, the Visuals do lead the pack of communicators. They love color and load their speech with descriptive terms. These types drink in the world with their eyes. Once you zero in on them, you will note that they frequently glance upward in order to access the information they need. That is because they are looking up into their mind's eye to see a mental image. Your words are creating a visual picture for them, and the more visual you are, the more comfortable they will be with you. Visual people also tend to speak faster, as images typically flash through their minds at a rapid pace and their words need to keep up with the pictures. When speaking with someone who is visual, you can help build rapport by occasionally looking up as well. This sends an unconscious signal that you are just like him.

Visual Terms

Can you picture that?
Just envision this.
This isn't what it appears to be.
It's a transparent deal.
Let me illustrate my point.
Here's what the plan looks like.
Our goal is in sight.
Can you see what I mean?
It's crystal clear.
Can you show me how this works?
Let's take a closer look at that deal.

Here's a demonstration of our product.
Look here, we have a lot to offer your clients.
You are a sight for sore eyes.
Imagine what we can do. (That's right. Imagine is a visual word, because when you say that, you are asking someone to see a photo.)

Auditory Communicator: I hear

Style: Talks to oneself; often hears thoughts

Go back to the beginning of this chapter and read the Hemingway quote again. Pretty clear which type he is, isn't it?

In an environment ruled by sight, the Auditory processes through sound. Try to describe something visually to an Auditory and you might meet with some stumbling blocks. You can build her a beautiful picture, but it won't be as potent; instead, you have to send your message in sound. Auditories are sending their message that way, and they are (unconsciously) asking you to reciprocate.

Have you ever gone to lunch with someone who cringed and complained that the background music—music you hadn't even noticed until then—was too loud? Or have you worked with someone who could tell you what a coworker in the next cubicle was whispering to someone else? Both were probably Auditories.

One of my friends can tell which actors are playing the characters in his kids' cartoon shows just by hearing their voices. Although his visual wife would recognize the actors if she saw them, she has trouble identifying those people by their voices.

These communicators will vary their rate of speech, their pitch, and their tone of voice more than Visuals. Their voices can be, well, musical and melodious.

Since they work better off sound, they might look in the direction of your face but perhaps slightly through it, because your face, regardless of how appealing, just might stand in the way of their understanding. They might turn away and look to the left or the right as they are trying to process what you are saying. In essence, they are trying to drift off to a level where they can process *words,* not *images.*

When I worked as a hypnotist, I learned the difference in a hurry. The language I used to relax a Visual did not always work well on an Auditory. It took some practice but eventually I learned to tailor a session to Auditories' needs. If somebody talked about what she *saw* in a dream, I knew she was a Visual and I would use visual phrases. If she consistently looked to the left or right, I knew she was *hearing* rather than *viewing* that dream. To this person, I would say something like, "You can hear yourself now. You can hear your words saying . . ." Once I could speak to the Auditory in her own language, it became easier to bypass her critical factor and connect with her subconscious. In addition, when speaking with someone who is auditory, you can build a better connection by also looking off to the side at certain points—again, demonstrating you are similar to your target.

Auditory Terms

Maybe we need to tone this contract down.
Hear me out, will you?
That sounds just right to me.
Listen to the plan I have in mind.
We can't whisper a word to anyone about this yet.
That has a ring of truth to it.
This speaks to everything we've been talking about.
We're going to announce this immediately.
Are you listening to me?
I can't recall the last time we were all together.
We all need to voice our opinions.
It's like music to my ears.
Your message is clear as a bell.
That strikes a chord with me.

Kinesthetic Communicator: I feel

Style: Emotional thinker; emotional speaker

The Kinesthetic is empathetic and emotional. These folks frequently look down when accessing their emotions.

As always, you need to evaluate the situation before you jump to conclusions. Someone who has just lost a loved one may look down out of sadness. That doesn't mean he is kinesthetic; it means he's human.

As *yes* targets, however, they are thinking of how it would feel to say yes, buy that product. Say they are considering buying a new car.

The Visual will glance up, imagining how the car will look speeding around a curve the way cars do in the television ads.

The Auditory will glance to the side, hearing the wind as the car whips around the curves.

The Kinesthetic wants to conjure up what it will feel like to drive that baby. How warm will those heated leather seats feel? How smooth to the touch is the instrument panel, the polished wood?

One of my friends works in a health facility and is very hands-on with her coworkers and patients. It's not just business for her, she says, and she means it. When speaking about her job, she frequently places her right hand over her heart. The way she communicates meshes with and enhances her job responsibilities.

Kinesthetics love to touch things, people, and themselves. If they are considering buying something, they need to feel that product. If they are selling something, they want to feel close to the *yes* target.

They are also comfortable being the first to reach out for somebody else. Touch says a lot about who we are. The more confident we are in ourselves, the more likely that we will initiate the touch. Once again, when speaking with someone who is kinesthetic, you can build a stronger relationship by occasionally glancing down to demonstrate you are feeling the emotion and by extending your hand out to him for a light touch, reconfirming that you are alike in your representational systems.

Kinesthetic Terms

This feels right.
Can you grasp this concept?
Are you motivated?
Before moving on, let's touch on this subject.
Here's the rough draft.
The plan is balanced and fair.

Let's try to stay calm here.
It's piercing the corporate veil.
The firm is stable, and our people have the experience.
This job is a challenge, but the rewards are fulfilling.
Get a grip.
I think the meeting went smoothly.
Let's let Jean cool off before we broach it.
Can you feel the excitement in the room?
This decision carries a lot of weight.

The two final communication types, **Olfactory** and **Gustatory,** are not primary systems. Do you really know anyone who processes entirely by speaking in terms of smell or taste? Occasionally, you might hear someone use a phrase such as:

This deal stinks.
Something about it smells fishy.
Did you get a whiff of that?
John is the only one who came up with a fresh idea.

Or:

I like the way that rolls around in my mouth.
This deal is so sweet it's giving me a toothache.
Don't be so bitter.
What a juicy story.
Don't be a sourpuss.

Although they are less important than the other three systems, olfactory and gustatory are still senses, and they are helpful in building rapport. Use them in context-specific conversations the way you would use salt, to bring out the flavor but not to draw attention to itself.

Now with that gustatory remark, let's see how you can use those two communication systems as secondary styles to turn a business lunch with a colleague or client into a *yes.*

Let's say your lunch partner and *yes* target is a Visual named Patrick. "How's your Southwestern salad?" you ask. "It *looks delicious.*"

Later in the conversation, you evoke the secondary stimulus of taste to enhance your message: "If everything goes the way I am sure it will, Patrick, we will be sitting here a week from now just savoring our victory."

That is the power of the spoken word. By simply changing your vocabulary, you can build rapport with someone that much quicker and make him comfortable with you.

ASK TONYA

Q: What kind of body language could I use in order to appear more confident speaking in front of groups?

Eye contact with your audience is incredibly powerful when speaking to a group. Use small gestures and keep your hands below your shoulders to avoid looking overly dramatic.

A: Take ten very slow, deep breaths right before going out. This will relax you by flooding your brain with additional oxygen and slowing down your heart rate, ensuring you are not shaky.

It will also ensure your voice is not high pitched, by relaxing your vocal cords to their normal position. Do not lean your body to the side; stand with weight balanced equally on both legs. Make eye contact with participants; this is incredibly powerful. Don't just glance at them—speak to them. Use small gestures, keeping your hands below your shoulders to avoid looking overly dramatic (unless, of course, overly dramatic is the goal of your speech). Keep your shoulders down and relaxed. Too many speakers I watch get nervous, and as a result, their shoulders lift toward their ears due to the tension. They wind up looking like they have no necks! Don't fidget, and don't keep anything in your hands except, perhaps, a PowerPoint clicker.

MIXING AND MATCHING COMMUNICATION STYLES: BLENDS AND PATTERNS

One of the most important takeaways of a discussion on representational systems is that these systems cross. Avoid the temptation of thinking of someone as a pure and total anything. That would make this business of communication a paint-by-number process, and it would make life a lot less interesting.

You might encounter a visual person who changes when discussing a kinesthetic situation. Or you might be able to do as we did in the last example (with the *yes* target's salad) use a gustatory remark to enhance a visual person's experience.

We aren't just one representational system, and we don't stay in just one system either. Think of the way you move from one representational system to another as mini-transitions between the senses. As you switch from one to another, your eyes follow the pattern and correspond with the system you are using. Suppose you are primarily a Visual and I ask you if you have ever cut yourself shaving.

"Of course," you say. "And by the way, that's a stupid question, Tonya."

"Sorry. But I really do want to know about one time you cut yourself shaving."

Your eyes dart down and right to remember the *feeling* of being cut. Then they move to the upper left as you assess a *picture* of the cut.

In order to move into another person's world, and in order to get that *yes,* you need to be looking at more than *what* she does. You must also look at the *order* of what she does.

ASK TONYA

Q: I am a pharmaceutical sales representative, and although I like and excel at my job, I can't seem to convince Jane, my district manager, to recommend me for a promotion.

I'm sure that I am part of the problem. Each time we meet, she intimidates the hell out of me. Right away, I've got my hands on my hips, and I can just tell that she wants to get away from me as fast as possible.

That diminishing attitude of hers shows up in her speech, as well. Even though my name is Melinda, Jane frequently calls me Melissa. Please help me turn this around and get the promotion I deserve.

A: You are right. Your manager does intimidate you. And you are compounding the problem when you place your hands on your hips. This is what is known as a broadside gesture. It's frequently used to dominate, even intimidate. Think of a parent looking down at a disobedient child. Do you really want to send that message to your district manager?

She, in return, is passive-aggressively bullying you by "forgetting" that your name is Melinda, not Melissa. You can change that, however. Start by adapting your body language. Drop the guard (translation: your hands).

OTHER VERBAL TACTICS

Yes Sets: Positive Rhythm

Yes builds rapport just as *no* destroys it. That's why we elicit the pattern of ***yes* sets.** They establish an unconscious pattern of agreement and thus compel the other person to go along with you. Once a listener has formed a consistent response of several *yes*es, he will experience dissonance if he breaks the cycle. For example:

"Hey." [*Head nod*] "Are you having a good day?"

"Yeah, I am."

"What's your name?"

"John Raphael."

"Is that R-a-p-h-a-e-l?"

"Yup, that's it."

"Well, John, it's a beautiful sunny day, isn't it?

"It certainly is."

"You picked a perfect day to purchase a convertible." [*Finishing off with a suggestion*]

"Absolutely."

This is your goal: Just keep those *yes*es coming. Most of us don't start there unless we're primed. Our first response is distrust, and we initially say no. "No, I'm not interested." "No, I don't believe that." "No, not right now."

Remember this: The target who starts in a *no* mode stays in a *no* mode. Once you can get somebody saying yes to you, it's more likely he'll stay in sync with that positive response. You want to get him on autopilot for *yes.* Get him nodding up and down instead of shaking side to side.

Truisms: Verbal Camouflage

Yes sets begin the process. Next come **truisms.** These are possible facts (but not absolutes) that you slip in after you have embedded your *yes* set to help solidify the affirmative pattern. You then follow the truisms with a similar statement that is, in reality, your own opinion. We see this technique all the time on television news. You get truism, truism, truism, *opinion.* Then, truism, truism, *opinion.* It sounds like the news, all right, but it's also somebody's take on the news.

Let's return to the job-interview scenario. You're speaking with the hiring person.

"So I would be working on this floor?" you ask, establishing a *yes* set.

"That's right."

"And I would primarily be handling customer complaints?"

"Yes, at the beginning, at least."

Now that you are sure the person is in *yes* mode, you move into truisms.

"You know, I worked in customer service at my last job. I can easily imagine myself doing that here at your company."

Two statements are true. The third is your opinion. They all blend into a positive path to *yes*. Near the end of that path, helping you close the deal or ace the interview, is the presupposition. Known as the presup to its fans, this is an underlying powerful inference or an implied assumption that your *yes* target will accept as truth.

Presupposition: *Yes* Is a Given

"My sister-in-law is the best cook in New York." Sure, you might argue with me about who is the best cook in New York, but you will probably overlook the less obvious statement that I have a sister-in-law or the unspoken implication that I am married or that I have a brother who is married.

Suppose you are trying to make a major sale to a married woman. Your presup is: "Lady, you are going to sign this contract today, come hell or high water." That is the message on which you are focused, but you don't blurt it out and send her running from the showroom.

Instead you say, "Do you want your husband to sign this, or are you the one who handles the paperwork?" You appear to be asking who signs the paperwork in the family, not whether or not you've made the sale.

As useful as the presup is, you have to respect your *yes* target and not bulldoze him or her, especially not too early in the process.

A friend of mine needed publicity shots taken and asked me for some leads. She went on to explain that she had called a local photo studio and asked about prices.

"When would you like to book your appointment?" the person who answered the phone asked.

"I have a few questions," my friend said. Translation: "How much do you charge?"

"Why don't we just book your appointment, and then we can answer whatever questions you have. What works best for you, morning or afternoon?"

This is too abrupt. The person who took my friend's call didn't build rapport and didn't ask meaningful questions. She just tried to get the appointment. Effective presups are more subtle than that.

Another colleague of mine attended a meeting for a possible consulting job. Her presup was: "I'm getting the contract." In the meeting (after the *yes* sets and the truisms), she asked, "So, do your attorneys have to review the contract, or can I just send it over to mine?"

Remember back when you created that unique selling point for yourself? This is the time you must take it out and study it. It's your basic list of presups. You already know who you are; the USP will help you focus your message.

Nominalizations: Slip Past the Critical Factor

Read the following three sentences and consider the first image that comes to mind.

> What a beautiful woman.
> What a beautiful dessert.
> What a beautiful dog.

Beautiful is nonspecific. The woman could be blonde or brunette, tall or short, Marilyn Monroe or Michelle Obama. The apple pie you imagined may be somebody else's crème brûlée. Your standard poodle could be my springer spaniel. In other words, the image is filtered through your own perception.

When someone uses a **nominalization,** we must ask deeper questions to fully understand her definition of a word (in this case, *beautiful*). That's because the word has no absolute definition. *Brick* can't be a nominalization. It's just a brick; it's tangible. To a single woman who has worked all week at the office, *tranquility* might make her think of lighting a candle, doing some yoga, and meditating. For a stay-at-home mom, it might be the few moments after she gets the kids off to school.

If you've ever been on a cruise, you know that the term *formal attire* means anything from "short and strapless" to "sweats and tennis shoes." At an office, *casual day* may be translated as "Dockers and loafers" or "cutoffs and flip-flops." A nominalization is hypnotizing because it forces someone to focus inward. She has to go inside to get her own frame.

President Obama's main theme was Change We Can Believe In. This is an excellent nominalization. Both the words *change* and *believe* have different meanings attached to different filters in our minds. The vague statement, however impassioned, offers each individual who hears it a different meaning, and all of those meanings are good.

When building rapport, use positive nominalizations to send your target inward. "Wow, this is such a *friendly* environment. I can see that I'd be really *comfortable* here."

The mind can handle only so many things at once. The *yes* target goes to his or her definitions of *friendly* and *comfortable*, and you slip in a command: "Knowing that I'm going to be working here makes me feel good."

Your target is already busy processing his definitions of friendly and comfortable, and when he hears *feel good,* your command ("Knowing that I'm going to be working here . . . ") goes right in under the radar.

Tag Questions: *Include,* Don't *Beg*

Tag questions are typically invoked to bring another into a conversation or to encourage a response from your target. They can also be used as a tool to make it easier for your target to agree with you, because if he or she disagrees with the tag, it puts a breach into the conversation. In addition, tag questions can be part of your *yes* set to help develop rapport.

Typical tag questions:

Can't you?
Doesn't it?
Aren't you?

Don't we?
Isn't it?
Can we?

With positive statements, the tag is negative most of the time. With negative statements, you need positive tags.

"It was a great meeting [positive statement], wasn't it [negative tag]?"

"We see eye to eye on this [positive statement], don't we [negative tag]?"

"You still aren't sure about this [negative statement], are you [positive tag]?"

"They won't listen to our side of this [negative statement], will they [positive tag]?"

As a rule, using tag questions is a dominant rapport builder. It can also be submissive: "We probably ought to accept his proposal, shouldn't we? Suddenly, the tag question isn't asking, Don't you agree? Instead, it's asking, Is this all right with you? Do I have your permission?

Tags are great, but only in the right pitch and context: "Looks like a great day out, *doesn't* it?" Speak your tag in a way that's strong, confident, and inclusive.

Now you are able to recognize and respond to different communication styles. These styles are the key to increased rapport. People will bond with you without being aware of why you make them comfortable. The next tool will help you create expectations. It's called priming, and you can do it with a single word.

SEVEN

PRIMING

Plant Positive Verbal Seeds

The tongue can paint what the eye can't see.

—*Chinese proverb*

Successful	Thriving
Respected	Appreciated
Confident	Loved
Energetic	Positive
Victorious	Secure

I just gave you a gift, and it's one that you can give to your colleagues, clients, and loved ones every day. Prime them with positive messages and the rewards will be immediate.

PRIMING

Priming is the process by which you activate specific associations in memory. Priming taps into clusters of neurons where information is stored. When a cluster is activated, surrounding clusters that store similar information come to the forefront of the conscious mind.

Beer commercials prime us to think of good times and sex appeal. It's not the beer we crave but the feelings the images evoke. In school, kids are primed to recognize certain symbols: the golden arches (McDonald's), the double *D* (Dunkin' Donuts). This priming is supposed to help them learn better. But what are they learning? That McDonald's is where you go when you need a break today? A place you deserve? Kind of scary, isn't it?

Priming is not mind control, and most primes won't last forever. I can't prime you today for next week, but I can prime you now for immediate results.

New York University students—unaware that they were subjects in a priming study—were asked to make four-word sentences out of a list of five-word sets. The sentences contained words to prime the students for thinking about old age: *wrinkle, bingo, forgetful, lonely, Florida*—and the word *old* itself. The priming was so effective that students left walking slowly, acting out the external demonstration of their internal priming.[13]

These findings underscore how open to suggestion we really are. The words you prime a colleague or manager with can change that person's mental attitude. It makes sense, then, to deliver a positive message.

Harold Kelley did a study in 1950 describing a guest lecturer who would be coming to talk to the class. Before the lecturer came, Kelley gave the students a paragraph-size description of him. Half were told, "People who know him consider him to be rather cold, industrious, critical, practical, and determined." The other half were told, "People who know him consider him to be warm, industrious, critical, practical, and determined." All the students then heard the lecture from the guest.

What was the priming effect? Fifty-six percent of the students who were told that he was warm were willing participants in the class. Only 32 percent of the students who were told he was cold participated in the discussion. In addition, those who were told he was warm rated him as more considerate, good natured, and humane than those who had been primed with the negative description. This demonstrates how significant that initial filter can be.

Prime Yourself to Others Ahead of Time

Use the buddy system to prime others who don't know you about what to expect. Go back to your USP. Suppose you want to be seen as enthusiastic, positive, passionate, and fun. That's what your buddy says. "Wait until you see how passionate she is. She's absolutely enthusiastic and positive."

In return, you carry information about your friend back to a group with whom you are acquainted. Plant those verbal seeds about each other and positive impressions will blossom for both of you.

Situational Priming

Although priming is usually thought of as a way to influence an individual with words, an environment itself can be a prime. In other words, when you walk into a particular place, you have certain expectations, and so does everyone else in that place, even if they're unaware of the fact. Those expectations change depending upon whether you are in a nightclub, a library, or a church, or at a political rally. Prepare yourself by knowing how the other people in an environment are primed, and what emotions—from introspective to outlandish—that prime will elicit.

False Memory

If you can't trust your own memory, what can you trust? Certainly not the people who might try to use that memory to their advantage. A study done by Loftus and Palmer discusses how language can alter our memory of an event. Their study demonstrated the power of perception. Two experiments were performed in which subjects viewed films of automobile accidents and then answered questions about events occurring in the films. When asked about the speed of the cars when they "hit," the subjects estimated speed as thirty-four miles per hour. When asked about the speed of the cars when they "smashed," the subjects estimated the speed as 40.5 miles per hour. *Smashed* literally carried more impact than *hit*.

One week later, those same participants were asked, "Did you see any broken glass?" The individuals who heard the word *smashed* were more than twice as likely to answer in the affirmative, even though there was no broken glass in the film.[14]

In a separate study, researchers found that faked video evidence could dramatically affect people's perceptions of events. Volunteers took part in a computerized gambling scenario and were given a pile of fake money to gamble with. They also shared a pile of money that represented the bank. The video footage of the session was tampered with to make it appear as if the research team member sitting next to each subject was not putting money back into the bank. One third of the volunteers were told that the person next to them was suspected of cheating. Another third were told that the person sitting beside them had been caught cheating on camera. The remaining third were shown the doctored video footage. Researchers asked all volunteers to sign a statement only if they had witnessed the cheating.

Almost 40 percent who had seen the doctored video signed the statement, and when researchers asked a second time, an additional 10 percent signed. Look at the difference with the group who were told the cheating had been caught on film but hadn't actually seen the video: Only 10 percent signed. And of the group who were simply told about the cheating, only 5 percent signed.

Although we know how easy it is to manipulate digital images, these images are such powerful primes that they can induce people to testify about something they never witnessed.[15]

Speaking of witnessing, I've seen, on a personal level, the astounding way false memory works. My neighbor's son went to preschool, which left his young sister home with their mother all day. When her son expressed his unhappiness about all the Mom time his sister was going to get, the mother said, "Oh, she's going to preschool too."

It was a well-meaning fib. Each day as they drove past the junior high, Mom pointed out the sister's "preschool." She mentioned her kind teacher with the long braids. As a result, the son was happy in his own preschool. Time passed, and everyone forgot the imaginary preschool, or so Mom thought.

When it was time for the son to attend junior high, he asked, "Isn't that where Lori went to preschool?"

"Lori didn't really go to preschool there, honey," Mom said. "There is no other preschool. I just told you that because you were so upset about your sister staying home with me."

"No," said Lori, "I went to that preschool, Mom. Remember the teacher with the braids who was so nice? Remember, we even celebrated my birthday there."

Without meaning to, my friend had created a false memory for her daughter. That's pretty scary. Be aware that this is a very powerful tool that people will use to manipulate you and your memory of a given situation.

Here is one of my favorite simple examples of priming that my children taught me. (*My kids* are teaching *me* approaches to influence.)

Say "silk" five times.

silk

silk

silk

silk

silk

Now spell "silk."

s-i-l-k

What do cows drink?

Did you say "water," the correct answer? Or did you say "milk" because you were primed with the rhyming combined with the cow-milk association?

Labeling Technique

This simple priming technique will help somebody else get in touch with his own ability and potential. You create a label for the other person based on a trait or ability and then make a request that will force the person to draw on that quality. In some work environments, many employees, including managers, doubt their writing ability. By complimenting someone when he writes an effective memo or letter, you attach that label ("effective writer") to him. Then when you ask him to write something for you, he has the tools to put aside doubt and live up to the label.

Criticism can keep us from growing. If you say to a colleague, "I could tell that was your first speech, Shannon. Man, you looked nervous," how is Shannon ever going to get past her fear? Instead compliment her on the one or two things she did right. Next time there's an opportunity, ask, "Shannon, would you lead this discussion group?"

Primed for Beauty

Priming can also be nonverbal. In fact, findings published in the journal *Emotion*, a publication of the American Psychological Association, described three experiments to investigate the preference for beauty.

The first study tested the idea that beauty can be assessed rapidly. Participants rated pictures briefly displayed on a computer screen of nonfamous males and females taken from three different high-school yearbooks and the Internet. Although those who participated reported that they could not clearly see the faces, they accurately rated the attractiveness of the faces they had glimpsed for less than a second. They were able to make an unconscious assessment of beauty.

Researchers also explored priming and whether or not seeing a pretty face makes us more likely to associate that face with positive attributes. Again, they briefly showed a face on the screen and followed it shortly thereafter with a word in white text on a black screen. They told participants to ignore the face and timed them on how quickly they could classify the word as either good or bad. Almost uniformly, response times to good words, such as *laughter* and *happiness,* were faster after viewing an attractive face.

They repeated the priming test using images of houses to see whether the beauty bias is a general phenomenon or one that is limited to socially important stimuli. In contrast to the experiment with faces, response times to good words were not faster after the subject viewed an attractive house. Our fascination with beauty appears limited to people.[16]

PRIMING FUTURE DOCTORS

By now you're starting to see how subtly priming can shape opinions. An article in *Archives of Internal Medicine* suggests that pharmaceutical companies actually prime medical students with free notebooks, ballpoints, clipboards, and calendars printed with the names of drugs. A study to discover just how influential the giveaway items are involved three groups of medical students. The first group comprised 154 students who attended the University of Pennsylvania School of Medicine. The school has a policy that forbids most free gifts, samples, and free meals offered by drug companies. The second group contained 198 students from the University of Miami Miller School of Medicine, which does not prohibit the common marketing practice of handing out promotional items. Students were asked to match drug brand names to their perceived attributes of the drugs.

By documenting the differences in reaction times, the researchers were able to measure the students' unconscious attitudes toward the drugs. Students also completed a questionnaire that asked them specifically to list which cholesterol-lowering drug, Zocor or Lipitor, was superior in terms of safety, efficacy, and convenience. They didn't know that the clipboard and small items they were given promoting Lipitor had anything to do with the study.

The third group, the control group, contained 171 students who were not primed by exposure to gifts advertising any drug. The students at Miami, where freebies from drug companies are allowed, demonstrated a much stronger preference for Lipitor after exposure to promotional items, while fourth-year students at Penn, where drug companies' promotional items are prohibited, had weaker preferences toward Lipitor than the control group.[17]

You need to recognize when you are being primed. When somebody is introduced as this spectacular individual, be aware of how you are expected to react. Maybe the person really is spectacular, or maybe the statement is just priming you to believe so.

Different environments will call for different primes. Visual primes such as letters of appreciation in a car salesperson's office mean more than top sales awards. However, a top customer-service award *is* a positive visual prime. Others might be awards or letters of appreciation from service groups such as Little League or Big Brothers Big Sisters. These lead you to see the businesspeople as good human beings.

On my first visit to meet with the woman who is now my chiropractor,

I noticed the visual primes in her office were in the form of letters from former and current patients. They all addressed her by her first name, and although I knew their purpose, I still felt better about my choice. Before we so much as met, those primes had made her more approachable than she had been before I walked into the waiting room.

JUST LIKE ME EQUALS *I LIKE YOU*

Studies have shown that people frequently marry others whose names, either first, last, or both, resemble their own. We are attracted to the familiar. Participants in one study were more attracted to people whose experimental code numbers resembled the numbers in their own birth dates and those whose surnames had the same letters as their own. They were also more attracted to those whose jersey numbers matched theirs.[18]

Do you think it's a coincidence that Dennis is the fourth most popular name among U.S. dentists? Could we be drawn to our professions by their similarities to our names?

ASK TONYA

Q: Do you have any tips for someone (me!) on how to control talking too fast while addressing others? I also have a tendency, when I do this, to interrupt in order to get my point across. As a result, I feel rude and clumsy when trying to establish rapport with another person.

A: Here are some tips for slowing down: Be self-aware. This is the most important one. Before each interaction, recognize that you have a tendency to talk too fast and focus on slowing down. Take a bunch of deep breaths, which will help to relax you before you speak to someone. Practice speaking slowly while you are alone. As with anything else, practice makes perfect.

FEELING WATCHED?

People are more honest when they're being watched, even if the eyes watching them are not real. Three psychology professors at Newcastle University conducted an experiment in their department's coffee area. Colleagues and students were able to help themselves to coffee and were asked in return to leave the equivalent of fifty cents for coffee and thirty cents for tea. For ten weeks, the professors alternated two posters—one of flowers and one of disembodied staring eyes—over the area. On the weeks the eyes were "watching" them, people contributed 2.76 times more money than they did when the flower poster was up.

In a similar study set on Halloween, mirrors were placed outside a house. Children were told to take only one piece of candy so that there would be plenty for everyone. When the mirrors reflected their images back at them, most children took only one piece of candy. Even when primed for honesty, 8 percent of the kids took more than their share. When there was no mirror and therefore no self-surveillance, 33 percent were dishonest.[19]

Priming is more than buttering up your *yes* target. It's conditioning and preparing your target for the best possible you. By using positive primes, you can elicit positive thoughts. By avoiding negative primes, you can avoid negative thoughts in yourself and in others.

Next, we're going to look at one of the most powerful combinations of verbal and nonverbal tactics, and you'll learn how to *lead* someone else by using mirroring.

EIGHT

MIRROR, MIRROR

"Life, like a mirror, never gives back more than we put into it."

—*Anonymous*

You're sitting with a colleague over coffee, happily engaged and not the least bit bored. He reaches up, covers his mouth with his hand, and yawns. Really big. Ahhh.

You yawn.

If a third person is part of this coffee meeting, *she* probably yawns as well.

As a matter of fact, you might find yourself yawning right now as you read this.

Or:

A business colleague, perhaps a friend, is assigned at the last minute to give a speech in front of a group of clients. She's absolutely lost. Her voice is too low. Her hands are visibly shaking, her movements robotic. Even in the back of the room, you can feel her fear. Suddenly, you are yanked back to *your* first public speech and how absolutely awful you were.

You sit through the torturous minutes, struggle with your colleague through every stutter, every mispronounced word, and hope she will improve. She doesn't. Sweat pours off her forehead. Her face is red now and, you realize, so is yours. Heat floods your cheeks.

WHAT'S GOING ON?

Your mirror neurons are at work, and you are unconsciously adopting the same behavior as the yawning colleague or terrified speaker.

Your **mirror neurons,** believed to be the root of empathy, are motor neurons—that is, nerve cells that control your muscles and, by extension, how your body moves. They make you more, well, human. We're evolutionarily built to bond with each other, and mirror neurons are an inborn order to do so. They have been discovered in primates and humans alike. What's amazing about these cells is that they make us react not only when we carry out an action but even when we just see, hear, or even suppose that someone is about to carry out an action. They make us literally *feel* that action in our body.

If you have ever felt yourself jerk back at a scary moment in a movie or cried during a Hallmark commercial, you've experienced your mir-

Family members mirroring each other.

ror neurons at work. Even the television networks make use of them by incorporating laugh tracks on shows to stimulate our mirror neurons so we laugh more easily at home. Laughing, just like blushing, is contagious. The mirror neurons in the right parietal operculum are the ones that map out other people's actions and help us sync with their movements.

In 1996, at the University of Parma, researchers Giacomo Rizzolatti and Vittorio Gallese defined this previously undiscovered class of brain cells. Neurologist Vilayanur S. Ramachandran, who is best known for his work with phantom limbs, autism, and synesthesia, believes that the discovery of mirror neurons "is the single most important . . . story of the decade." More than that, he "predict[s] that mirror neurons will do for psychology what DNA did for biology: They will provide a unifying framework and help explain a host of mental abilities that have hitherto remained mysterious and inaccessible."[20]

So what does this mean to you as you work toward achieving that *yes*? Well, most important, if your brain *unconsciously* forced you to mirror another person, that means you can also *consciously* mirror him. And what good will that do? Mirroring is particularly useful in establishing rapport, and rapport leads to trust. Why does it work? It turns out we can be pretty simple creatures—we learn as children to be most comfortable with people who are just like us. So, by mirroring behavior, you encourage others to think that you're just like them and, by extension, to unconsciously trust you.

No doubt you've been mirroring other people's behavior most of your life without realizing it. I have a wonderful friend who whenever exposed to someone with even the slightest accent will immediately incorporate the accent and feed it back to his target. The first few times I witnessed this, I silently wondered if he did it on purpose. After knowing him for years, I now recognize that this is just his way of unconsciously bonding with others. It doesn't matter what accent it is; within minutes, he can perfect it and use it in its subtlest form so you hear hints of it—just enough to make his target unwittingly comfortable.

Usually, you will find mirroring happens naturally with those who make you feel comfortable, and even, at times, with those you dislike. It's almost second nature. Yet when using mirroring in a targeted fashion, as a way to establish rapport with your *yes* target, it feels like magic. It certainly did the first time I tried it.

When I first learned about mirroring, the concept sounded pretty simple: Just match someone else's behavior in order to establish a subconscious connection. It wasn't until I tested it that I realized the immense power that mirroring both verbal and nonverbal language could carry. At the time, I simply wanted to see if it worked. No way was I going to try it out on my boss or client, though. I'm sure you've figured out that it is best to practice these techniques in line at the bank and work your way up to the boardroom.

So, here I was, having lunch with an associate, one who already liked me, so it was okay if this little experiment flopped. She made a reference to something visual, and I followed her lead, feeding something visual back to her. The conversation was light and easy. We were making jokes. We commiserated about a troublesome client. I noticed that her breathing was shallow, and so I matched my own to hers. I watched her posture. She had an open frame; I had an open frame. She gestured low; I gestured low. She was smiling; I was smiling. She lifted her right hand; I lifted my left hand. It was working!

To confirm my hypothesis I had to see if she would mirror me. You see, when mirroring is in full effect, your subject will unconsciously mirror you back. Without warning, I picked up a pen that was sitting on the table. Immediately, she picked up her fork. Just like that, the pendulum swung to a *yes* position. In fact, she wouldn't have even had to pick up the fork for me to know that I had her. A subtle twitch of her hand would have indicated the same thing. We were on the same wavelength, and I had guided her there. In formal terms, this is called **leading**; it's the process by which you usher your subject, your *yes* target, into matching your actions. And once she's there, you can be sure you've established a harmony that brings you one step closer to *yes.*

Student and teacher mirroring.

So let's recap, because I am sure you can see the power here:

- First, we connected verbally. I matched her representational system: She said something about *seeing,* and I said something about *seeing.*
- Next, I followed up by commiserating with her about something troubling her, a pesky client.
- Finally, I mirrored her body movements for a few moments. She sat up straight; so did I, and so on.

Voilà! In sync.

MIRRORING IN FIVE STEPS

Now we're going to focus on going from mirroring to leading, and from there to *yes.* We'll start with body movements and move on to facial expressions, breathing, voice, and blinking. Finally, you'll see how to incorporate language for total mirroring. Before we start, though, it's important to understand that successful mirroring is not just mimicking the other person. The moment someone feels you're playing monkey see, monkey do, the game is over, and you lose.

Step 1: Body Movements

Begin with the body, because that's what you see first. Does the person talk with her hands? You can do the same. High gestures or low gestures? Check it out—it makes a difference. He crosses his legs; you do the same. She smoothes her hair; you run your fingers through yours. She tilts her head when making an important point; you tilt and nod in agreement. Of course, you want to mirror the movements and connect with the unconscious mind—not with the conscious. That means you need to be subtle; if you're over-the-top, you'll attract attention to your actions and end up looking like a desperate stalker (which will have the opposite effect you're going for!).

Cross-mirroring is less obvious than body mirroring. You don't need to replicate *exactly* what your *yes* target is doing. He taps his foot; you could tap a finger. She puts her hand through her hair; you adjust your eyeglasses. Another strategy is pretending your subject is the mirror image of yourself: She lifts her left shoulder; you lift your right.

Step 2: Facial Expressions

All humans have a core set of five facial muscles that are believed to control our ability to produce a set of standard expressions. However, as I mentioned earlier, Paul Ekman found that there are actually forty-three muscles in the human face that can be combined to make many, many expressions.

You already know that smiles are contagious. That's probably one of the reasons we are attracted to positive people. He smiles with his lips together; try doing the same. Stay away from the fake, pasted-on grin, however. You are not a mime; you are a mirror.

Strive to stay in tune with the other person's feelings, not just what she is doing. If the *yes* target is serious, so are you. If she is frustrated or angry, you facially share some of her frustration by knitting your brow and blowing out air in exasperation. Is he confused? You tilt your head in perplexity. The goal is to share the same animated expressions, achieving facial harmony.

You do this not to make her more frustrated or angry, but to connect with her and move her into your frame. You've already learned how to reframe experiences. Moving another person into your frame requires rapport and trust.

She says, "Can you believe I was stuck in traffic for twenty minutes on the way here? I'm furious!"

"Twenty minutes," you reply. "Can you believe these streets?"

You **don't** say, "Sorry to hear that, now let's look at this big fat contract I want you to sign."

If you move too fast, you might notice some signs of hesitation. Your *yes* target bites her lip. Is something you're saying making her uncomfortable? Is she biting her lip while you're smiling? Well, then you are not in the same place. You are disregarding her frame of mind. Part of the mirroring process is subtly acknowledging her current emotion, and slowly changing the topic of conversation; steer her into a better frame.

Step 3: Breathing

As a hypnotist, I know there is no bigger rapport builder than matching breathing. The success of group hypnosis stems from getting the group to breathe in sync. When I work in large settings, I always instruct a group, "When I count to three, everybody breathe in through the nose. Great. Hold it. Exhale now." Once I've done that six or seven times, I have trained them to breathe in unison. Everyone senses (and hears) everyone else breathing. Unconsciously, they fall into sync and drop down into a much deeper trance because they hear the other participants' repetition of breath in unison.

This is another technique that you can practice while in line for your next latte. You need to baseline the *yes* target's breathing pattern. When we're nervous, we breathe faster, so give it a few minutes before you try to mirror. Watch the rise and fall of an individual's shoulders. That will give you an indication of his or her breathing style. Does the person breathe shallow or deep? Rapid or slow? Don't deplete your oxygen supply trying to figure it out; just practice matching the depth and frequency of his breathing. It's a very subtle tool, but synchronized breathing is extremely effective in creating connections.

Step 4: Voice

Tone, pitch, rate, and volume are extremely important for building rapport in a face-to-face conversation, but absolutely essential for making a connection over the phone. Extroverts, dominant personalities, and alphas speak more loudly than others. Regardless of where your personal volume control is set, adjust your tone to the other person's.

If the voice is soft, slightly lower yours. If it is varied with an up-down, musical cadence, try varying your own speech. Slow talkers have a difficult time building rapport and keeping up with fast talkers. Fast talkers, on the other hand, can become frustrated by those with snail's-pace speech.

Listen to the rhythm. Observe the pace. Then mirror.

Step 5: Blinking

Blink rates say volumes about us. How frequently we blink is a key to our state of mind, and it is another action you can learn to mirror. One study found that during the 1996 presidential debates, Bob Dole averaged 147 blinks a minute, which was several times above normal. President Bill Clinton averaged ninety-nine blinks a minute, but when asked about increases in teen drug use, which was a sensitive issue at the time, Clinton's blink rate increased to 117 times per minute.

I know. Right now, you're probably saying, "Tonya, how am I even going to hear what this person is telling me when I'm trying to do everything from mirroring his breathing to figuring out how many times he blinks?" Here's my answer: Take your time. You won't become a mirroring master overnight. Don't even worry about blinking until you are comfortable with the other four techniques. Once you are, doing a baseline reading of your *yes* target will come easy. Then you'll be ready to move on to blinking.

To begin, gauge the person. People typically blink eight to twelve times a minute. Ideally, you will just keep up with the blink rate. If he blinks three times a minute and you blink ten times, bring your blink rate down. If he blinks ten times and you blink three, bring your rate up.

And now you sigh heavily and say, "Tonya, I told you I don't have the time to count how many times someone blinks."

Maybe you don't right now, while you are in learning mode. Start simple. Just decide if your target is fast, medium, or slow. That's all. You just want to be similar to him, not identical. It's not a blink-off.

Once you have mastered your five steps, it's time to try **leading.** That's what I did when my colleague at lunch picked up her fork that day. What a feeling when you see that this technique really works and that you can do it! It takes only practice and, most important, awareness of the other person.

After several minutes of mirroring your *yes* target, you make a move that is out of sync. Pick up your pen, as I did, or touch your hair. If the other person follows with a similar movement, you know that you are no longer mirroring; you are leading. You're on your way to *yes.*

Verbal Mirroring

Mirroring doesn't stop with expressions, gestures, carriage, voice, and breathing. You can also mirror communication styles. The same caveats apply. Be careful, and don't turn your mindful mirroring into bad theater. If your *yes* target uses dialect, you can't recklessly feed it back to her. Softening your tone and speaking in a less clipped manner can accomplish the same goal.

At one time it seemed as if corporate America had sent a mass memo informing managers to get more folksy with their speeches. Barack Obama did his version of folksy in 2008 when he was accused of being too intellectual and out of touch. His speech patterns changed. He softened his voice and used that ubiquitous "You all" when addressing voters. If the polls are accurate, his attempt to mirror the way much of America speaks (or thinks it speaks) worked.

Remember when we talked about representational systems in Chapter Six? The three primary ones are **visual, auditory,** and **kinesthetic.** If you are speaking to someone who uses visual terms—as I was in the example with my female colleague—such as, "I *see* what you mean," you can adjust your responses to include her mode of processing to something like, "I'm glad you *get the picture*." Answering with, "I'm glad you *feel* that way," puts you out of sync with your *yes* target; your systems will clash, making rapport much more difficult and an instant connection impossible.

Another way to quickly build rapport is to use the same kind of language your target does, such as unusual catchphrases. If a colleague talks about how boring a meeting was and refers to the participants as "glazers," you can respond by using the same reference.

Speaker: "Didn't Sarah realize that she was speaking to a bunch of glazers?"

Response: "You looked like you were glazing yourself, Joe."

This mirroring is especially powerful when the word is one not used in everyday language. Shared original jargon makes a strong bond, which is probably why professions ranging from medicine and law to sales and journalism develop their own insider vocabulary.

Years ago, a colleague I respected used the phrase "Not to be fresh" whenever she said anything critical of a coworker. More than fifteen years later, I am still using that phrase, and I make special note when others use it around me. Because it is unique, and I am aware of language patterns, when someone I'm talking to uses this phrase, I automatically recognize that rapport is blossoming.

Of course, you cannot continuously match your *yes* target word for word. To engage in mindless parroting would make you appear insincere, to say the least. Use word matching sparingly and rely most of the time on word *patterning.* Word matching is using exactly the same words or phrases. **Patterning** is simply using the same types of words as the speaker—visual, auditory, or kinesthetic.

Word matching:

"Yes, Mr. Parrot, this is a huge event for us, and we want a speaker who can motivate our team in a big, big way."

"What a huge opportunity, Frank. I'm really up for this big, big opportunity."

If you've ever dealt with a really bad salesperson, you have probably endured conversations like this one. You also probably work with people who mirror the patterns of higher-ups. I'm sure it irritates you, and that's because it's so transparent.

I once worked with a charismatic manager who would say, as she walked through the office, "Okay, team, *vamanos.*" It fit her; it worked. The statement became part of who she was. Another manager, slightly higher on the corporate ladder but with far less charisma, stepped out into the hall one day and blurted, for all to hear, "Okay team, vamoose." Everyone made eye contact with each other and silently groaned. This manager so much wanted to capture the magic of the other one that he uttered the phrase first thing every morning. When he did, it was a fingernails-on-the-blackboard moment for all of us.

Even though others in the office could have gotten away with that parroting, this manager could not. The first manager was a true alpha who radiated charm and confidence. She could have uttered any phrase and made it work. The second would have done better to develop his own style and try to find his true Alpha Self instead of absorbing someone else's.

Types of Speech Patterns and How to Match Them

- **Visual communicator:** As we discussed identifying your own system in Chapter Six, visual communicators seem to see pictures in their heads. To bond with them, match visual words and phrases with those of your own: *illustrate, look, sight, clear.*

For example, your manager says, "I can't picture your idea."
"If you have a minute, I can make it crystal clear," you say.

- **Auditory communicator:** If the speaker tends to look to the right or the left side without moving the head up or down when remembering something, or uses auditory words or phrases, reply with other auditory phrases: *hear, ring, listen, whisper.* See the checklist in Chapter Six for more.

Your coworker tells you, "That contract you have been working on sounds like it could be trouble."
You say, "I'll tone down the areas you are concerned about."

- **Kinesthetic communicator:** If the speaker seems to be an emotional person who tends to look down while speaking, respond with kinesthetic terms: *grasp, rough, touch, calm.*

Your client tells you, "I feel really good about your meeting."
"I feel the same way," you reply. "It's going to be smooth sailing."

SURVIVING THE ROUGH SPOTS

The road to *yes* has a pothole or two along the way. No path is entirely smooth, and verbal mirroring is no exception. I could write an entire book about this chapter alone. Give yourself time to digest the information, as well as to practice each technique.

Here's a quick review.

Start with the bank teller, the deli clerk, the postal clerk, even the people you make small talk with online, at the salon, at the basketball game, in line for the bathroom. In other words, any- and everyone who does not directly affect your career should be considered practice.

Go easy. Cartoonish gestures and giant winks won't get you to *yes*. They'll only get you filed under "D" for "desperate to fit in."

Be aware of the other person. It's not enough to mimic. You have to understand the meaning of the gesture.

Care. This is about empathy. If you're crassly trying to use another person, and that's all you're doing, it is going to show. Sincerity is the name of the game.

ASK TONYA

Q: I'm in sales and I have a hard time trying to convince someone that my product is better than product X. I'm not shy, but I don't seem to have the right tactics down. What is the quickest way to close the sale?

A: Well, since you don't mention what you sell, I will give you a generic answer: Gain trust. I can't emphasize enough that trust is one of the most significant traits an individual has to offer. People can be very suspicious of anyone trying to get their business and change their minds. You need to convince your clients/customers that you are genuine, knowledgeable, and in for the long haul. What does this mean? It means you must know your facts. You must know all the information about your own product as well as your competitors' products. Give them a reason to listen to you and have confidence in you—and your sales will go up. Building trust is also sharing commonalities and making your target laugh. If you can demonstrate a shared interest and build rapport, he will trust you. For example, if your target mentions that he works on Wall Street, and you have a friend, sibling, client, or know anyone who also works on Wall Street, bring it up. Familiarity helps build trust.

NINE

ANCHOR THE MOMENT

"We all have our time machines. . . . Those that take us back are memories. And those that carry us forward are dreams."

—*Über-Morlock in* The Time Machine

An anchor can steady a ship in choppy water, and it can do the same for you. Your emotional anchor is the link between a memory and the physical reminder of that memory. The easy definition of an anchor is a stimulus that is associated with a physiological state. When the anchor is activated, the associated physiological state is triggered.

Years ago, I had an assistant named Jim. Every morning, he would say, "I'm going for a cup of coffee, Tonya."

Then, I would call out, "Oh, Jimmm. Get me a cup of tea, will you, please?"

It became a joke for us, an anchor. Part of it was the repetition. The rest was my tone. Even if I said it in the afternoon, I wouldn't have to ask him for the tea. I would only have to call out, "Jimmm?"

"All right," he'd reply, "tea."

We did it completely by accident, and it demonstrates how easily you can anchor someone else.

The technique of anchoring has been compared to Pavlovian conditioning. As we all learned in high-school psychology, Ivan Pavlov conditioned his dogs to salivate the moment the food bell rang, not the moment they tasted or smelled the food. Few remember that the initial intent of the experiment focused on neither food nor ringing bells, but on the gastric function of dogs.

Pavlov discovered that the dogs salivated *before* they tasted the food. No longer interested in the chemistry of saliva, he changed his study and focused on what we know as the conditioned reflex, and that is the reason we still know his name today.

The anchor I just described with "Jimmm" was a nonverbal as well as a verbal one. Although it was verbal because I spoke his name, the paralanguage (tone, pitch, and longer stress) I used added a nonverbal component. We can combine paralanguage with any of the representational systems.

Anchors fall into the categories of the five representational systems. You hear, smell, taste, touch, or see something and it brings you back—you are connected to a memory from your past. Perhaps you hear theme music that instantly recalls the experience of watching a film that had a big impact on you, such as *Psycho* or *Jaws*. How long before you were comfortable showering when you were home alone? And did you stay a little closer to shore when swimming in the ocean? The smell of apple pie gets your olfactory system geared up and perhaps makes you think about Grandma. The taste of malt liquor reminds you of your first encounter with alcohol. The warm sand under your feet makes you think about that summer in the Hamptons. You've probably heard that if you tie a string around your finger, it will serve as a reminder. That's visual and kinesthetic. You see the string, and you feel its presence.

A quick way to learn visual anchoring is to study comedians. Most have a specific area on their studio sets, the way David Letterman or Bill

Maher do, that's anchored to millions and millions of fans. Others need only an expression. Chris Rock will tell a joke, and then will open his mouth and widen his eyes like, "Get it?" Everybody laughs, and that face becomes an anchor for the crowd. All he has to do is make that same face, anytime, anywhere, and everybody will laugh.

Chris Rock. We're primed to respond to his expression.

Dave Letterman had his share of embarrassment in 2009. After a blackmailer attempted to extort money from him, Letterman needed to tell the public about his relationships with female coworkers. So the talk-show host went on the air to set the record straight. He began speaking as his blink rate went up and up and up. His palms were in the upward, submissive pose. He told the audience that he had received a letter saying he had done bad things. The audience burst into laughter. He was serious. He began discussing the fact that he'd had sex with coworkers on the show. Again, the audience laughed.

He was being completely serious, opening up. As he said, "Yes, I have. I have had sex with women who work on this show," the audience not only laughed but they also applauded his disclosure. He covered his mouth with a finger, looked down momentarily, and then continued. His downward gaze suggests that he was experiencing shame and embarrassment, yet the audience still exploded with applause and laughter. After his confession was over—more laughter.

David Letterman at the Ronald O. Perelman Heart Institute dedication and opening. We're conditioned to laugh, even when he's serious.

What was going on here? Was it an unsympathetic audience? No! Not in the least. Letterman chose to make his very serious announcement from the "joke chair," the chair that is anchored to humor. The chair in which he is a comedian. It's the place he sits when he's being funny, and his audience was conditioned to laugh, regardless of what he actually said.

Spatial anchors are equally powerful. Through the political spectrum, every president uses spatial anchoring. Kennedy did. Reagan did. Clinton did. A recent example is one of President Obama's speeches about his healthcare plan in 2009. Please don't think I'm maligning Obama. The man is a magnificent speaker, and his anchoring was so intense in that speech that it was beautiful to watch. In general, when he spoke about the benefits of his plan, he used his left hand. When he talked about the criticism opposing his plan, he used his right hand. He didn't do it all the time—that would have been too obvious.

In this photo taken on June 27, 2009, in Washington, D.C., Barack Obama anchors his points by using his hands.

But most of the time, he anchored all his positive comments on his left hand. At the end of his speech, he used the left hand to rally the crowd. He called on them to support him with the same hand he had used to point out positive aspects of his plan. This comes across naturally, as he is left-handed. It makes sense that he would use his dominant hand to talk about positive aspects as this is what people normally do unconsciously. This sort of spatial anchoring is easily adapted to both your professional and personal life.

"You think this is manipulation?" I might tell my audience as I walk to one side—let's say the left.

Then, as I walk to the right side, I say, "You have no idea how powerful and beneficial this can be."

The left side is where I'm going to be shooting all of my negative comments from. The right side is where I'll talk about the positives. At the end of the speech, I'll make sure I end up on the right side of the platform. I want to be associated with all of those great feelings I've been generating.

POWER ANCHORS LEAD TO *YES*

You can link memories for others as well by sharing a positive emotional moment with them. Then touch them on the shoulder or forearm and raise your voice. Make them associate your gesture with their positive feeling.

Suppose a friend tells you about a trip she took.

"What was your very best experience?" you ask.

"It was when we walked inside Notre Dame in Paris, and there were all these candles," she replies. "There was just darkness and all of that flickering light. And I realized in a way I hadn't before that I really was in France."

You touch her arm and say in a lower and deeper-than-usual tone, "Wow. That sounds magnificent."

Anytime you want to connect her to that moment of excitement, you can repeat the same touch and use that same lower, deeper tone.

You can anchor somebody else's movements to you. Before I give a speech, I might approach the person who is introducing me and make small talk: "Anything exciting happening in your life?"

As he tells me his story, I watch.

He touches his heart. "Oh my god, my daughter got married last week."

Later, I will drop the anchor back on him.

"Oh, my god [*heart touch*], this is going to be such a powerful event." That anchor becomes much more positive than anything I could make up, because it came directly from him.

ANCHOR YOURSELF

Just as you can use anchors to connect others to positive feelings, you can use them on yourself. I have a friend on the California coast who walks at dawn every single morning. Weather has nothing to do with it. Nor does time involved in trudging through all of that sandy beach. When I asked her how she managed to get out of bed before dawn every day, she said, "I take a mental photograph." Yes, she admitted, she had to fight herself all the way to roll out of bed in the wee hours of the morning.

However, once she had walked for several minutes, the endorphins kicked in, and she felt in charge.

How could she motivate herself to walk every day? By taking an emotional photograph of this moment. By reminding herself of how good she could feel once she just did it. In this case, at the height of her euphoria, my friend touched her ring and emotionally "photographed" her feelings and sensations. The next time she was tempted to sleep in, she consciously touched her ring in order to bring back that moment. In doing so, she connected a powerful emotional experience to a gesture.

You can use this technique and instantly connect yourself to your past successes, whether small victories or enormous feats: the way you felt when you turned in that laborious report; the satisfaction of resolving a conflict with a coworker; the elation when that client you'd been trying to win over finally said yes.

Anchors work with each of the senses. You *see* an image of yourself crossing the finish line, winning an award, clinching the speech, or maybe you even see yourself two summers ago in jeans a few sizes smaller. You *hear* the sound of your name spoken by someone who cares about you. You *smell* the coffee shop where you wrote up your last big deal; it's the smell of success. You *taste* the Dom Pérignon with which you toasted your first big deal. You *feel* the supporting back pat of a colleague.

"Okay, I get it, Tonya," you might be saying. "Anchors are everywhere, right?"

They sure are, and that's one reason you need to be sure which message you're anchoring. Just as these techniques can reap positive results, they can also lead to negative connections.

Picture a married couple. The husband comes home and sees that his wife has a scowl on her face.

"What's wrong?" he asks.

"I'm not sure how we can pay the bills this month," she says.

Immediately, he feels the blow to his self-esteem.

A week or two later, he comes in and again sees that scowl.

"What's wrong?" he asks.

As he suspects, she says, "Money. We have more going out than we have coming in."

The anchor is set. The next time this guy sees his wife scowling, he's going to think *money* and what a lousy provider he is. And worst of all, she might be scowling for some completely different reason. Perhaps she just didn't sleep well last night. Maybe she fell down a flight of steps and twisted her ankle that day. It won't matter. The moment she scowls, he'll think about how he can't provide.

Each of us constantly anchors negatives. We don't mean to, but we will continue to do it until we are aware that in doing so, we are transmitting powerful messages to others.

Take me, for instance. If I'm even remotely upset, my eyebrow will lift—not very high, but enough for my husband to notice.

He walks through the door, sees me, and just like that, demands, "What's the matter?"

"Nothing," I lie.

"Tonya, I see it. What's the matter?"

Not every husband analyzes his wife's every expression as carefully as mine does, but you'd better believe most of them do notice, and are affected by your anchors—they see the eyebrow and suddenly feel anxious, knowing that something not so good is up with you.

Anchoring can have a negative effect on each of us. Once you've worn a jacket to a funeral, how often do you reach for it again? How do you feel when you hear that song that played so often when you and your former spouse used to fight all the time?

One of my colleagues was chased by a turkey when she was very young. Now she hates birds. Even the sound of flapping wings can raise her hackles and cause her to hunch her shoulders. Another coworker had a terrifying experience on a plane that suddenly made a crash landing. Now each time he flies he breaks out in a sweat when the plane hits turbulence; the feeling forces him to relive the experience of almost crashing.

This is random anchoring, and it is the way most anchoring occurs in life. That song just happened to be playing. That ocean breeze just happened to drift in. The man just happened to be wearing that scent. Now it will always remind you of that time and whatever you were doing and feeling. You can break these anchors by becoming aware of what they are and what reaction they elicit in you or in others around you. Once you recognize the trigger as well as the response, change that response. Use the steps listed above and create a new reaction to the stimulus. It might take some time to do, but it's worth it.

TEST IT ON YOURSELF

In addition to these naturally occurring anchors, there are many ways to surreptitiously manufacture power anchors in yourself and others. A power anchor is something you create to generate your desired response.

This tool is so versatile that it can be used for everything from weight loss to smoking cessation to mood enhancement. Let's try it right now.

Remember a time when you felt a strong positive emotion: elation, confidence, success, victory. You decide. Reexperience the event through your own senses. How did it look to you? How did it sound? Give this memory everything you have; make it really vivid.

Now, as your emotions become more intense and you start to feel what you felt then, touch your ring or squeeze your thumb and forefinger together for a moment or two. Then think about something completely unrelated (such as your phone number). Repeat the gesture several times, if necessary, to be sure you have captured the moment. If you can't instantly reclaim that experience, go through the capturing process again.

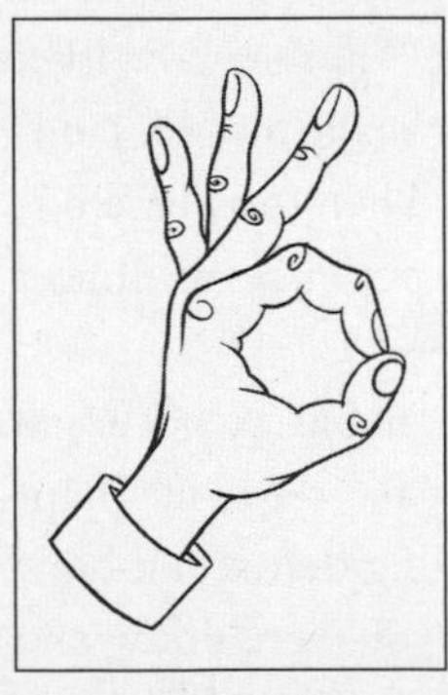

Anchor a thought by pressing finger to thumb.

Now you've created an authentic, wonderful, vibrant memory for yourself. And you can go there anytime you need to access it—all you have to do is repeat that gesture.

In the back of the book, you'll find a game plan for how to break this down. Don't expect to try twelve new tactics the first two days. You need to layer tactics on top of each other. If you piece them out, practicing a little bit at a time, the program as a whole will become second nature.

I still have to remind myself sometimes that I can't fall into autopilot. When you do that, your defenses go down. And when your defenses go down, you're going with the flow, and you're open to other people's manipulation as opposed to directing the encounter yourself. If you aren't the one making the move, somebody else will be.

COUNT THE *F*'S

Read this sentence:

Finished files are the result of years of scientific study combined with the experience of years.

Now count the *F*'s in that sentence. Count them only once—*only once.* Do not go back and count them again.

There are six *F*'s in the sentence. Many find only three. There is no catch. Many people do not see the *F*'s in the word *of.* It has been argued that the human brain tends to see them as *V*'s and not *F*'s.

It takes a long time to make a new neural pathway and a new habit. I never tout this as an overnight process. It's just too much information. So use the plan and really internalize each step.

LAYERING ANCHORS

Suppose a campaign you designed for a client succeeds? You clap your hands together and say, "That was brilliant. You rock." (Assuming, of course, that your client is the "you rock" type). Repeating the gesture and statement in the future will connect your client to his (and your) victory.

You just layered anchors—a gesture and a statement. For maximum benefit, combine anchors in this way. Speak. Touch. Give a visual response, a smile or a frown. Use more than one representational system at a time.

Let's go through another example to demonstrate the power of layering the anchors: Come up with an emotional state that you would like to be able to reach at any time. I think a big one is confidence. Perhaps you are uncomfortable walking into a roomful of people you don't know at a party, bar, or social gathering. Confidence might assist you in doing that. The first thing you need to do is come up with memories of absolute confidence. Perhaps it was last year when the big boss gently punched you in the arm and told you your proposal was the best and he was going with your idea. Great! Not only did that make you confident, but you had the added benefit of an immediate rise in status witnessed by your colleagues. Powerful.

Now, the easiest way to set the anchor is to choose the moment during this experience in which you felt the climax of emotion. In this case, it's when the boss punched you in the arm and congratulated you. Then you need to choose your anchors. I might choose seeing the letters *C-O-N-F-I-D-E-N-C-E* in my mind as my visual anchor; whispering "confidence" as my auditory anchor; and gently tugging my ear as my kinesthetic anchor. Layering all three anchors together will make the effect much stronger each and every time you use it. With your anchors in place, you recapture the experience and go through it second by second, and as soon as the boss offers his congratulations—*bam*. Activate all three anchors simultaneously. Feel the confidence. Repeat this process until you can walk into that roomful of people like a rock star!

Take a look at what you've done here. You have taken the basic idea of anchoring and used it as a tool to "photograph" certain moments and motivate yourself. You have also learned how to go from random anchoring to power anchoring in order to bond with the *yes* targets in your life.

As exciting as this technique can be, it's not without pitfalls. First of all, I don't have to tell you to be careful about how and where you touch business associates. You are looking for rapport, not a slapped face, a proposition, or a trip to HR. Furthermore, if you do touch someone, it needs to be somewhere that isn't constantly triggered. A handshake is not a strong anchor unless it is in some way unique. But remember, it is usually the first connection you share with another person.

Also, you, I, and anyone (including your *yes* target) can smell an insincere anchor a mile away. You're no dummy. If a salesperson asks you how you *felt* when you bought your first car, then waits poised as an eager cat waiting for a mouse, you will know what's going on. So will your *yes* target. For your power anchor to work, you must feel the other person's excitement and emotion yourself.

Instead of asking how you felt, a smart salesperson might ask *why* you bought your first car. What made it special? Asking that gives the impression that the salesperson is trying to find what value that car had, thereby connecting the dots to what you, the customer, think has that same value. "What made that car so great?" This smart salesperson is really covertly asking you to relive that experience so that he can feed back that information to you without looking like the Cheshire cat. It's all about the wording.

Finally, a power anchor is most effective when your target is actually experiencing a moment of extreme emotion, not just recalling one. This occurs less frequently in business than it does at home. But it does occur, and you have the power to incite that same emotion by being excited yourself.

Now that you know how to use power anchors, you will find the opportunities. Keep up with your clients' personal lives. Even by just making small talk, you can elicit great stories and emotions. One of my favorite studies is about Joe Girard, who, according to the *Guinness Book of World Records,* was the world's greatest car salesman for twelve consecutive years. His secret was amazingly simple: All thirteen thousand of his former customers received cards from him every month. The cards were signed by him and carried the handwritten message, "I like you." His buyers always came back to him. Why wouldn't they?[21]

If you are a professional in any field and someone returns to you, you're doing something right, and it's probably something you are doing to make the encounter a personal one. I take notes after a speaking engagement so that when I reply to my host I can mention all of the personal details we talked about.

Perhaps your host went on a cruise. He's a Braves fan. When you write back to him you say, "Thanks so much. By the way, the Mets won that night. Just wanted you to know how jealous I was that you went on a cruise." When he gets that e-mail, the link between you tightens.

You'll find many opportunities to anchor at home, as well. I've discovered that sharing meaningful, fun anchors with my family makes the time we spend together that much more precious. We are movie buffs, and many of our instant bonding moments come from films we have enjoyed. Whether it's repeating a well-known line from a movie, hearing part of the sound track, or using one of the gestures that a character exploits, anchors connect us not only to a movie, but to the joy we shared watching it.

MOTIVATION

Anchoring is a very potent way to self-motivate, as you can associate a positive emotional state with your words or movements. Anchor a feeling of success for yourself so that when you are feeling down, you have a quick pick-me-up. Let's say you are in the middle of a great workday. You are fully immersed and energized—in short, you are in the zone. Either give yourself a verbal cue, such as a word that you like, or perform a gesture, such as putting your thumb and forefinger together. (Do this under the table or desk.) Stay in that place for a few seconds while you repeat the anchor over and over again. This anchor will now be associated with that mental state, and you can use it whenever you feel the need.

If you're a manager, you are probably constantly challenged with how to keep people on track. Even team members need to be able to motivate the other people in their group.

Critiquing an individual is a tough job. The most important aspect of motivational criticism is to stay positive. In Psych 101 we learned to sandwich a positive and then a negative, and close with a positive. "This is a great sales proposal you wrote, Jane; you've really improved since the last one. I think we need more details about our competition and why we are the clear choice, though. Add that, and this will be close to perfect."

Think of criticism as an Oreo. The two cookies are the wonderful things the individual is doing, and the cream is the negative. (I know, you're saying to yourself, When could the cream ever be negative? It's just a metaphor.) Show the person you're critiquing how much you care about him. After all, you wouldn't share Oreos with just anyone, now, would you?

Also make sure you criticize in private. I try not to even reprimand my children in front of each other. Their self-esteem couldn't handle the humiliation of being admonished in front of others.

Criticism should help the person come to a solution. For example, if his numbers are down, what can he do to improve them next time? What negatively affected the past performance and how can it be eliminated in order to get those numbers back up?

Be careful that what you're putting out there isn't a disconnect. Although I will later talk about how finding a common enemy can be a key component to building rapport with another, I don't advise you to gossip or speak ill of others. And I don't suggest you spend time with those who do.

Recently, I talked to a new friend about a project another person and I had done previously. When I said I had been less than thrilled with it, my new friend prodded for more information. I wasn't sure how to answer her request delicately, but then before I could, she stunned me by saying, "Never mind telling me about the negatives. What could we do to make the outcome different?"

She wasn't interested in idle gossip; she was interested in getting to "done" and improving my experience in the process. This is the sign of a person you can trust—someone who motivates, not denigrates.

People who are team builders and who motivate are those who carry the traits of charisma, enthusiasm, and confidence. They recognize the power of working together and allowing everyone to feel important. Team builders and leaders think in terms of appeal to that which is important to the other group members. Motivating others occurs when you target an individual's aspirations, ambitions, goals, and hopes.

A motivator needs to be powerful without being overly emotional. He must convey a sense of passion without demonstrating weakness or vulnerability. Think of the role of the president. He must be a figure of authority without demonstrating his Achilles' heel. When President Obama spoke at a healthcare rally and brought up the letter from Ted Kennedy in which Kennedy requested the letter be read after his own demise, the crowd was silenced, and many were brought to tears. Obama was able to ignite emotion in others while maintaining composure himself.

Howard Dean's shouted concession speech following his third-place finish in Iowa's 2004 Democratic caucuses.

Now, think about Howard Dean and the speech that essentially ended his political career. His passion was so intense that people feared he would not make rational decisions in office.

By offering respect to others, you command respect yourself. People tend to like to be around those who make them better and valued. A powerful motivator is one who always builds up the self-esteem of others.

One of the reasons you'll love anchoring is its warm-fuzzy factor. It helps you share and connect with another person's big moments. It makes the *yes* target—and you—feel good. What better way to conduct business?

Now it's time to get acquainted with the nonverbal aspects of communication.

ASK TONYA

Q: I am a caterer. Although the pay is not great, I love my job. Some of my customers give me big tips. Some simply pay the cost of the event. I treat everyone with warmth and respect. I make small talk and listen when they tell me about their lives. How can I get the non-tippers to tip?

A: Right now you are depending upon the generosity of your clients, and that's not enough. You might try being more proactive. Make one additional small dessert (free of charge) that can be eaten the next day, but don't take it out. Consider the good-bye moment. When your work is over for the night, extend your hand and say, "I am so glad that I could be of service to you." Then, the ace in hole: Hand your client the beautifully wrapped dessert and conspiratorially whisper, "I made this little gift for you to enjoy tomorrow," wink, wink.

Studies have shown that waitresses who touch customers when they return change or charge slips to their tables are more likely to receive bigger tips. If instead of placing dinner mints on the counter, the server hands a patron a mint, the tip goes up. If she hands a mint, starts to leave, then turns, smiles, and hands the customer another mint, the tip will increase 23 percent.[22]

In another study, when librarians touched borrowers for a half second when returning their cards, the borrowers liked them—and the library—more. Believe me, your parting impression will influence your tip. Don't be afraid to touch.

HIS SIGNALS/HER SIGNALS

Touch Equals Power

Even a slight touch packs a punch.

In a 2004 study, eighty-seven male and female university students viewed one of three videotapes of a male and a female having a conversation. The videos were identical, except for the beginning and end. In one, the male touched the female on the shoulder. In the second, the female touched the male. In the last, neither touched the other. The subjects used seventeen adjectives to rate the individuals in the videos. The female was rated most dominant (stereotypically male) when she did the touching, and the male as most passive (stereotypically female) when the female touched him.[23]

PART III

THE NONVERBAL ADVANTAGE

TEN

BODY LANGUAGE ESSENTIALS

"The less you talk, the more you're listened to."

—*Abigail Van Buren*

You will get to *yes* quicker when you understand what your target is really saying, and, surprisingly, the most effective way is to watch him or her. After all, studies demonstrate that the majority of our communication is nonverbal. That's why by combining verbal and nonverbal techniques you can become a communication wizard.

Earlier we looked at the role the brain plays in communication. I think it's important that you understand how it all works so that you know this is not just my opinion; it is science.

Here's what's going on the first time you see someone. During that first one-tenth of a second, you make your initial judgment about a person and his attractiveness, his likability, his trustworthiness, competence, and aggressiveness. This happens on a regular basis, sometimes hundreds of times per day. The results of these encounters become part of our autopilot system, our own little database that determines which characteristics make an individual a *yes* or *no.* Of course, even though these initial judgments take place, if an actual encounter occurs, the next few moments become vital to the impression. How does this work? Your midbrain (amygdala) registers the immediate impression of the person. Is he safe, nonthreatening? How does he rate on the criteria above? Then in comes your neocortex with a more analytical evaluation. Based on your prior experiences, your own little database of filters, your brain click-clicks over the person's approach style, tone of voice, his handshake, his spatial recognition, his smell, his smile—every bit of available data is input and compared with our life's experiences and a *yes* or *no* spits out. That's it—the first impression is now formed. It might not be the correct impression. But an impression is made nonetheless.

FIRST IMPRESSIONS: THE MORE POSITIVE, THE BETTER

As we already discussed, scientific evidence has long supported the theory that the right hemisphere of the brain processes emotion. A second, newer theory suggests that how it does so depends on which emotion is being processed, and whether that emotion is positive or negative.

In a 2009 study of eighty psychology students, researchers found that not only is the right side of the brain more effective in processing emotions, but it processes some faster than others. After looking at a face for only one hundred milliseconds, subjects could detect expressions of happiness and surprise faster than those of sadness and fear. If the results of the study are correct, we may actually process happiness faster than we process sadness, and surprise faster than fear.[24] Just another reason to smile when you're making that first impression.

ASK TONYA

Q: My boss is right-handed. He tends to cross his right leg over his left whenever one of my coworkers speaks during a meeting. I believe that this is his way of telling the coworker he does not like his ideas, because right-handed people never do this naturally.

A: Although statistically speaking more people do cross left over right, 30 to 40 percent of the population (left- and right-handed) cross right over left. You need to norm your boss and determine if this is something he does on a regular basis.

Just as others make instant evaluations of you, your brain is evaluating *them.* So the million-dollar question for all you skeptics out there: Are you receiving accurate information, or has the person you're talking to learned how to convey a favorable impression and hide his true motives? Here's a way to tell.

Study everyone you encounter—longtime colleagues and friends, and strangers you meet on the street. Take notice of their expressions, movements, stance. She might be smiling and putting out her hand, but where are her feet pointing? If it's away from you, she can't wait to get out of there.

"What if that's just how she always stands?" you might ask. "What if you just cross your arms over your chest because it's the way you've always done it?"

That's where this next technique comes in handy.

30 SECONDS TO BASELINE

Everyone I know has made at least one major mistake because he trusted the wrong person. The financial planner who said your money was safe (ahem); the HR director who insisted that what you had shared was confidential; the salesperson who smiled and said those jeans made you look soooo slimmm—liars, all of them.

Right now I'm going to teach you a technique that will forever help to protect you from the liars of the world. It will also help you detect when someone is nervous, upset, or feeling something entirely different from what he is saying. This technique is called baselining, also known as norming, and I mentioned it in Chapter One. I'll bet you've been baselined before. I know I have. In baselining you detect an individual's deceit signals by first detecting his truth signals. Put simply, a truth signal is the way somebody gestures or acts "normally," when not under pressure and not trying to sell himself.

So what does that mean? Well, your goal is to notice someone else's signals when he is calm. How is his handshake—dominant, neutral, or submissive? How is the person standing? What is the position of his trunk and torso? Does he orient toward or away from you? What type of gestures does he use—high upper gestures or lower gestures? What is his neutral facial expression? What about his eyes? Does he maintain eye contact while he speaks, and how often does he seem to blink? Finally, what is her normal eye position when speaking and remembering? Ask innocuous questions that are straightforward and fact based.

During a nonthreatening conversation, casually ask a question that will make her try to remember something visual and factual. "How many years has the company been in business?" "Who is the vice president of the firm?" "What's the circulation of the newspaper?" Watch her face as she answers. Does she look up? Down? To the right or the left?

Soon you'll be aware of how this person recalls facts. Now when you want to test if she's telling the truth about something, you can put your observation to use. Go ahead, ask whatever you want to know. If she has been looking up and to the left when recalling facts, she will probably look up and to the right when fabricating a story. Why? Because she needs to access a different part of the brain to construct a lie than to recall actual details.

Job interview: "How many floors does this company occupy?"

Social interaction: "Oh, so you are a vice president of a bank now? What did you do before you joined Merrill Lynch?"

Parent-to-parent dialogue: "How old is Katie?"

"She's six."

"So is Jaidan. When does Katie turn seven?"

Now that you've baselined your target, you can also determine her representational system. Is she a Visual, Auditory, or Kinesthetic? People tend to move their eyes when they are thinking. When we watch for the movement, we are offered an insight into whether they are thinking in pictures, sounds, or feelings. Do you realize how valuable this information is, how powerful? When you know someone's representational system, you understand her world.

Visuals tend to move their eyes upward. Auditories, on the other hand, usually move their eyes to either side. Kinesthetics frequently direct their eyes downward. A person can "tell" you how she thinks just by how she moves her eyes.

In addition to eye movement, tone of voice is a revealing tool when determining if someone is in a state of agitation. Even a salesperson, someone you've never met, can give away his approach by the tone of his voice. That's what happened to a colleague of mine who ordered an expensive dining-room set. The salesperson told her the furniture would arrive in six weeks. It didn't.

When she called back, the salesman said, "Oh, that's going to be twenty weeks." His tone was condescending. She could tell that he didn't care about resolving her problem.

"That's not what I was told," she said. "My husband is furious. I'm going to cancel the order." (We all have outs. For parents, the out is usually the kids. For those without kids, the out is usually the significant other.)

She finally had the salesperson's attention.

"Let's make this right," he said. It was a male-dominant, Big Daddy voice. "I'm so sorry this happened that I'm going to throw in protective table pads for you." Picking up on the role he had assumed—macho and condescending—my friend intentionally played back to him, specifically to his need to be the dominant one in the conversation. She thought to herself, Does this man actually believe that ninety days of waiting for a dining-room set is worth no more than protective table pads? But did she say that? No; instead she performed her role as a woman in need.

"This is really a problem because my husband thinks this deal is canceled. I need your help here." (People like it when you ask for their help.)

"Okay, then, I might be able to knock off four hundred dollars."

"I'm sorry," she said. "Four hundred isn't going to cut it."

"Five hundred?"

"Please listen to me. I need your help because my husband is going to flip out if I don't have my money back. I did wait an extra ten weeks."

"Six hundred?" he asked.

"My husband . . ."

"I can't knock off any more money," he said. "Is there any other furniture you need for the house?

"Well, I could use a new sofa."

She got a new sofa and six hundred dollars off the dining-room set. Why? Because she baselined his voice and tailored her negotiations accordingly.

If he had been a different personality type, say submissive and apologetic, my colleague might have used the alpha dominant approach—direct and to the point. "Listen, Charlie. You're taking four hundred dollars off the price, and still I don't feel that this is a win-win situation. In every transaction, both parties should walk away feeling good, and I don't feel that way." However, because he assumed the alpha role, that approach would not have worked here. Recognizing this, she played into what he wanted to hear. She said she had "a real problem," and asked for help.

Although to some her approach might have looked submissive, in the end you have to read your audience in order to come away dominant. That's what she did, and she is now sitting on her new sofa.

Baselining changes the way you deal with people. It gives you a head start. Next we'll discuss the steps to take after you've baselined someone.

ELEVEN

THE ANATOMY OF GESTURES

Body

We've all heard the expression "She talks with her hands." Actually, we all talk with our hands. And our feet, and our entire bodies. More important, we enhance our messages by using gestures.

The body never lies. It gives away what you're feeling.

In August 2009, Bill Maher made an appearance on *The Tonight Show with Conan O'Brien.* Soon the topic moved to President Obama's proposed health plan. O'Brien was visibly uncomfortable. Maher's mouth was tense. "What we need is a progressive party in this country," Maher said.

"We don't have it." This was followed by a tight lip compression aroused by his anger.

O'Brien looked down, palms up in a submissive pose, shoulders hunched and downward mouth conveying defeat and submissiveness. He paused momentarily, wondering where his power had gone.

"Did I hurt you?" Maher asked, while pulling the ultimate power play, gently touching him while leaning forward in a pacifying gesture. "You look crestfallen." O'Brien responded, "No, no, you didn't hurt me. I have my own views." Too late, however; O'Brien had already lost his power.

The context of a gesture determines the meaning. For instance, a forward lean into someone else's space is seen as aggressive most of the time, especially in a business setting. But in a different frame—let's say a man wanting a woman to like and bond with him—it takes on an entirely new meaning.

THAT FIRST HANDSHAKE: *"LET'S CONNECT."*

During the Clinton-Lewinsky media fest, *Newsweek* magazine reported the following: "Among staffers at the White House, where she arrived in June 1995, Monica Lewinsky was known as a 'clutch.' If an important person shook her hand, she wouldn't let go. Her determination to enter the inner sanctums of the White House was exceptional, even among other starstruck young interns."

I don't know the legitimacy of that claim, but I do know the power of the handshake. This gesture momentarily connects us—like glue—to another person. It's typically the first form of intimacy that two people share with each other. Of course, we don't want to be cemented there; nor do we want to be manipulated by that first touch.

I'm sure you've shaken hands with someone who has consciously or unconsciously tried to show you that he is dominant, by either giving you a tight-gripping handshake or making sure his hand is pressed down over yours. Didn't work, did it? You didn't feel connected to that person. That's because an arm-wrestling attempt is not a way to bond during an initial connection. The goal is *yes,* not a defeated opponent.

Don't be a clutch or a manipulator, and keep the business handshake less than three seconds. Use your right hand, never your left. Extend it horizontally. Your palm should meet the other person's (no finger shakes), and your grip should be comfortable. Point all parts of your body toward your target, and shake the entire arm, not just the hand.

Limp and bone-breaking handshakes are equally off-putting. Limp handshakes give the impression of insecurity and make the other person extremely uncomfortable. Conversely, if you grab the hand of someone wearing a ring, you will make an instant impression, all right, but only in the person's flesh. Practice on a friend until the gesture feels natural and spontaneous.

Keep in mind as well what your target does for a living. Is he a surgeon? An artist? A pianist? If he works with his hands, his shake might be intentionally limp, but his personality strong.

THUMBS-UP: *"YOU GO! GREAT! I'M FINE WITH ME. WE'RE TOGETHER ON THIS ALL THE WAY."*

Thumbs-up signals confidence and acceptance—nothing wrong with that. Use it to bond, express optimism, and communicate congratulations. He got that new client. Thumbs-up. You and your colleague are committed to the new plan of action. Thumbs-up.

Here's the only problem: That gesture has been used so frequently by public figures, from John F. Kennedy to Bill Clinton, that it can come across as clichéd and insincere. Don't use it if you don't mean it.

SELF-CLASPING HANDS: *"OKAY, LET'S GET STARTED."*

This gesture is a clap that signals, "Let's wrap it up now." Quite often it is followed by a quick palm-to-palm rub to get people's attention. You're trying to begin something or end something. You might even be trying to compel an individual to do something.

PALMS UP: *"HEY, HERE I AM, NOTHING TO HIDE."*

This is a "trust-me" gesture, and thus a favorite among dishonest people trying to scam you. Former FBI agent Joe Navarro says that he would be highly suspicious of someone who used this gesture while proclaiming his innocence. Stating your innocence isn't affirmative—you are asking to be believed instead of insisting that you are telling the truth; therefore an upward palm would mean that you are insecure about your own answer.[25]

Actor Tom Cruise attends the *Valkyrie* red carpet premiere at Cinemex Santa Fe Mall in Mexico City on January 5, 2009.

Of course, an open palm can also be a gesture that demonstrates submission, goodwill, and openness. You should read it accordingly unless you have reason to assume otherwise.

MAN HUG: *"HEY, BRO."*

At one time considered inappropriate behavior, the man hug has become a familiar greeting. The way men hug each other has little resemblance to the way they hug women. The one-armed hug is probably the most common. Varieties include two arms with a back pat, one arm with a back pat, and one arm with a shoulder bump. Sometimes you'll see two men shake hands as they hug. The handshake provides a barrier so that they can combine the formality of one gesture with the affection of the other.

Michael Ballack and Per Mertesacker of Germany celebrate their 1–0 victory over Austria in a UEFA Euro 2008 Group B match on June 16, 2008, in Vienna, Austria.

FIST BUMP: *"WE'RE CONNECTED."*

When two people bump fists it is a sign of cohesion. Typically, it's a way to show solidarity, affection, or connection with another person in a very prideful way. It's not a submissive gesture.

HIGH FIVE OR HIGH TEN: *"AREN'T WE GREAT?"*

If a high five is good, a high ten is great. High ten is used when we are congratulating each other. Strike palms and we connect. Extended high fives or high tens are semi-equivalent to handholding and are a playful way of touching the opposite sex and testing the waters for a possible relationship.

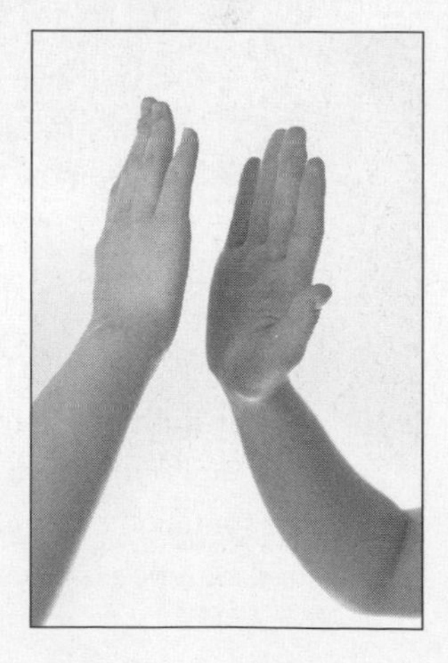

CROSSED ARMS: *"GET OUT OF MY SPACE."*

This manner of shielding the body from others may be comforting to you, but it appears defensive and shut off to others. As an experiment, try it on a friend in a conversation, and watch him back away.

Although usually perceived as a negative signal, crossed arms can also bond when the gesture is used to mirror. You might notice college students talking outside the student union with arms crossed and books against their chests. They are probably not in disagreement but bonding by mirroring each other's gestures. Besides, those books are heavy. However, studies show that crossing your arms does tend to close you off to new ideas, so try to keep as open as possible.

THE POINTED FINGER: *"STOP." "GO."*

Depending on how it's done, the point can be a tool for building rapport or destroying it. If you point your finger away from someone else, either to direct someone's gaze, to emphasize a point, or to help someone understand a concept, that's fine. However, finger-pointing is a universal symbol of aggression and disdain.

Often, the finger-point is used by someone who is lying and exaggerating his anger in order to divert attention. It's a sign of anger as well as eagerness to lead someone in the opposite direction, not a sign of honesty.

ORIENTING RESPONSE

We naturally move toward those things we like. You may realize you've relocated within five feet of this person you find interesting. If you see that somebody has made eye contact and he moves closer to you, that's a good sign he's interested.

THE SHOULDER SHRUG: *"I DON'T KNOW."*

When you shrug your shoulders, you are conveying that you are unsure of what you or someone else is saying, or you're trying to demonstrate indifference.

Most of the messages of this gesture imply uncertainty, whether about someone else's messages or your own. The shrug is an unconscious attempt to make yourself appear smaller and vulnerable and therefore more likely to be forgiven. If used frequently, it makes you look perpetually uncertain. Watch for it used with a positive statement. "Oh, I completely know the answer to that." Big shrug, which telegraphs self-doubt. Be sure that you don't shrug when making power statements.

THE CHOP: *"NO WAY." "MY WAY." "THIS IS HOW IT IS."*

The chop is one of those gestures that, like winks and eyebrow raises, travels in packs. If you're chopping out accompaniments to your gestures and words, you had better be the person in charge. Only the boss, the authority figure, or the big-spending customer will be able to get away with all this posturing.

President George W. Bush uses a chopping motion.

You will bond better if you aren't so aggressive. You can keep the emphasis and remove the bully effect if you perform this gesture with an open palm on top of another open palm.

COUNTING ON FINGERS: *"STAY WITH ME HERE."*

People often do this when they're feeling cocky, confident, arrogant. However, it can be used effectively when teaching someone, because finger-counting can be an anchor. In addition, it helps convert someone to *yes.*

RUBBING HANDS TOGETHER: *"BRING IT ON."*

This is also known as the expectancy rub. The tactile contact between two hands somehow gets things in motion. The palms are sensitive to pressure, and the heat that is created when rubbing the hands together can literally warm us up to an idea.

PALMS DOWN: *"THIS IS THE WAY IT IS, AND THIS IS HOW IT'S GOING TO BE."*

While open palms are beseeching, palms down demonstrate that you are in control.

This gesture trivializes the other person's contributions, and it may make you appear condescending. You are looking for *yes,* so use this gesture purposefully and cautiously.

HANDS ON HIPS: *"DON'T MESS WITH ME."*

When two cats square off against each other, their fur stands on end; their tails look five times their normal size. Each is trying to take up as much room as possible. Placing your hands on your hips and facing the other person directly does much the same thing for your authority.

Square your shoulders, place your hands on your hips, and look directly at your target. This is extremely effective in a situation in which you are demonstrating your dominance. This is a position I have often noted Rahm Emanuel to keep when he is standing by the president's side, that of a man ready for action. This stance is one that most use for defense, not offense. Don't use it unless you are trying to come across as dominant.

Hands on hips. Actress Sandra Bullock arrives at the 2009 MTV Movie Awards held at the Gibson Amphitheater on May 31, 2009, in Universal City, California.

STEEPLE: *"I'M IN CONTROL."*

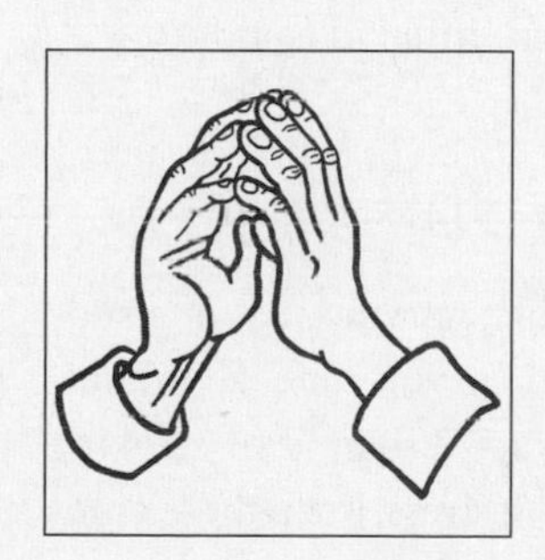

This gesture of touching the fingertips together and pointing up conveys confidence. It is generally used by someone who's in a position of authority. It also conveys one's position on the corporate ladder or even the social ladder. When you are with a peer, you might steeple. Your manager will steeple in front of you but might not in front of the vice president.

HANDS BEHIND THE BACK: *"YOU DON'T INTIMIDATE ME."*

Remember the photo of Angelina Jolie? When you assume this posture, you are also saying to another person that he is no threat to you, and you are no threat to him. You are exposing your entire body without fearing an attack. It is a demonstration of confidence and superiority.

Clasp both hands behind your back. Make eye contact. Smile. Without the smile, this gesture can be read as a warning not to come any closer.

NAIL BITING: *"I'M INSECURE."*

This ranks right up there with picking your fingernail or biting your lip on the list of turn-off gestures. If you are interviewing for a job or negotiating a deal, don't telegraph your nervousness. Keep your hands away from your lips. Of course, on the flip side, biting your nails can also be done intentionally to signal coy playfulness.

PIGEON TOES: *"PLEASE DON'T LOOK AT ME."*

This happens when someone is feeling vulnerable or shy. The toes point inward. You (or your *yes* target) feel like a scared little kid again.

HAND-WRINGING: *"I NEED COMFORT."*

The conversation changes. You're uncomfortable, nervous. All of a sudden, you lace your fingers together, prayerlike. Or you squeeze the fingers of one hand with the other. Dead giveaway! Wringing or stroking your hands telegraphs low self-confidence or high stress. Keep these emotions to yourself by keeping your hands apart.

SCRATCHING: *"HUH?"*

People scratch when they aren't certain. At one of my speaking engagements, I had a conversation with one of the directors. I asked him a question and, as he answered, he turned his head and scratched his neck. He really didn't know the answer to what I was asking. His words became irrelevant.

TOUCHING THE NECK: *"I'M STRESSED."; "I'M INTERESTED."*

Our hands move to our necks when we're feeling stressed. Protecting the neck area, even minimally, is a sign that the brain is communicating stress or uncertainty.

Make note of when someone else does this, as it could indicate which issue under discussion is putting pressure on him. Avoid using it yourself, especially when negotiating.

A powerful way to tap into the erogenous power of the neck is to delicately stroke the suprasternal notch, the neck dimple in the front of your neck, between the collarbones. It's a disarming gesture that says, "I'm open."

PREENING: *"LOOK AT ME."*

You brush invisible lint off your shirt. You sweep back your hair. These are attraction gestures that are more appropriate in social situations. They don't belong in the business world.

HANDS IN POCKETS: *"I'M NOT OPEN."*

Quite often this position is a comfortable pose for men; however, it comes across as being insecure or secretive. The impression is that the person is hiding something. Hands are typically the way we communicate. When we hide them, in essence we partially stop communicating. Keep them out to demonstrate your personality.

THUMBS OUT: *"I'M FEELING POWERFUL."*

As the digit that distinguishes primates from the rest of the animal world, the opposable thumb is our most powerful finger and, as such, a potent tool for expression. Make sure you keep these digits out on display.

TOE TAP: *"I'M EXCITED."*

We are always so concerned about keeping our block face that we don't pay attention to our lower limbs. When we hear good news, we tend to tap our toes. Our excitement leaks out through our feet.

ANXIOUS FEET: *"I CAN'T CONTAIN MY EMOTIONS."*

Just as there are happy feet, there are also anxious and angry feet. When we are feeling anxious—good or bad anxiety—we will usually "jazz" our feet or quickly heel-bump up and down. In anger, we whack our feet against the solid ground to blow off steam. Stomping must be instinctive, as blind and deaf children are found to stomp their feet in anger as well.

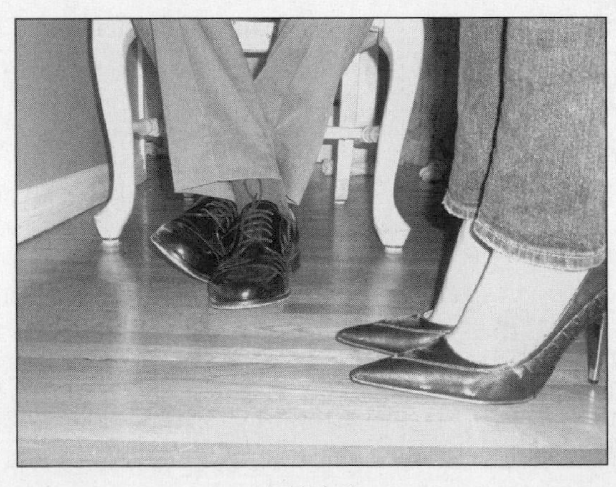

Ankle lock.

ANKLE LOCK: *"I DON'T AGREE WITH YOU."*

Closed-off ankles tell a story, typically that an individual feels closed off, defensive, or uncomfortable in a situation.

You close yourself to the experience. In business environments, the same thing happens. It's a covert way of saying, "I don't agree with you."

HIS SIGNALS/HER SIGNALS

What the World Needs Now Is Touch, Sweet Touch

I believe we can improve our lives one touch at a time.

All relationships have their peaks and valleys. Some people go into that valley, figure it's no fun anymore, and head for a divorce attorney. The goal is to recognize that there is a peak up ahead someplace, and to hang on to each other, both physically and emotionally, until you get there. One of the most important ways to do that is constantly touching somewhere on your lover's body. Doing so will help to keep the spark in your relationship and always make you a sight for sore eyes, a constant anchor of happiness locked in each other's minds.

STIFFENED MOVEMENTS: *"I CAN'T GIVE MYSELF AWAY."*

You're happily talking away to a prospective employer, animated and clearly on your way to making a great impression. The conversation moves to references, and you reply that yes, Jim over at ABC Corporation will give you an excellent one.

"ABC," he says. "Do you know Ellen Smith, who used to work there?" He has just named your archenemy from the past. "She's a friend of mine."

"Ellen Smith? No, doesn't sound familiar," you lie.

Now, look what's happened to your body. Your animation has deserted you. Your hands are frozen; your arms are stiff. This sudden freezing up is your brain's attempt to avoid a blunder. Its very abruptness can halt the good impression you were making, even if the interviewer does not know anything about nonverbal communication.

HIS SIGNALS, HER SIGNALS

Expansive and Diminutive Movements

When in a challenging situation, a man takes a deep breath to expand his chest. He opens his legs when standing and puts his hands on his hips. Obviously, he's not going to do this at the breakfast table. He might do it when he's with his girlfriend and an attractive guy walks by. He'll puff up his chest to show the woman how big and attractive he is. The girlfriend doesn't even have to be there—he may also do this when just walking by another man.

Women use the same gestures to show skepticism. Men do it to take up space and demonstrate dominance, but when women want to appeal to men, they make themselves appear smaller, vulnerable, and childlike. They don't tend to sit with their legs open; rather, they may cross their legs instead. They also keep their elbows tucked in. Men are wired to like smaller women and, consciously or not, women realize that smaller gets the guy.

FIG LEAF: *"I'M VULNERABLE."*

The gesture of the hands over the genitals signals vulnerability. It is a gesture that helps to protect oneself from pain, whether physical or emotional. It offers a sense of security because you're protecting what is es-

sential to you. The fig leaf is not just done with the hands; it can be done with a briefcase or a pocketbook as well—anything that protects the lower body from exposure and risk.

MEASUREMENT GESTURE: *"THIS BIG."*

This is also known as power palms or parallel palms, and you can use it two different ways. When you separate your hands, as if saying, "It was a fish this big," you are emphasizing the enormity of something. You can tell when someone is lying if the spread doesn't match the words.

Watch for expansion of the hand movements. "I got a raise that was so good." [*Hands six inches apart*] "But poor Paul. He really got screwed." [*Hands twelve inches apart*] Your hands are saying that Paul was the one who got the big raise, and you are the one who got the paltry one.

Parallel palms can be used with one hand to chop or two. One palm might be used to emphasize every single word. Two chopping palms is a movement used to reinforce your verbals and demonstrate your emotional fervor about your ideas. Typically, the deeper the passion, the higher and slower the chop forms from top to bottom. In addition, parallel palms with slightly bent fingers can be used to demonstrate holding an idea within your grasp.

BODY ANGLING: *"THIS CONVERSATION IS OVER."*

We tend to directly face people that we like. When we don't like a person, we exhibit body angling, also known as cutoff. You use it consciously to let someone know you need to leave, and if you see someone else using it, you should back off fast. By turning your body to the right or left, you cut somebody's body away from yours. The greater the distance, the less rapport you share with the person.

Body angling can also occur unconsciously, indicating hesitation, uncertainty, or conflict with the other person. You can usually sense right away if someone is intentionally angling away from you, even if you don't consciously process that thought. Sometimes cutoff can be a strong indication of dislike, but keep in mind, at times people are also shy or uncomfortable with frontal exchanges.

In my trainings, I frequently ask people to role-play in pairs. Usually, I hand each in the pair a card. One card reads, "Your job is to continuously *build* rapport." The other reads, "Your job is to continuously *avoid* rapport." Neither person knows the other's goal. After they converse, I ask the couples to come up to the front of the room and explain what they experienced.

As they discuss their mixed signals, they make statements like these:

"He kept backing away from me."

"That's because you were invading my personal space."

"Not until you started moving away."

"No, you were in my face from the start."

They demonstrate how, when we are focused on only our own goals in an encounter, we completely miss the slowdown signals from the *yes* target.

Focus not only on your goals, but on any closed-off signals you may encounter.

You must be tuned in to those turnoffs at all times. I'm usually really open to listening to people, as it is the quickest way to build rapport, but a while back I was approached by a casual acquaintance at a show I was doing. She wanted to talk about her new job, her new boyfriend, her new boobs, and anything else that would revolve around her. (As I mentioned earlier, the quickest way to bond is to let others talk about themselves. That's what they love to do anyway.) Based on our previous conversations, she knew I would listen, and listen, and listen, and listen, and then she would ask me tons of questions, which I would be more than happy to answer. On this particular day, however, one of my babes was not feeling well and I was in a mad rush to get home to them. I needed to leave right then. This woman was holding me up from getting home to my babes.

I found myself gripping the wall, a sign of literally trying to pull yourself out of a situation. My feet were completely angled out the door. I tried to take a step, and she touched my arm in an attempt to keep me there.

"Yeah, yeah, I see your point, oh, yes, I completely agree. We'll talk more next time I see you. Right, no, I think you are completely justified. Okay, yeah, right. See you soon." As I walked away, she followed me out, down the hall, and into the bathroom. I had to hide in the stall and wait for her to leave first. She just didn't get it.

I had sent her every possible cue: gaze avoidance, feet pointed away, lack of response, even a verbal cue. She had not picked up on any of them.

When the conversation is over, it's over. Read the cues. Maybe you've said something wrong, but just possibly your *yes* target needs to get home to her kids. Or she has another appointment. Or maybe she's just been working since early morning and needs to chill. Continuing to pursue your goal without reading what you see in another person's body language will destroy any hope you have of swinging that pendulum to *yes*.

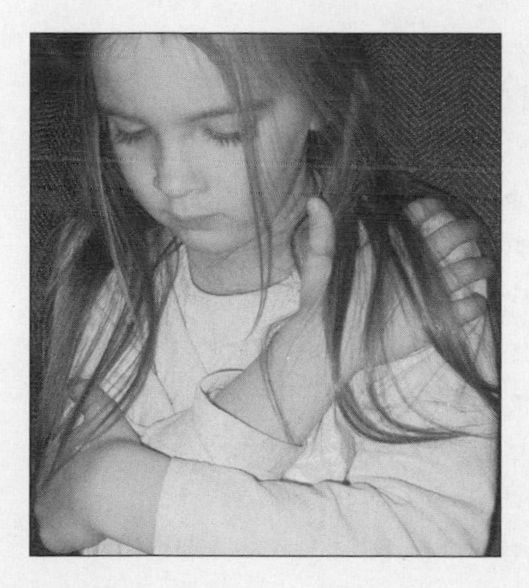

SELF-STIMULATING OR PACIFYING GESTURES: *"I'LL BE OKAY."*

On certain places on our bodies, we have more nerve endings than others. For instance, you have tons of nerve endings in your inner thighs, and you may stimulate them, almost in a sexual fashion, by crossing and uncrossing your legs.

When you touch or rub yourself, in essence you are giving yourself mini-hugs. You are nurturing you, and it can be powerful. The more intense your apprehension or anxiety, the more vigorous the self-stimulating or pacifying gestures will be. Self-pacification can come in the form of touching the face, lips, or neck, stroking the arms, wringing the hands, caressing the face (especially the forehead), rocking back and forth, playing with the hair, massaging the neck, rubbing the thighs, kneading the fingers, even stroking the ears.

BODY LANGUAGE LOCKDOWN (WITHDRAWAL OR ABSENCE OF GESTURES): *"I'M LYING."*

Typically when individuals are holding something inside that they do not want released, they instinctively lock down their nonverbal cues. They believe that in doing so, their lie or secret will not leak out. Of course, the individual trained in nonverbal communication will recognize this shift from movement to lockdown and identify it as a cover-up. People are under the impression that if they avoid movements, they will not give themselves away. This is also known as the freeze response, because as the brain recognizes the threat of being detected, we freeze so as to be invisible to others.

ASK TONYA

Q: I have heard you mention body language lockdown. Can you explain what that means?

A: Quite often we attempt to shut down our nonverbal signals in order to avoid disclosing information about ourselves. It could be an attempt to convey our disappointment in someone, or it might stem from our effort to avoid disclosing a potential secret. In other words, lockdown is when you won't allow your feelings or intentions to leak out of your body.

SITTING IN SPRINTER'S POSITION: *"I'M READY TO HAUL."*

The body is leaning forward. Hands are on the thighs. This person is ready to leave. That's not a comfortable position, so when she's doing it, what she's really saying is, "Let's pick this up another time." Or, "I'm not interested in what you have to say.

TWELVE

THE ANATOMY OF GESTURES

Head and Face

NODDING: *"YES."*

Nodding shows your interest, your comprehension, and your agreement. Slow down, pay attention to what the person is saying, and nod only at appropriate times. Otherwise, you might come across as saying, "Come on, come on, hurry up." Studies show that women tend to nod whenever a person speaks, whether they agree or disagree; men tend to nod when they agree with what someone says. Just some food for thought.

HIS SIGNALS/HER SIGNALS

Women Nod More

A study published in the *Psychology of Women Quarterly* found that women in college classrooms nodded more than men, and students nodded more to professors speaking than to peers speaking. Female and male students nodded equally to professors speaking but men nodded less to peers speaking. Thus, both men and women reacted to the status and not the gender of the speaker.[26]

WELCOME/DEPARTURE KISS: *"I LIKE YOU."*

Sometimes called the air kiss, this is usually done cheek to cheek. In my opinion, in the U.S. a kiss at the beginning of an interaction with someone new is never appropriate.

When I was doing a photo shoot for a public event, I worked with a six-person team of makeup artists, image consultants, and photography assistants. They were a warm group, and we hugged as if we had known each other for years. The only person on the team with whom I did not spend much time was the coordinator. He wasn't there for most of the shoot, and we didn't have a chance to interact.

When we finished, I kissed and hugged the first five. Then there stood the coordinator. There was this awkward pause, and I didn't know what to do. Finally, I said, "It was great meeting you," and put out my hand. I regretted it instantly.

I should have hugged him, and if I felt restraint, I could have given him the shoulder bump and stepped back. If you're kissing the first five people good-bye, you're going to have to do the same to the sixth. Go ahead and admit that this is an awkward moment. Just put it out there and say something like, "Look, I happen to be a touchy-feely person, so you're going to have to hang with this hug." Then, if you need to, you can always soften the gesture. Don't do what I did and single out one person in a group for different treatment.

HEAD NEGATION—THE HEAD SHAKE: *"NO, NO, NO."*

Your target disagrees with whatever you've just said. This often minute movement shows what someone's subconscious is saying. A person who doesn't believe or agree what you are saying *or* what he himself is saying may unconsciously shake his head. I've seen this numerous times in politicians and celebrities I've analyzed on television.

When you have verbally disagreed with somebody and want to reinforce your opinion, you can shake your head slowly. You can also use this gesture when you want to let someone know he has pushed your limits. Limit your use of this gesture, however, and be sure you aren't shaking at your own statements. If you are, you're sending conflicting signals.

HAND TO NOSE: *"I'M UNCOMFORTABLE WITH THIS CONVERSATION."*

You probably have heard that people who touch their noses are lying. That may be true, but good liars have probably learned by now techniques to avoid the behavior. "The Pinocchio Effect" can occur in any stressful situation. Perhaps you're waiting for your annual performance review, or you're interviewing for a promotion. When you experience sudden anxiety, your blood pressure increases. This causes your soft tissue, including that on your nose, to swell. Your skin tingles, and you are frequently unconsciously compelled to touch or scratch your nose.

Consider the situation when identifying this gesture. The person touching her nose may be using the touch as a pacifying behavior to comfort herself, not necessarily identifying herself as a liar.

ROLLING THE EYES: *"WHATEVER."*

This aggressive gesture, which is sometimes called the "eye shrug," is often accompanied by a large sigh, demonstrating that you're bored or disinterested. It is a provocative signal that demonstrates contempt, sarcasm, and a lack of respect for your target.

BOWING THE HEAD FORWARD: *"I'M DEFEATED."*

This gesture is derived from our ancestors' protective crouch when attempting to hide from animals. When you bow, you tuck your chin and end up looking smaller and more vulnerable; it's a nonverbal plea for pity. It is a signal that someone is in trouble, and it signals that the person will accept whatever you're going to hand him.

DOWNWARD GAZE: *"I CAN'T LOOK YOU IN THE EYE."*

This is a submissive signal. It can also indicate lack of certainty—or defeat, guilt, shame, or embarrassment.

"I feel really strongly about that," you say, but you are looking down at your desk. Strength and confidence? I think not.

Of course, this gesture is context-dependent. It could also signal that you are accessing your emotions.

POUTY LIPS: *"I'M VULNERABLE."*

The lower lip comes out. This is what a child does when sulking. A female might pout to tug on a man's paternal strings; it can be a flirtatious gesture as well.

WINKING: *"HI, HONEY."*

This is flirtatious, friendly, conspiratorial, and secretive. It's also a way of sharing something or connecting with another. I was asked to analyze Sarah Palin's winks for a segment on *The O'Reilly Factor* and found that she winked five times during an approximately thirty-second video clip. The problem was the frequency of those winks. When you overuse a gesture—almost any gesture—it loses its initial intention, and is more comedic than sincere.

CHIN TUCK: *"I'M ANGRY."*

We tuck our chin to look down our nose at others in disdain or to demonstrate anger. In anger, we tend to tuck our chin in order to protect it, as it is one of our vulnerable areas. Women occasionally use this gesture to indicate delicacy; it can come across as quite endearing to a man because it makes a woman's eyes appear wide, innocent, and childlike.

CHIN LIFT: *"I WIN."*

The person who uses a chin lift exposes his neck as a sign of strength and pride, demonstrating that he is not vulnerable but confident and resilient. This stance communicates that he has the upper hand in the situation, while simultaneously elevating his height.

People tend to punctuate a point by lifting up their chin as if to say, "Hmpf, I win." The chin lift is the ultimate smug gesture.

LOOKING OVER YOUR GLASSES: *"ARE YOU KIDDING ME?"*

This is a gesture of disdain and contempt. If someone peers over the top of his glasses at you, don't be surprised if you feel as if you are being examined under a microscope. Gazing over your glasses at another conveys a judgmental attitude and can be seen as standoffish and aggressive. Typically, the results will be unfavorable.

COMPRESSED LIPS: *"I'M HOLDING IT ALL IN."*

This is a sign of anger, guilt, remorse, or shame. When we feel these emotions, we seal the mouth off. President Clinton made lip compression notorious when he demonstrated it to the world during the discussions of Monica Lewinsky. Nothing that can hurt us can get in, and we are trying our best to let nothing come out.

George Bush with compressed lips.

The muscles involved are the same that you use for biting. You hold in your anger. It's that good old reptilian brain getting you ready to fight. You've seen this on a number of philandering politicians. When an angry person looks at you this way, part of his brain is, literally, trying not to bite you.

INWARD LIP ROLL: *"I'M EATING MY WORDS."*

This conveys a similar meaning as compressed lips: frustration and keeping secrets. You have probably seen numerous photos of Katie Holmes doing it. Typically, you're feeling the pressure, bottling everything up. This is usually a sign of tension or frustration. Some people do a lip roll when they concentrate, but it comes across as indecisive, nervous, and even somewhat deceptive.

THE ONCE-OVER: *"YOU INTEREST ME."*

Men and women don't look at each other the same way. A man will stare directly, like an animal in hunt mode. A woman will check out a guy in a quick glance. Because women don't have to look directly at a man, their once-overs are not as obvious and may go unnoticed.

THE BALLAD OF MILEY AND NICK

On one of my television segments, I analyzed an interview Miley Cyrus did with Barbara Walters in 2008.

As Walters began talking about the breakup between Cyrus and Nick Jonas, Cyrus closed up her entire body. She crossed her legs, she crossed her arms, she leaned her body forward toward the floor. She even did a lip pucker. All in all, her unconscious attempt was to make herself appear smaller, which ultimately resulted in her also appearing more vulnerable.

"This is what he had to say," Walters told her. "'It comes down to a good friendship.'"

Miley Cyrus arrives at the 2009 MTV Movie Awards held at the Gibson Amphitheater on May 31, 2009, in Universal City, California. When interviewed by Barbara Walters a year earlier about her breakup with Nick Jonas, her extended eye closure and inward lip roll telegraphed that she didn't want to hear what Walters was saying.

Cyrus responded with an inward lip roll and extended eye closure. She didn't want to hear what Walters was saying. With this extended gesture, nothing can get into your eyes because you're keeping them closed.

Extended eye closure is a blocking mechanism that protects us from what we find unpleasant. When we hear or see something that offends us, harms us, or insults us, or something we don't agree with, our eyelids tend to close longer than they would during a normal blink. This is an involuntary reaction that typically goes unnoticed to the average individual.

SQUINT: *"DON'T LET ME SEE THIS."*

The squint is an eye block. It protects the unconscious mind from really seeing anything unpleasant, be it shame or embarrassment. When you cover your eyes during a scary movie, you are blocking the brain from seeing the horror because you don't want to take it all in at once. That's what the squint does.

In 2009, former Atlanta Falcons quarterback Michael Vick gave an exclusive *60 Minutes* interview, his first since serving eighteen months in prison for his illegal dog-fighting operation. I analyzed his body language in an *O'Reilly Factor* segment.

> **Michael Vick:** The first day I walked into prison, and he slammed that door, I knew, you know, the magnitude of the decisions that I made, and the poor judgment, and what I, you know, allowed to happen to the animals. And, you know, it's no way of, you know, explaining, you know, the hurt and the guilt that I felt. And that was the reason I cried so many nights. And that put it all into perspective.
>
> **James Brown:** You cried a number of nights.
>
> **Michael Vick:** Yeah.

In twenty-five seconds, Michael Vick used "you know" five times. We typically repeat phrases when we feel vulnerable. He also used an eye block and licked his lips three times. He was talking about shame for what he had done to the dogs but my impression was shame and contempt for having been judged, not for having inflicted pain.

PURSED OR PUCKERED LIPS: *"YOU EXPECT ME TO BELIEVE THAT?"*

This expression of pulling your lips into a circular position gives the impression of disagreement, contemplation, or consideration and is frequently paired with narrowed eyes. The person isn't buying what you have to say. The pendulum is moving away from *yes* to *no* or *maybe*. It's time for you to stop, reassess, and try a different approach. Of course, on a brighter side, your target might also be puckering up for a big, juicy kiss—in which case, rock on.

HEAD TILT: *"I HEAR YOU." "I'M TRUSTWORTHY." "I'M SEXY."*

This is usually a sign of vulnerability, an animal sign of submissiveness. One study suggests that if you tilt your head to the right, you will be perceived as more trustworthy. People who tilted their heads to the left were perceived as more attractive.

Either way, the head tilt is done to demonstrate interest, build rapport, imply coy flirtation, and even reveal shyness. It is a positive gesture when listening but a submissive gesture when speaking. When speaking, your head should be in the neutral position.

BITING LIP OR INSIDE OF CHEEK: *"I CAN'T HANDLE THIS." "I WANT TO PLAY GAMES WITH YOU."*

People who bite their lips are usually viewed as embarrassed or shy. It's a childlike gesture, a universal signal of vulnerability that tells the world you don't have much self-confidence. The lip nibble can also be a flirting technique, as it comes across as very young, shy, and innocent. This works well only if you nibble the lower lip. The upper-lip bite demonstrates true anxiety.

TONGUE TO TEETH OR LIP LICK: *"I'M STRESSED."*

This gesture involves running the tongue along the front of the lips or teeth. Our tongue swipes our lips from right to left or left to right. Or we lick our lips up and down. During the fight-or-flight response, less saliva is produced, which helps explain why people who are experiencing high levels of stress (such as one might experience during a speech or a fabrication) suffer from dry mouth. When your nervous system is activated, that arousal causes you to lick your lips. In the nervous lip lick, the tongue quickly darts out of the mouth, swiping at the top lip on the way, and then curls under to swipe at the bottom lip on the way back in.

LIP TOUCHES: *"I'M THINKING." "I'M FEELING INSECURE." "I'M FLIRTING."*

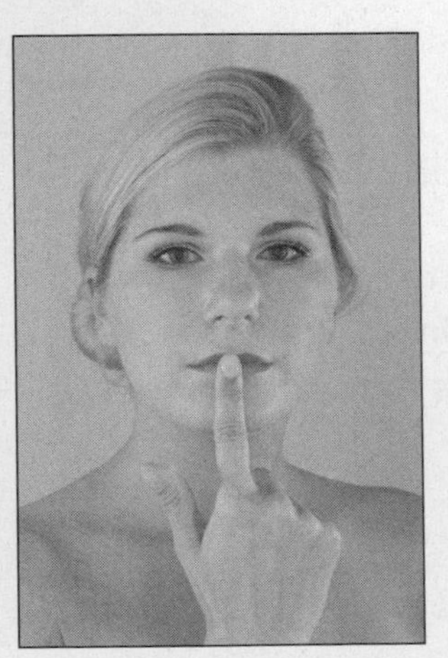

The lips are extremely sensitive, and manipulating them is a self-stimulating and pacifying behavior.

Quite often, we cover our mouth with our index finger and combine that with a momentary pause, which results in a contemplative gesture. Some people like to touch and rub their lips when they're in deep concentration. That extra bit of self-comforting helps them focus better.

Women and occasionally men will also playfully suck on their fingers as either a pacifying gesture or a flirtatious one. In addition, we sometimes stroke our lips as we ponder an idea. Occasionally, placing the hand to the mouth—including fingers to lips—corresponds with telling fibs.

CHIN JUT: *"I SEE YOU, BUT I'M TOO COOL TO SPEAK."*

Bill O'Reilly agreed to demonstrate a chin jut. It indicates recognition and acknowledgment and is usually a way of saying hello to people without having to actually speak to them.

This signal can indicate recognition and acknowledgment and is usually a way of saying hello to people without having to actually speak to them. It is typically used by a dominant individual as a means to communicate superiority, fearlessness, and arrogance.

DILATED PUPILS: *"I'M INTERESTED." "I'M ATTRACTED."*

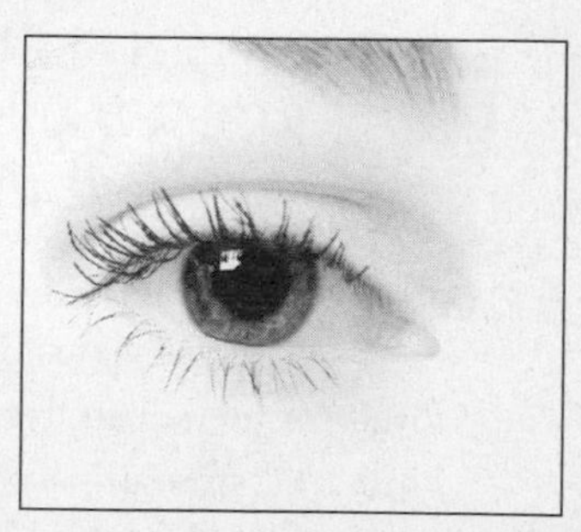

If the lighting remains constant, and you see a change in pupil size, use that as a cue that a person may be interested.

Pupil size is a covert yet readable physiologic response that can vary from pin size to pea size depending upon the situation. Pupil size can be a strong "tell" of interest or disinterest. If the lighting remains constant, and you see a change in pupil size, use that as a cue. Dilated pupils convey affection, friendliness, interest, and attractiveness, while constricted pupils expresses dislike or boredom. Poker players wear sunglasses when playing so that other players can't distinguish a good hand from a bad hand.

STROKING THE CHIN: *"DECISIONS, DECISIONS."*

Like pursed lips, this is a thoughtful and evaluative gesture that suggests pensiveness and concentration. The most important thing you can do is watch for the next gesture. If it is a positive sign, such as a forward lean, the pendulum has probably just swung into the *yes* position.

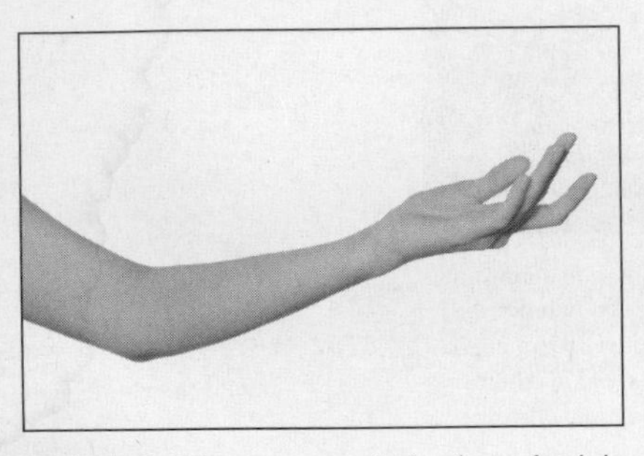

Wrist flash. When a woman flashes her palm, it is a gesture of interest.

FLASH OF THE WRIST FROM A WOMAN: *"YOU MAY APPROACH."*

When women flash their wrists to a man, it's a very seductive pose, as the inside of the wrist is a vulnerable area as well as an erogenous zone. A woman flashing her palm is a sensual gesture and a gesture of interest.

MEN WITH SLEEVES ROLLED UP: *"I'M VERY APPEALING."*

Women find men who roll up their sleeves sexy; it shows their forearms, demonstrates masculinity and strength, and implies physicality.

Rolling up your sleeves shows your forearms and demonstrates masculinity and strength.

BLOWING AIR OUT OF YOUR MOUTH: *"I'M FRUSTRATED."*

When you fill your cheeks with air and then blow it out of your mouth, you are indicating your disapproval and/or uncertainty in a situation. Depending upon the context, blowing air out might suggest you are resigned to your fate and to whatever is going to happen next. When you hear this burst of air from someone else, this person is intentionally letting you know that maybe she isn't happy with whatever you've suggested.

HANDS SUPPORTING CHIN: *"I'M BORED."*

This gesture is typical of an individual who is either feigning interest or is openly bored or tired. Usually, when an individual lightly holds his chin up, he is trying to appear interested in his surroundings. When the face falls heavier into the hands, the more likely he is fatigued or bored.

FINGER MOVING UP THE CHEEK: *"I DON'T THINK YOU'RE THAT IMPRESSIVE."*

This motion is also an evaluative gesture; however, the difference is that as the finger creeps up the cheek, the intention is often one of critical thought or judgment.

TONGUE SHOW OR DISPLAY: *"YUCK."*

Thrusting out the tongue is a negative exhibition. It is a signal of deceit, agitation, and unhappiness. Similar to the shoulder shrug, it can contradict the spoken word and demonstrate disagreement.

JAW CLENCH: *"I'D LOVE TO SINK MY FANGS INTO YOU."*

This is similar to what Bill Maher did in the interview I described earlier. The muscle in the jaw that prepares for biting contracts, and you clench your jaw in anger or pain. A clenched jaw will invite either fear and opposition or anger and aggression in your target.

BLUSHING: *"I'M EMBARRASSED."*

The hot, red rose that rises up your body typically stems from insecurity, fear, anger, or shyness. When your fight-or-flight response is activated, your sympathetic nervous system kicks in. From there, the blood vessels dilate and your face, ears, neck, and chest can redden, acting as an antenna broadcasting your embarrassment.

Once you're aware of the messages your gestures are sending, you can replace the negative ones with others that will build instead of destroy rapport. Just as important, you'll be able to see behind what other people are saying and read their true intentions.

Nonverbal communication isn't just about gestures and facial expressions, however. It is about how we use—and sometimes abuse—each other's personal space.

THIRTEEN

ADVENTURES IN INNER SPACE

"Conversational distance—don't you hate these people that talk to you? They talk into your mouth like you're a clown at a drive-through?"

—*Jerry Seinfeld*

Remember the Close Talker on *Seinfeld*? He was the guy who went around invading everyone's personal space. No one feels rapport with a Close Talker, yet sometimes we have difficulty determining how close is too close. That's because we're usually not aware of our effect on someone else's space. We're aware only when someone like the Close Talker invades our own. We are all encircled by our own safety bubbles that keep us comfortable with others. When that bubble is penetrated, we feel violated.

As our status increases, so do the size and firmness of our territorial boundaries: from cubicles to offices to executive suites; from public housing to private condos to penthouses; from the bus to the train to first-class air travel, with its private lounges and spacious seating areas. Like lions in their wild kingdom, the people with the highest status have vast amounts of territory that they consider their own.

People feel better about themselves and others when they aren't crammed together as if they were on an airplane or in an elevator, where their personal space is negligible.

Yet we still balance this desire for privacy with an equally strong desire to connect. Our personal bubbles of space expand and contract to suit our moods, our relationships, and the situations in which we find ourselves. They also bounce off other people's expanding and contracting bubbles. We might feel perfectly comfortable standing shoulder to shoulder with a colleague on the elevator—but once the doors open, what happens when one of us follows the other a bit too closely and the other person scurries away, desperate to escape to her office?

Recognizing where those spaces are and how we can ensure comfort with others is monumentally important. Shifts in space zones happen constantly, and experts have found that how we handle these transitions can tell a lot about people's status. One study was designed to find out if gender had any impact on whose space was violated within a larger public space. In a bustling public area, the researchers had multiple sets of people of both genders (female/female, male/male, and female/male) sit facing each other in chairs about twenty-six inches apart. The idea was to see how often each group would be "interrupted" by people passing through. They also left about twenty-one inches of space behind each chair, to provide the people approaching them the option of walking around each pair. The results were astounding. Of the 1,181 people who passed the couples, the vast majority chose to go around them. But when people chose to go in between them, 53.3 percent of the time they walked between the two females, 29 percent of the time between a male and a female, and only 17 percent of the time between two males.

This study shows how people will react to each other differently within space, and invade certain people's space more often than other people's based on perceived status. The researchers commented that the fact that women's personal space was invaded much more often than men's personal space shows that women are still considered to be of lower status than men.

In general, people feel better about themselves and others when they aren't crammed together as if they are on an airplane or in an elevator, where their personal space is negligible.

We stake out our territory with anything we can, such as towels on chairs at the pool or backpacks on desks at school. Once you define your territory, you don't want anyone messing with it. Think of students in a college class: If someone sits in their space, they're not happy. It's the same in a business meeting. Unless someone consciously forces everyone to change their seats, it's not going to happen. In my years in the corporate world, I recognized how people stake out their territory with folders, notepads, and cups of coffee. In meetings, people tend to mark their territory and then feel they have the right to return to that marked territory whenever they enter the same meeting room. Sometimes they become flustered if they can't remember what seat they took at the previous meeting or, even worse, if someone else is sitting in their formerly staked-out territory. They get annoyed when another sits in their seat, even though it is open seating.

One of the funniest stories I know came from Debbie, a friend with whom I shared a study about how each time we sit at a table with another person, the space is broken out fifty-fifty. Debbie decided to try it out. She and her date went out to lunch, and as they ate, she slowly but continually pushed either a napkin, a dirty plate, or a fork over onto her date's side of the table. Each time she moved something onto his side, she would note his slight agitation and realize that after a few seconds, he would subtly move the item back onto her side. After she had been playing this game for a while, he suddenly became quite annoyed and finally said, "Why the hell do you keep putting all your sh*t onto my side?" His side? The table belonged to the restaurant. Neither Debbie nor her date had a "side," yet he recognized instantly that she was invading his territory, and he couldn't tolerate it.

In 1955, Swiss zoologist Heini Hediger, formerly the director of the Zurich Zoo, described four different types of interactions between animals: flight distance (the distance to where the animal could safely run), critical distance (the distance needed to escape attack), personal distance (the distance between the animal and noncontact creatures such as swans), and social distance (intraspecies communication distance).

His theories became a basis for the work of Edward T. Hall, who in 1966 coined the term **proxemics,** which is still used to describe the study of measurable distances between humans. Hall pointed out that different cultures have different comfort levels regarding personal space. In Nordic cultures, people are uncomfortable standing close to each other. In Latin cultures, the personal-space zones are much smaller.

We've all sat on a crowded bus or train with a bunch of strangers all too close. What do you do when that happens? Typically you bury your head in a magazine, hunch over your phone and check your text messages, avert your eyes, wait patiently to exit. In contrast, if you were in the lobby of a large hotel and these same strangers were standing far away, you wouldn't experience any discomfort. Hall defined four spheres of personal space: intimate, personal, social, and public.

The intimate sphere. This is the sphere for whispering and touching, and when it comes to my husband, Kenny, I'm all for that.

INTIMATE SPHERE

The intimate sphere is six to eighteen inches. This is the sphere for whispering and touching. It's where you interact comfortably with your spouse or partner, your children, and your close friends. This zone forces you to be aware of every aspect of your target: her scent, her skin tone, even the energy her body gives off. People tend to be wary of others who attempt to bond with them by entering this zone too quickly.

During my trainings, I will always invite a participant up to the stage for a demonstration on proxemics and how space affects us. I typically invite two men and one woman up individually and ask them to stop me when they feel I have violated their personal space.

In training after training, the same thing happens. The majority (which means not all) of the men will let me literally get nose to nose with them, and they'll smile both excitedly and nervously as they declare they are not intimidated by a woman invading their space. Of course, their ears redden and, on occasion, a bead of sweat rolls down their face. At times they even turn their face away from mine, but they have proven their point. They allow me into their intimate zone. The women, on the other hand, will usually stop me when I hit the two- to three-foot mark, admitting when I am too close for comfort. And it goes both ways. Remember, others will feel the same way about you if you attempt to enter their zone too early. I am a hugger; I love to hug people. For many people in a number of professions, it's the standard greeting—friendlier than a handshake and less personal than a kiss. But it's still touching, and not everyone wants to come into contact with people outside their intimate sphere.

The same is true of leaning close to whisper into someone's ear. Colleagues frequently whisper at work out of necessity. Don't be the first to do it. Be sure the other person is comfortable being that close to you. The complications and mixed signals of people of opposite sexes hugging, whispering, or otherwise sharing intimate space are pretty obvious. It can happen in same-sex encounters, as well—you're taking a chance if you get close before your *yes* target has indicated her comfort with that.

PERSONAL SPHERE

The personal sphere is two to four feet.

This is the friends-and-family sphere. It's coffee with a friend, a drink with a colleague. If your shoulders brush, or one of you pats the other on the back, no big deal. You've been there and done that before, and you are comfortable interacting within the personal sphere. You'll find that although we can communicate from this distance without the fear of touching, people still tend to use barriers such as pocketbooks or briefcases in this zone to maintain their bubble if they are uncomfortable.

During one of my hypnosis seminars years ago, I witnessed a man trying to interact with a woman. He approached her while she was seated at a typical school desk (the kind you have to slide into from one side) in the back of the room. He walked up to her on the side of the desk that was open and essentially locked her into place at roughly the two-foot mark. On top of that, because she was sitting and he was standing, from her perspective he appeared rather menacing. His approach was intended to be casual, he would later tell me. However, as it unfolded, she began to scan the room like a trapped wild animal in need of an exit. Typically, in that situation she would have experienced an increase in heart rate, a rise in blood pressure, tingling in the skin, and heightened brain activity.

The close phase of the personal sphere is two to four feet.

Although I could not hear the conversation from where I stood, I recognized the intensity on her face and immediately walked over to them. As I approached, he opened his position in order to include me in "the group." She noticeably flooded with relief, as if he had let her out of a cage.

SOCIAL SPHERE

This sphere is four to twelve feet, and it is typically considered to be close enough for professional relationships but slightly distant for personal conversations. It is the acquaintance zone. It's the ideal space allotment for the professor in the classroom and the sales representative pitching a client.

PUBLIC SPHERE

This sphere is twelve to twenty-five or more feet. This outer range of Hall's "reaction bubble" is the distance used for public speaking. It's the distance between a performer and his audience, a politician and the public, a celebrity and his or her adoring fans. It is the zone that allows you to be seen and heard, but not touched. I work within this zone when I speak to sizable groups or walk into large conferences.

Public sphere. The Pope greeting crowds at the Vatican.

Your body language will help determine how people perceive you. Make eye contact. Smile. Demonstrate excellent posture. When you walk as if you have a purpose and are important, you'll be identified as such.

Personal space is someone's emotional home. You can't just go barging through the front door unless you know it's okay. Our bubbles are quite fragile and are subject to a number of different influences such as age, status, attractiveness, and gender. It's not often one will verbally tell you, "Hey, you invaded my personal space. I don't want to bond with you." But he will always tell you nonverbally, in very subtle ways.

He might flinch at your too-close approach. Perhaps she'll take a step back. He might angle his body away from you. If you're sitting at a table, she may pile books or papers between you or lean back. People may tap their toes, cross their arms, stiffen in the chair, refuse to make eye contact. All of these gestures are screaming, "Move away from me."

He takes one step back. You take one step forward, and the dance of the body invasion begins. Become aware and learn to see the signals. The moment you read hesitation in the other person's body language, you need to note it, lower your voice if you are speaking, and slowly back away. Don't pull away too quickly; doing so will make you look submissive. Refrain from what you now know is aggressive behavior, and remember sometimes size counts. Comfort zones are not one-size-fits-all. Some are bigger than others.

In July 2009, President Obama and Vice President Biden had their high-profile "beer summit" with Harvard professor Henry Louis Gates Jr. and Police Sgt. James Crowley in the Rose Garden. Two weeks earlier, Crowley had arrived at Gates's house to investigate a potential burglary and arrested Gates for disorderly conduct, which Gates said was racial profiling. Obama's comment that police had acted "stupidly" further increased racial tensions.

I analyzed their body language for the New York *Daily News.* Obama had made it clear that he wanted the meeting to build rapport and bring the men closer together. I wasn't surprised that they were sitting at a round table. The president and vice president were both in shirtsleeves without ties, which underscored Obama's emphasis on a casual meeting over beer and snacks. His nonverbal message was: *I'm going to be the good guy, roll up my sleeves, and show that I'm just another working fellow.*

Repeatedly, the president leaned and pointed his shoulder toward Crowley, as if trying to build rapport. Crowley, however, didn't orient himself toward the president. When the president wasn't leaning toward Crowley, he was leaning back.

Crowley's posture seemed to be saying that he was the alpha, and he was still going to remain one, even when sharing a beer with the president of the United States.

Now you know how to navigate personal space, but there's more to learn that involves choosing where you sit, whether in the boardroom, the office, or the corner coffee shop.

FOURTEEN

TAKE A SEAT

Establishing Your Authority

"Man is still the most extraordinary computer of all."

—*John F. Kennedy*

You walk into a meeting or the office of a client. Where you chose to sit and where others sit says a lot about the dynamics of the group. In every situation, you have your choice of seats: position of authority and power, position of interest, position of neutrality, and position of invisibility. This has a tremendous impact on social dynamics. Whether it's the office, the party, the bar, or the first date, you can learn a great deal about a situation by noticing where people sit. In many situations, you can encourage the other person to sit in a particular place to elicit the emotions you want him to feel.

POSITION OF AUTHORITY

At the traditional rectangular table, the leader sits at the head. This is where everyone automatically turns for direction. It is the singular posi-

The position of authority is at the head of the table in traditional rectangular seating. Power positions are at the head's left and right sides.

tion, and it gives the most powerful the most space. Everyone else has to fight for arm room.

Twelve jurors go into a room. Typically, the one who sits in the power position is going to be voted the foreman. It just tends to be the place we look to for guidance. He or she is going to be expected to talk the most, to offer the most direction.

Sitting at the opposite end you'll see the second in command. If the leaders are equal in status, so are the seats. If Mom sits at one end of the table, Dad sits at the other. If Microsoft's chair Bill Gates is at the head of the table, CEO Steve Ballmer will sit at the opposite end.

POSITION OF INFLUENCE

In the absence of a seat of equal status opposite the head of the table, the two seats on either side of the head honcho are the stardust chairs. They are close enough to the leader that some of the stardust falls off on them. If the leader needs a pen, the second in command can quickly hand one over, and his status shoots up. Others sense his superiority by association. We crave, desire, *need* to be around and surround ourselves with powerful people. Two types claim these chairs—people of influence and wannabes.

The top manager might sit to one side of the president. A wannabe alpha might sneak into the chair on the other side. If the group is made up of peers, everyone knows who is there to kiss up and sit next to someone in power, as if that person's energy is going to rub off. If the group members don't know each other, all they see is that somebody is sitting next to their chief.

POSITION OF NEUTRALITY

This position is located on the other side of each stardust chair. In this easily overlooked seat, you won't be expected to participate, and you'll be surrounded by alphas who are trying to get attention. This is the blend-in chair, where you have no contact with the main attraction unless you choose to.

POSITION OF SECONDARY INFLUENCE

This is located about dead center of the table, after the position of neutrality. Humans like symmetry. It's easier for us to rest our eyes on the middle. Grab one of these chairs if you want to be seen as somebody who is really participating in the group. This position isn't as powerful as the stardust chairs, however. The leader isn't going to shout, "Hey, you, two seats down. Do you have a pen?"

POSITION OF INVISIBILITY

When you walk into a meeting room, you see the table, and then, lined against the wall, are the second-tier chairs. These are positions of invisibility. They aren't even at the table. If you want to be a participant, avoid the second tier.

Suppose it's a small meeting room with only a table? The neutral seats I just described become the seats of invisibility. You really don't have to play if you don't want to. You can doodle and withdraw.

OTHER SEATING ARRANGEMENTS

Team-Style Seating

This round table is the best when you want everyone on equal footing. It is usually selected by a manager who is geared toward teamwork. The message is: "Right now, regardless of your position in this company, we are all equal." You feel less intimidated by the round table. If you are unaware of the power people, you can pick them out by how much room they take up. They'll come in, put down their cell and notebook, then spread out their stuff in the biggest possible area. Because they can.

Side-by-Side Seating

This is known as the best possible position in order to work out a problem or plan effectively with someone. Your message is: "We are on the same side," and you are. You're not making direct eye contact, which can sometimes be confrontational. Position yourself on the other person's right side to convey a sense of trust and cooperation.

Across-the-Table Seating

You don't want a barrier separating you and the *yes* target when you're trying to work things out, and the width of a table between you makes it difficult to have a conversation. You can't see the person's bottom half, so you don't know what's going on. We're taught to control our upper half, but the truth leaks out through our legs and feet.

I can tell you from experience, this position reminds people of being interrogated. A couple of times in my career, someone has interviewed me on a sofa while sitting on a chair to the side of me. What a change from sitting face-to-face doing an interview across a desk. The seating took some of the pressure off.

If you are forced to sit this way, turn your body at an angle to get rid of the confrontational stance. Shift in the chair a little bit so your right eye lines up with the other person's.

Right-Angle Seating

This is an intimate, win-win position. There's no real barrier between you. You can literally touch one another if you want to. You're looking

Right-angle seating is ideal for bringing you closer and allowing you to view another's body language.

off from one eye. That means you have no intense eye contact. In addition, you can observe the other person's lower portion—how she's moving, if at all, and which direction her feet are pointing.

Restaurant Seating

The restaurant is a circus of activity: attractive people walking by, servers dropping trays, silverware clattering. You, of course, know that your target needs to feel as if he is the only thing going on in the entire world. It is all about him, and you are fully attentive. He doesn't know this rule, but you do; you cannot lose focus.

We are motivated by movements. Our eyes go to what's happening, and unless the restaurant is crumbling around you, there's little that's more disrespectful than breaking eye contact. Since you are "in the know," you won't make this mistake.

Instead, you'll make certain that your *yes* target is seated facing the wall. It's important that you are the one facing the crowd. You never want to give your target an opportunity to become distracted. The goal is for him to have no other visuals except you and the wall.

I learned this lesson from my first boss. We went to lunch and he took the wall seat, so I faced only him. Then he leaned across the table in a contrived submissive pose with his elbows on the table. He folded his

In a restaurant, sit with the wall behind you so that you are your target's only focus.

hands the way schoolchildren do, continuing to shorten the distance between us. The waitress appeared. Without breaking eye contact with me, he asked, "What would you like?"

This was how we spent the entire lunch. There was metaphorically no one else in the room but the two of us. It was a series of carefully plotted steps geared toward triggering a powerful bonding mechanism, an automatic reaction. It was pure dominance—a form of magnetism he skillfully used to create a feeling of attachment and loyalty to him. He nonverbally let me know (or led me to believe) that he found me fascinating. He wanted me to feel important, and I did—until I learned the game.

At work, you want to be the alpha 24/7. This won't happen if you don't plan ahead, and that includes where to sit. Never disregard the importance of scouting out your territory. Arrive at the restaurant fifteen to twenty-five minutes early. Head directly to that status-appropriate seat you want in the boardroom. Put your energy in that chair, and make that room your own.

FIFTEEN

THE POWER OF YOUR VOICE

"Don't look at me in that tone of voice."

—*David Farber*

Open your mouth to speak and you define yourself. Your voice is a strong part of your identity. The sound of your voice can soothe, excite, impress, or annoy. The nonverbal elements of language that convey emotion and other bits of information are known as **paralanguage.** Paralanguage reveals the emotion that lies directly beneath linguistic communication. These nonverbal components include pitch, rate, and tone. Is someone male or female, older or younger, short or tall, heavy or thin, higher or lower on the social scale? Your voice gives away secrets you didn't even know you were keeping.

Voice is so powerful you can even hear a smile over the phone. Think I'm kidding? When we smile the vocal tract is shortened, with the effect of raising the resonances.[27] A pleasant voice is associated with personality traits such as dominance, competence, sensitivity, and warmth.[28] Vocal cues are among the many ways you use your paralanguage to convey who you are.

During my own first speech, I experienced such an anxiety attack that I almost fainted. My mouth instantly filled with cotton, and I could see only roughly two feet in front of me. Shortly thereafter, my mentor insinuated that he thought I had sucked pretty badly on that first occasion and might not be able to make the cut. I still have that first trial speech on DVD, not that I would ever watch it again. That would be too painful. I keep it as a tangible reminder that the only things that can limit us are our thoughts.

VOICE CHEMISTRY

Your voice isn't just a sound. It's a timbre and pitch. It's also a shortcut for anyone to figure out who you are.

Pitch

This is how high or low your voice is. When you are nervous, your vocal cords lengthen, thin out, and stretch tighter; your pitch gets higher. To tame this beast, try doing some deep diaphragmatic breaths when nerves hit you. For men, low-pitched voices are considered more powerful, and they are seen as more attractive, pleasant, and persuasive. For women, a higher-pitch voice is seen as sexier but not professionally dominant. High pitch can tell people you are excited but it can also lead them to believe you might be deceitful or insecure. Both men and women who demonstrate greater variety in pitch are seen as more dynamic and extroverted. People do not enjoy listening to monotony for long. Think Ben Stein here in *Ferris Bueller's Day Off.* Learn to vary your sounds and you will instantly change the way you are perceived by others.

Rate

How rapidly or slowly you speak is somewhat dependent upon your locale, but it also reveals if you are high energy (fast talker) or lower energy (slow talker). Emotions affect your rate of speech. If you're angry or excited, you might speak faster, and if you're sad, you will speak slower.

Studies show that people who speak faster are more persuasive and credible, and we believe them to be more intelligent and more knowledgeable than the rest of us. Faster talkers seem to have achieved an unconscious competence whereby spewing out facts becomes second nature. Of course, we often allow their ideas to bypass our critical factor, as we don't always have time to process what they're saying. Being able to churn out information in nice, bite-size chunks gives others the impression that you are the expert.

Intensity or Emphasis

What words are you emphasizing in your speech? "*I* think this is an excellent deal for you." (Emphasis is on you and not the other person.) "I *think* this is an excellent deal for you." (But I'm not sure.) "I think *this* is an excellent deal for you." (Immediate—this deal right here.) "I think this is an *excellent* deal for you." (Emphasis on the adjective; this deal is excellent.) Each colors the meaning of the message.

Emphasis Self-Test

Even a statement as direct as "What are you doing here?" can have any number of connotations. Read the following sentences aloud. Then decide which emotion the emphasized word conveys.

"*What* are you doing here?"

"What are *you* doing here?"

"What are you *doing* here?"

"What are you doing *here*?"

Pay attention to the underlying content in your communication and ensure you are transmitting the correct message when you speak.

Volume

Strong volume equals confidence, but you don't want to shout anybody out of the room or sound as if you're talking to someone who is hard of hearing. Nor do you want people in public places shooting you dirty looks.

Research has shown that extroverts and dominant personalities speak more loudly than others, so use that high volume—but check the body language of others to be sure it isn't causing them to back off.

One of the most powerful men I ever knew spoke in a soft, low-pitched voice, close to a whisper. (Think Clint Eastwood in *Dirty Harry.*) Because of the respect he commanded, no one missed a word of what he said. He was a dominant alpha individual.

Keep in mind, however, that often a soft voice can convey shyness, insecurity, and weakness, so speak up. Projecting your voice is not just making it louder; it's making it bigger. You can achieve this by:

Changing your breathing
Changing your tone
Changing your reach

Avoid strident speech, and force yourself to keep anything judgmental, such as contempt, sarcasm, or pretension, from your voice. Some years ago, I had a manager who would sarcastically use the phrase "you don't say" whenever an individual brought up an idea that the manager was already aware of. That was her way of insinuating the person speaking was an idiot.

PAUSES, PREGNANT AND OTHERWISE

Media personalities frequently use the term *dead air* to refer to silence on the airwaves. Everything on the radio is sound: music, commercials, talk, more music, more talk—anything to fill the silence. We do the same, filling the gaps with all types of pause fillers such as *um* and *ah.* Typical pauses are roughly five-tenths of a second in general conversation. Unfortunately, we often feel the need to fill those five-tenths of a second with nonwords like the ones above. When we do this, we interfere with the fluency of our speech, and fluency is one of the best predictors of competence and persuasiveness.

A confident, dominant individual recognizes the significance of silence, its various meanings, and the dominance it conveys. Don't be afraid of pauses—captivate your audience by demonstrating that you are comfortable with silence. A pregnant pause, which is merely a beat or two longer, is suggestive of anything you allow it to be: power and confidence or weakness and insecurity. Few people are confident enough to find solace in silence, and those few will reap the benefits of being deemed authoritative, self-reliant, and trustworthy. Invoking a pregnant pause in your communication will actually boost your status.

You might also take the opportunity to observe how others fill the pauses. Quite often you can use this to your advantage as you note where in their conversations they become insecure and invoke nonlanguage.

DIALECT, ENUNCIATION

In the musical *My Fair Lady* (and the George Bernard Shaw play *Pygmalion*), phonetics professor Henry Higgins makes a bet with a friend that he can teach a cockney flower girl to speak as a lady, and in doing so, pass her off as a duchess. Sure, Eliza Doolittle's transformation is over the top, but it demonstrates how the way we speak defines us.

Not long ago, I was in a salon and heard a conversation in the next booth. The man's diction was straight out of an Italian mob movie. Interesting, I thought, and immediately conjured up what he looked like while I tried to guess what he was doing in a salon.

"Yeah," he said in that accent. "I'd like a manicure and pedicure. And lemme know if you could take a little bit off my eyebrows and wax 'em." I had never before heard a man ask for an eyebrow wax. A manicure, yes—but a mani-pedi and a wax? Well, that left me with some impression. When I left, I made sure to check him out. What I saw didn't match the dialect. He was a nice-looking older man elegantly dressed in what could have been an Armani suit. Okay, I prejudged based on his accent, but that's what people do.

You don't want to sound like the man in the above example, Armani suit or not. Enunciation and pronunciation make a difference. And if English is not your first language and you are uncomfortable speaking, or others frequently ask you to repeat yourself, invest some time in practicing certain phrases. Speak slower than usual and lower your pitch. Record your own voice and play it back. What could you improve?

Although some accents are believed to convey sophistication, the first rule is clarity. Don't risk making your target strain to decipher what you are saying, no matter how elegant or charming your accent.

Pronunciation and Articulation

A friend of mine was a finalist for a public-information position in the state-college system. She lacked a master's degree and was convinced that would eliminate her. "You've gotten this far," I said. "Forget about the master's, already. Get it after you land the job." To compound her worries, her plane was delayed and she arrived at the college only thirty minutes before her interview. I'd be understating the situation to tell you she was a nervous wreck.

The interview went well, until one of the panel members asked what she knew about the job. She blurted out that she knew she would be working on the alumni publication. Only she pronounced the word "aloomni" throughout the interview. "That's when I knew I had lost it," she told me later. "They didn't hear anything else I said."

She was right.

THE UNLUCKY THIRTEEN

Words You Should Not Mispronounce

Oriented, not orientated

E*lec*toral, not elec*tor*al

Espresso, not expresso

Brusketta, not brushetta

Etcetera, not excetera

Youth, not yute

Regardless, not irregardless

Mischievous, not mischieveeous

Preposterous, not perpostereous

Offen, not often

Jewelry, not jewlery

Nuclear, not nuke-yu-ler

Pronunciation, not pronounciation

I'm not being picky here, and I've had my moments. During one of my early speeches I made the mistake of saying the word *impenetratable* instead of *impenetrable*. Shortly thereafter I received a note from a participant wryly advising me of my mistake. How you say it makes a difference. If you were an HR person, would you really want to hire someone who told you he was sales orientated or that he wanted to conversate with you? Or that he was from the state of *Warshinton*?

TURN TAKING

He starts to speak, and so does she.

"Oh, I'm sorry," she says. "Please, go ahead."

"No, please go on."

That's not exactly a bonding moment, is it? It's almost a disconnect because you can't get in sync. Turn-taking signals let you know when it's your turn to talk.

There are specific turn-taking cues, such as tilting the head, increased eye contact, slow nodding, and m-hmming, that demonstrate that we are listening and the floor still belongs to the other person. On the other hand, cues that indicate we would like our turn to speak include decreased eye contact, squinting, very fast nodding, and quicker *m-hmms*. It's important to keep the back-and-forth fluent; it builds feelings of rapport and allows both parties to come across as well versed and intelligent.

Each may also interrupt and talk over the other person. If you're a fast responder, look for these signals:

Ums and Ahs

The other person might be trying to fill the space so that you know not to jump in.

Increased Volume

He is letting you know he isn't ready to be tuned out or that he wants his turn.

Stop Gestures

She might hold up the stop-sign hand.

Slow responders are perceived as less knowledgeable and confident. Try to increase your speed, and look for these signals:

Time

If it's been more than three seconds, you need to speak up.

Head Tilt

The other person is waiting for your response.

Stare

The other person stops and looks right at you, as if to say, "What's up?"

FEELING THE VOICE

When you're happy, your pitch and volume will rise. You'll also speak at a faster rate. When you are sad, your pitch might drop, along with the rate of your speech.

Anger will cause you to speak faster and more loudly, and your pitch to increase. If you are extremely angry, and practically ready to throttle someone (or at least dump the jerk), your pitch might drop and your speech might slow. Fear will cause your voice to lower in volume while the pitch and rate increase. Disgust and contempt will cause pitch, volume, and rate to drop. Make note of these vocal changes in yourself and you will start recognizing them in others.

Can you see how crucial your voice is on your path to *yes*? It is the music that gets you through the door, the varied rhythms that communicate how important you are, how trustworthy. Or not.

Your voice is only part of the package, however. In the next chapter, you'll learn how to make the most of your oldest and, some would say, most powerful sense.

SIXTEEN

THE SCENT OF SUCCESS

"Don't wash / I want a week's worth of you wet / I want the same underwear the same sour smell / layers of it thick / the soak and musk of you."

—*Letter to Josephine from Napoléon*

The smell of the rain falling on meadow grass. Chocolate-chip cookies baking in the oven. A whiff of a long-forgotten shampoo. Our noses have strong memories, and a scent can evoke any number of emotions. Smell is our oldest sense and evolved as an early system of detection. We could smell our enemies (or our next meal) from a distance.

When you inhale, molecules in the air dissolve or mix into the mucus at the top of your nasal passages. Epithelial olfactory receptor cells in the lining of your nose have cilia that dangle in the mucus. These cilia can detect different types of molecules, and the smell is processed in the basal ganglia. In a fraction of a second, we can identify any of approximately ten thousand different smells.

Both men and women emit **pheromones,** chemical signals that, although we cannot detect them consciously, have a strong effect on others. Pheromones may be in our bodily fluids, including our sweat, saliva, and blood. If smell really does play a role in sexual attraction, that could explain why those who have lost their sense of smell frequently report losing their sex drive as well.

Many animals who sense danger warn others by releasing chemicals. Can humans do the same? Male subjects in a Rice University study wore gauze pads in their armpits while viewing films with fear-inspiring topics. Female volunteers were then fitted with a piece of this same gauze under their nostrils. Then they viewed images of various unlabeled faces that were either happy, fearful, or ambiguous. Participants didn't know which emotion was ascribed to which face, but were asked to press buttons on a computer to indicate which category they thought the image fit into. For the most part, while wearing the gauze they interpreted the ambiguous expressions as fearful. The findings provide evidence that human sweat contains emotional meanings.[29]

A study by University of California–Berkeley scientists found that smelling a chemical found in male sweat raised levels of the stress hormone cortisol in heterosexual women. The study, reported in *The Journal of Neuroscience,* provided the first direct evidence that humans, like rats, moths, and butterflies, secrete a scent that affects the physiology of the opposite sex. It was the first time anyone had demonstrated that a change in women's hormonal levels is induced by sniffing an identified compound of male sweat.

Noam Sobel, associate professor of psychology at UC Berkeley and director of the Berkeley Olfactory Research Program, found that the chemical androstadienone changed mood, sexual arousal, physiological arousal, and brain activation in women. Although this chemical is found in male sweat and is an additive in perfumes and colognes, there is no proof that humans respond to the smell of it in the way many mammals and even insects respond to pheromones. Many people argue that human pheromones don't exist, because humans don't exhibit stereotyped behavior; however, androstadienone did cause hormonal as well as physiological and psychological changes in women.[30]

HIS SIGNALS/HER SIGNALS

Women are apparently much more sensitive than men to smells. Approximately 60 percent of women can identify their personal odor. Less than 6 percent of men can identify theirs.

ASK TONYA

Q: Guys used to always turn their head to look at me, but it has slowed over the past few years. Now it seems to have just stopped. I am still the same weight, and I still feel the same. You talk a lot about someone being attractive. Does "attractive" end when someone hits forty?

A: Everything starts to change after you hit your twenties. Research tells us that an individual's ears continue to grow throughout their lifetime and we look to the ears as a sign of youth. As we mature, the pores of our skin get larger, and we lose elasticity. We look in the mirror every day and might not notice the slow aging process. Keep in mind your personality can make you just as attractive as your external appearance; you just need to know how to apply the right "foundation." Here are some quick tips to help others find you more appealing: Maintain eye contact, smile often, let others speak while you listen intently, never get into someone's personal zone, maintain good posture, and finally, keep yourself in shape.

Sweat has been the main focus of research on human pheromones, and in fact, male underarm sweat has been shown to improve women's moods and affect their secretion of luteinizing hormone, which is normally involved in stimulating ovulation. Other studies have shown that when female sweat is applied to the upper lip of other women, these women respond by shifting their menstrual cycles toward synchrony with the cycle of the woman from whom the sweat was obtained.

So how is any of this information relevant for us? Well, the power of smell is another nonverbal cue to keep in mind. Think about it: When you interact with someone, you inhale. And while a sour smell is revolting and a sweeter one is appealing, the research above suggests that things go deeper. Smell, like the other senses, has a deep psychological and biological impact on our behaviors.

Some researchers even go as far as saying that smelling each other's faces or hands can be likened to a type of greeting. According to researchers Barbara Sommerville and David Gee of the University of Leeds in England, the Eskimo kiss is not just a rubbing of noses but a mutual sniffing.[31] Of course, most of us don't touch nose-to-nose, but when greeting we do quite literally sniff each other out, connecting with or avoiding people whose olfactory chemistry is pleasing or displeasing to us.

There are also the scent maskers and detractors to consider—deodorant, perfume, hair gel, aftershave. Everyone has worked with a fragrance junkie. He shows up wearing cologne you can smell a block away. She waltzes in on a cloud of floral notes. They buy only the best and think it makes them stand out in a crowd, and it does that, all right. You can tell when they've been in a room because whatever fragrance they showered in that day still lingers. You want to whisper your arrival, not shout it with heavy, overdone fragrances.

In fact, studies have shown that the brain fires off positive sexual cues if we are smelling someone's natural scent, and negative cues if we are smelling a manufactured scent. Although we might think we like the smell of a certain cologne, our body actually turns off. Just something to think about before you spritz!

HIS SIGNALS/HER SIGNALS

When Like Does Not Attract Like

Do you like your lover's natural scent? If not, your sex life might suffer. A cluster of immune-system genes known as the **major histocompatibility complex,** or MHC, detects bacteria and viruses in your body and affects the production of body odors. In one study, women were asked to sniff and rate the scent of T-shirts that had been worn several days by unidentified men. Overall, women preferred men whose MHC was least like their own.[32] The average couple shares 20 percent of their MHC variants, and some have more. In another study, researchers at the University of New Mexico questioned approximately fifty couples about their relationships and sex lives. The more MHC variants a woman shared with her partner, the more turned off she was to him sexually. These women were less aroused during sex, fantasized about other men, and resisted their partners' sexual advances more often. Some had relationships with other men.

Remember anchors? Well, as we've already discussed in Chapter Nine, olfactory anchors are strong—the scent you're wearing could elicit feelings of mystery, intrigue, and fascination, but it also might induce cues of disenchantment, repulsion, and disgust. You may think you're acing the sale and that the manufactured masculine cologne you've splashed on that day makes you seem strong and protective. The only problem is it's the same scent your client's former husband wore, and she thinks neither "masculine" nor "sold" when she smells it.

The choice is simple for your first encounter with a *yes* target. Either go naked and allow your natural scent to make a statement, or layer on a neutral scent, such as musk oil, vanilla, or lavender for women, and sandalwood or herbal notes for men. Fragrance changes with body chemistry and intensifies with heat, so use even less in warm weather.

HIS SIGNALS/HER SIGNALS

Scents They Fall For

What fragrance do you think most arouses men? Musk? Amber? Gardenia? Tiger lily? Pumpkin pie? At Chicago's Smell and Taste Treatment and Research Foundation, subjects were exposed to the aromas of various foods. Then researchers measured the blood flow to their nether regions. More than 40 percent of the males were physically aroused by the smell of pumpkin pie, especially when it was combined with lavender. Other turn-on fragrances were vanilla, strawberries, cinnamon buns, black licorice, and popcorn.

For women, the turn-ons included baby powder, pumpkin pie, chocolate (what a surprise!), and banana nut bread. Want a subtle but surefire concoction for your next night out? Layer your body with musk, vanilla spice, and baby powder. That combination works like fine wine, with wave upon wave of scent. It also telegraphs that you need to be protected and cared for and triggers all of the hardwiring in males.

Men should apply scent with a light hand to avoid giving off signals of coming on too strong. Neurologist Alan Hirsch suggested that wearing baby powder would evoke a maternal instinct in women.

PART IV

Putting It All Together

SEVENTEEN

THE BASICS OF BONDING

Now you have the tools you need, both verbal and nonverbal. In this section, you'll learn how to put them together to get a *yes* from anyone—anyplace and anytime.

COMMON GOALS: LET'S JOIN OUR VOICES

Common enemies unite us, and a common goal seals the deal. At a 2009 march protesting taxes, in Washington, D.C., the crowd was led by a

Republican who encouraged the group to chant, "Don't tread on me. Don't tread on me."

"Can you say it with me?" he shouted. "Don't tread on me. All together now," he continued until he had the entire group reciting the mantra in unison. In a situation such as this, you're bonding with everyone. You feel tremendously important because you share these common feelings, and you are not alone.

Participants in a peace rally will chant something like, "What do we want? Justice. When do we want it? Now. Whose streets? Our streets." Hearing your own voice magnified by the chant of the crowd is euphoric. Any type of group chant is trance inducing and extremely powerful. "The *people* ... *united* ... will never be *divided*." This mild hypnotic state of groupthink empowers everyone en masse.

Whether it's hating a common enemy or pursuing a common goal, people like being part of a group. Runners always acknowledge one another with a quick hello or nod of the head. People who drive the same kind of car honk at each other. On an episode of *Curb Your Enthusiasm*, Larry David, who is bald, commiserates with a friend who has accidentally gotten his head shaved.

Larry talks about being discriminated against and says, "I get support from my bald brothers." When the friend questions him, he says that yes, they nod to each other, smile at each other, and give each other support, as if there is a weekly meeting where all bald people hang out. The concept is funny because it resonates with the way we feel about those with shared beliefs, ideals, and values.

COMMON ENEMY: LET'S HATE HIM TOGETHER

Find a common enemy and experience instant bonding. It starts when we're kids, with the boys versus the girls. Then it's our team versus their team. In the world of work, we engage in sales contests against the other group; we bond together to beat our competition. We build rapport by making someone else the bad guy. We commiserate, complain, and plan victory. And perhaps more important, we connect in the process.

Sometimes negative bonding can get out of hand. A friend of mine is an intern for a newspaper where a columnist is pitted against the columnist at another paper. These two have a reason to hate each other; they have conflicting philosophies and they're fighting for readers. Each of their editors hates the other as well. Even my intern friend hates the columnist at the other paper. When I mentioned I was going to analyze an entertainment figure, she said, "I hate him."

"How can you possibly?" I asked. "What's to dislike about him?"

"Well," she said. "Maggie [the columnist at her paper] hates him."

BUILDING CREDIBILITY: BECAUSE I SAID SO

Credibility opens doors, changes minds, makes sales, and wins admiration. When you're credible you are perceived as authoritative and trustworthy.

Put a white coat on a man and his credibility immediately soars. Put a Ph.D. after a woman's name and what she is telling you suddenly makes much better sense. We communicate credibility with our competence, friendliness, appearance, sociability, body language, and paralanguage.

A doctor's white jacket increases the degree of credibility and trust.

In an experiment conducted in Australia, a visitor to a college classroom was introduced as a student from the University of Cambridge. To another class, he was introduced as a demonstrator. So it went with three more classes, in which he was presented as a lecturer, senior lecturer, and professor. When he left each class, students were asked to guess his height, and he literally rose in stature right along with his credibility. Each elevation of status gave him an extra half inch of perceived height.

In another study, done at a hospital, a researcher made the same phone call to twenty-two nurses' stations on various wards. The caller, posing as the hospital physician, instructed each nurse to give twenty milligrams of Astrogen (an unauthorized, fictitious medication) to a patient. Even though the maximum "dose" for the fictitious drug was ten milligrams, 95 percent of the nurses did as they were told and prepared the dosage. In another study of thirty-three nurses and student nurses, only two said they would have administered the drug. Perhaps these nurses were not aware of how much they were influenced by the word *doctor.*

TEARS

Multiple studies across cultures show that crying helps us bond with our families, loved ones, and allies. By blurring vision, tears reliably signal your vulnerability and that you love someone, a good evolutionary strategy to bind people emotionally to you, said Tel Aviv University evolutionary biologist Dr. Oren Hasson, of TAU's Department of Zoology.

"Of course," Dr. Hasson adds, "the efficacy of this evolutionary behavior always depends on who you're with when you cry those buckets of tears, and it probably won't be effective in places, like at work, when emotions should be hidden."

SMILES

Disqualifier: I'm Probably Not Interested

Little turns us off as much as someone who is emotionally needy. Using the disqualifier can make you appear more desirable because you aren't ready to leap on an offer.

A playful example was used by a friend of mine the first time we met in person after working together on the phone for several months. We went to lunch and when he placed our order, he said, "My future ex-wife will be having the Caesar salad."

At first it sounded like a compliment until I realized what he was really saying.

Needless to say, the disqualifier is a useful tool in getting your target closer to *yes.* We're always attracted to a challenge. His approach was effective because he wasn't falling all over me; he didn't come across as needy.

You might use it in a casual social conversation to attract the opposite sex, as my friend did above by referring to me as his future ex-wife. That was his way of sending the innuendo that it would never work out between us. He was disqualifying himself indirectly.

A disqualifier would fit in well for a consulting gig you might be offered. "I really like what I know of your company, and I think I can do amazing things for you, but I'm not sure that I would fit into your budget. If not, I have a former student in mind who I think would do wonderfully and still fit your budget."

Or if you're being sought after by a headhunter: "I really love my job with XYZ. It would take an amazing opportunity to convince me to leave."

SITUATIONAL ANALYSIS: IS THE SETTING APPROPRIATE?

You need to take the situation into account before making determinations about individuals. Recognizing the appropriateness within the current environment will help you establish rapport and keep you from looking as if you don't get it. You simply ask yourself, What is appropriate in this situational context?

On the job, you and your colleagues may be serious and low-key in a meeting. At a football game later that night, you and your coworkers will be drinking beer and cheering on the team. With that same crowd of people, you are a whole new person. At the annual Christmas party, you sometimes see coworkers doing things that make them practically unrecognizable from the person you met with to discuss your healthcare benefits earlier that day. Context changes everything.

THE SOUND OF A LIE

Thus far, we've been talking about people who have positive intentions. Not everyone does. Liars may be able to look at you with earnestness, but their bodies and voices frequently leak the truth indicators. Once you know what to listen and watch for, you can recognize a liar almost every time.

SIGNS OF LIES

Higher Pitch

The person's voice will suddenly rise in pitch as the lie is told.

Liar's Lilt

Frequently, someone who is lying will finish the sentence with a tag question coupled with a higher-pitched intonation at the end of the sentence. "It's true, I did have lunch with someone from XYZ Corp. We've got to keep tabs on the competition, you *know*?"

Nonwords, Throat Clearing

Listen for those *uh*s, *um*s, and throat clearings. When we experience great anxiety, our vocal cords thin out and stretch, which in turn makes our voice higher.

Shorter Responses

She wants to get into the lie and get out.

More Speech Errors

He may change tenses, speak in the third person, or repeat stock phrases.

More Inclusiveness

She uses words such as *always, everyone, no one.*

Distancing Language

Liars want to keep the accusation as far away as possible.

Hard Swallows

Swallowing is mostly an involuntary act. However, when we become stressed, emotionally anxious, or embarrassed, our throat muscles tighten, causing us to swallow harder or gulp.

Mark McClish, author of *I Know You Are Lying,* defines **statement**

analysis as putting yourself in the shoes of the suspected liar. Ask yourself what you would do in a similar situation. How would you answer the same questions? To detect deception in a statement, you must be a good listener, McClish says.

Each word has meaning, and you need to listen for specific words. Everything a person says is significant. Even though it may sound as if someone is telling the truth, if you listen carefully, you can determine what that person is really saying based on his specific language. This will help you to determine exactly what he is saying.[33]

LINEAR LYING

Liars are not retrieving information; they are inventing it, frequently as they go along.

"Why did you miss the eight o'clock staff meeting?"

"Well, first I had coffee with Joe. He's considering increasing his order. After that, I had to stop for gas and wash my car because I'm taking Brenda to lunch to pitch her on the June promotion. About that time, I got a phone call from Tom about that damaged shipment. Then I realized it was already eight thirty, and I didn't want to come in late. So I stopped at the office-supply store to pick up some supplies and on the way, I popped in to visit the new account I signed last week."

Here's how you can tell if it's a lie. Ask the person (indirectly) to tell you the story out of order. "What did you say you did right after you talked to Tom on the phone?" You'll probably hear a pause while she tries to mentally go through the story and stop at the appropriate portion of the lie. She is trying to retrieve the made-up story. In linear lying, you can actually witness the thought process as it happens, because it's not flowing naturally. Since it never actually happened, it's not stored in memory.

Having said that, I think it's important to point out that there's a fine line between anxiety and deception. The same high-pitched voice I described earlier might be used by someone in a job interview, not because he's lying, but because he is nervous.

Don't write off someone as dishonest at the first "well, uh." Spend some time learning to recognize these cues, as well as the verbal cues I listed earlier.

THE LOOK OF A LIE

"No, those pants don't make you look fat."

"Of course I've never loved anyone this much."

Some lies are harmless. They make other people feel better and keep conversations flowing without emotional speed bumps.

Other lies are designed to harm.

"Sure, I'll pay you back next week."

"Honest, I've never been married."

Forget the words for a moment. Here are some of the nonverbal cues that will help you spot deception before you get hurt.

Some signals are involuntary while others are just unconscious habits. Occasionally, when we lie, we recognize we are putting ourselves in the precarious position of being caught. Thus in some circumstances, our flight-or-fight response will kick in as adrenaline and other chemicals are activated. Observable physical symptoms include: shallow, rapid breathing, dilated pupils, flushed skin, sweating, and increased swallowing.

Dilated Pupils

Although dilated pupils may also show arousal, pupils will also dilate when a person feels in danger. When a liar feels trapped, he will be unable to control this physiological response.

Increased Swallowing

The liar's mouth gets dry, and he tries to take bigger gulps of air. When anxiety sets in, blood is diverted away from the inner organs, which slows down the digestive process and causes the mouth to dry up.

Rapid, Shallow, Irregular Breathing

With any lie, there is a chance of being caught. This risk causes the deceiver's breathing to speed up and allows his body to take in more oxygen— to metaphorically run faster and not get "caught" in the lie.

Flushing—Anywhere on the Body

Anxiety causes the blood vessels to dilate and rush closer to the surface of the skin, causing the blush. Evaluate this response in terms of the social situation, as well as what other signals are present.

Sweating

Anxiety causes the body temperature to rise, and the body produces sweat in order to avoid overheating. If you see sweat above the lip area or by the brows and there's no reason for it, you may be witnessing deception.

Increased Blinking

As we become nervous, the brain works quickly to come up with a story. Remember, an increase in blinking is an indicator but by no means a telltale sign. Most people can't control their blink rate, as it is typically correlated with the brain's processing of information. We might blink faster as we become emotionally aroused and as we form and evaluate our thoughts prior to delivering our message.

Hands to Mouth, Fingernail Biting

Some liars touch their lips. Others place their fingers or hands over their mouths. It stems back to childhood. Remember? Children cover their eyes and think they're invisible. They cover their mouths so that Mom can't see the lie. As we grow older, we learn to adjust our thinking. However, some may still bring their hands to their mouths in unconscious attempts to cover up their lies.

Touching Nose

Those nasty blood vessels again. The person lies, and the nose starts itching. Pinocchio Effect, big time. Pay attention.

Fewer Body Movements

It's called the freeze response, and if you've baselined the person, you'll know this one the moment you see it. The deceiver feels if he moves, the lie is going to leak out.

Increased Body Movements

These include twitching and self-touching. The other person is unconsciously distracting himself in the hopes that all of those movements will distract you away from the lie.

Mixed Signals

A shrug combined with an emphatic statement such as, "I absolutely agree," indicates uncertainty.

Less-Frequent Eye Contact

If you've baselined a person and know that she usually makes frequent eye contact, and suddenly that changes, it could be because the person isn't being honest with you. Conversely, a person who makes little eye contact in everyday speech may use a stalker stare when trying to deceive.

Time-takers

Sometimes even a second or two will provide the liar with enough time to deceive you. He will adjust his glasses, which will both give him a good reason for breaking eye contact and shutting up for a beat or two. The deceiver may fake a cough or pretend something is in his eye.

Dealing With Deception

Some of these nonverbal signals are within a liar's control, and others are not. Keep in mind, an experienced liar knows how to play the game. Knows not to avert his eyes, knows not to use self-pacifying gestures, and makes sure that he maintains necessary eye contact. In order to keep from being deceived, look for more than one signal.

Block Your Own Emotions

Some call it poker face. I call it block face. Keep that expression glued onto you until you're sure about the other person. Suppose you and a colleague are having a conversation. She's trying to lie to you. You're unconsciously giving signals of distrust. Crossing your arms, perhaps. Biting your lip. She unconsciously picks up on these signals and (again unconsciously) adjusts her behavior in the hopes that the new signals will be more believable. Once you omit those signals of skepticism, she will keep giving off the lying cues consistently and won't think to adjust her body language accordingly.

ASK TONYA

Q: I think my coworker stole money from me. How can I tell if she is lying when I ask her if she knows what happened to it?

A: There is no guaranteed way to discern deception, but you probably know what your coworker's normal behavior patterns are and can therefore distinguish atypical behavior. Does she cross her arms or legs? Does she stiffen her movements or bring her hands to her face? Does she slightly shift her body away or physically move away from you? Does her voice pitch get higher or end on an upward inflection? Does she suddenly start to flub her words? These are a few of the signals of deception, but you must first know how she regularly behaves before you can begin to make a determination.

EIGHTEEN

IMAGE

Putting On Your Professional Costume and Making It Fit

"If men can run the world, why can't they stop wearing neckties? How intelligent is it to start the day by tying a little noose around your neck?"

—*Linda Ellerbee*

You spent hours shopping for the perfect suit for that interview, so many hours that you didn't bother correcting that mushy handshake. You looked great coming through the door, but you lost the *yes* target at hello.

Or: You perfected your handshake and eye contact, but when you meet your *yes* target, your mouth was so dry that you could barely speak and the little spittle around the edges of your lips glowed white.

Or (and I know that *you* would never do this): You didn't bother to polish your shoes or your briefcase, and your status is diminishing as you pass every individual with your new sexy eyeglasses, which you didn't take care of and that now have thirty-seven obvious fingerprints on them.

You can't be the Alpha You until you take all of the verbal and non-verbal cues we've talked about and put them together into one powerful package, the *yes* package. When I speak to a group, I sometimes ask those attending to do a little activity where everyone gets to write their first impressions of everyone else. When I share that information, the group members frequently are shocked to see how others perceived them. They have no idea that they may be projecting the exact opposite impression than they intend, or, better, that they come across as stronger than they ever imagined possible. Since I started doing this, I have witnessed grown men cry at the input, managers go hysterical laughing at what their underlings say, and some get real eye-openers as to their mode of dress. One woman, upon getting her feedback, had a fit: "Nice jugs—try covering them up once in a while." Thank goodness the comment was anonymous.

Every day, most of us get up, look in the mirror, and rate ourselves about a seven on a scale of one to ten. If that were true, we would all be average, with no bottom tier and no top tier. I have news for you: There are plenty of twos, threes, and fours out there as well. You want to be the Alpha You, and that means being aware of the image you convey. Image is a combination of the way you look, the way you dress, and the way you relate. It's everything from the tone of your voice to your shoes. Each and every thing on your body makes a statement about you. So take a look and ask yourself, Is this really what I want to say to the world?

Dress one step above the individual you will be meeting.

Alphas of both sexes need to own the room from the moment they arrive. But that doesn't mean your wardrobe needs to shout, "Look at me!" Calling unnecessary attention to yourself just won't do the trick. I believe you should dress one step above the individual you will be meeting. Go neutral on the accessories the first time you meet someone so that you can more easily form a social bond. If you walk into a client's office with a big gold religious symbol around your neck, what happens if the client is of a different faith or no faith? Immediate bonding? I don't think so. Instead of nonverbally screaming the differences between you and your *yes* target, going neutral allows you to get a feel for and sort through your target's ideas, beliefs, and feelings and find the commonalities you share.

POSTURE

Researchers found that men six feet tall earned almost one thousand dollars more annually than men who are two inches shorter.

In the work world, taller is better. How much better? Well, in an Australian study reported in *The Economic Record* in 2009, researchers found that men six feet tall earned almost one thousand dollars more annually than men who were two inches shorter. Over the course of a long career, this could add up to some serious dollars. Other studies in the U.S. and UK estimated the extra earnings at almost that much per inch! According to Arianne Cohen, author of *The Tall Book*, tall people earn $789 more per inch per year.[34]

So, what if you aren't tall? Successful people come in all sizes. *Stand* tall or make sure you have the credibility and authority to be perceived as tall as we discussed in the study above. Show with your body language that you are an alpha. Elongate your neck. Keep your shoulders back and down and your chest high. Keep your spine straight and your weight on both feet.

WAIST-TO-HIP RATIO

This magic number is interesting for any number of reasons. Women with a waist-to-hip ratio of 0.7 or less are not as susceptible to cardiovascular disease, ovarian cancer, and diabetes. Men with WHRs of 0.9 to 1.0 or less are not as likely to contract prostate and testicular cancer.

You can find your WHR by dividing your waist measurement by your hip measurement. For women, a WHR of 0.7, in which the waist is seven-tenths of the hips, is considered most desirable by the opposite sex and therefore what you should strive for—for both good health and the leverage of desire. So for someone who has a waist measurement of 29 and hip measurement of 33 the calculation would be as follows: 29/33 = 0.88 (unhealthy for a woman). Measurements of waist 27 and hips 36 would be: 27/36 = 0.75 (healthy for a woman). Doctors are now using the WHR as a stronger indicator of cardiovascular disease than the body mass index.[35]

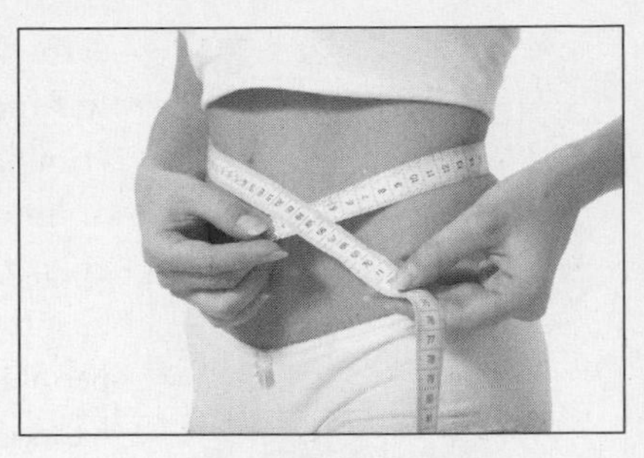

Women with a waist-to-hip ratio of .7 are less susceptible to cardiovascular disease, ovarian cancer, and diabetes.

At the University of Texas at Austin, men were shown line drawings of twelve female figures. The men ranged from ages twenty-five to eighty-five, and the figures varied in terms of weight and WHR. The majority of these men preferred the figures of normal weight with a curvy .7 WHR.

Evidence suggests a link between an hourglass figure and fertility. In a Harvard study, women with lower WHRs were three times more likely to conceive than less curvy women of the same age.

THE EYE OF THE BEHOLDER

It's not enough that tall people earn more. According to the Federal Reserve Bank of St. Louis, beautiful people earn about 5 percent more than their average coworkers. After factoring out education, experience, and other variables, researchers found that the premium for beauty ranges across all occupations. And jobs requiring more interpersonal contact have higher percentages of employees whose appearance is above average.

What's beautiful? The answer: symmetry. Although the equation varies slightly from culture to culture, the symmetrical face is the one that attracts us. And these lovely people tend to earn more than anyone else.

Researchers also found that employees with below-average looks

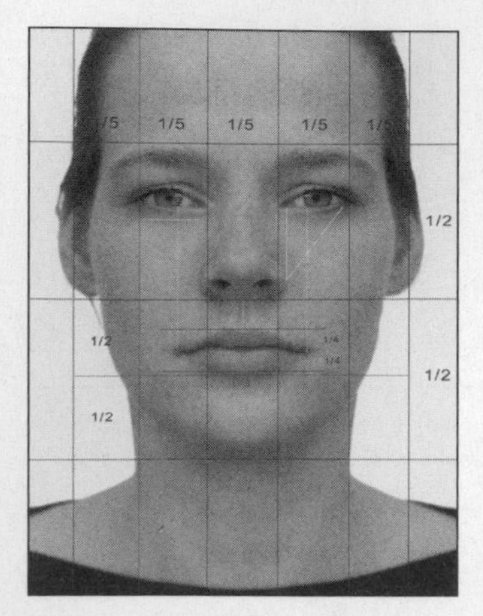

A so-called perfect face, the expected result of cosmetic surgery. The lines show the perfect proportions of the human face.

earned 9 percent less an hour. Is this because self-image affects self-confidence, or is it discrimination? Whatever the cause, and regardless of how attractive you are or aren't in your own eyes, my suggestion is to be your best and most beautiful self inside and out. We've all known people who are not traditionally beautiful or handsome whose commanding presence and self-confidence make them the focus wherever they go. Their exterior looks take a backseat to their interior disposition. In other words, they are their Alpha Selves. This applies to many in the entertainment industry and political field as well. Furthermore, once someone has seen an individual several times, the brain is trained on what it has seen, and a person will become more attractive through the familiarity effect. This is really beneficial for those of us who believe we are a seven on the attraction scale but are really only a four or a five.

But remember that beauty is also about how you carry yourself. So, as just one of many examples, a comfortable, healthy weight is key in keeping your confidence up. And that's not just vanity speaking! Economists have found that women considered obese in terms of their body mass index earned 17 percent less than women within their recommended BMI range.

SIGNS OF BEAUTY

For Women

High forehead	Small jaw
High cheekbones	Small chin
Clear skin	Big eyes
Full lips	Small nose

For Men

Smooth skin

Straight nose

Strong jawline

Big eyes

It's vital that after all this work you don't let anything detract from your intended message. Sometimes it's the little things that slip past us. The flake of dandruff on the shoulder. The picked fingernail polish. The too-strong aftershave or perfume. As we've discussed throughout this book, these minor oversights can detract from your intended message. Plan in advance: Know what you're going to wear, how you're going to go through every part of the meeting and greeting. Don't leave anything to chance. Here are a few commonsense pointers:

WALK

A man I knew who managed a surgical-supply house invited every potential employee he interviewed to tour the facility with him. Clerical workers, salespeople, accountants—they all got a walk around Don's company. Although they didn't know it, Don was watching how they moved. If they slumped, moved too slowly, or didn't show interest, they were out. If they moved briskly and with purpose, yet stopped when intrigued, they had a much better chance. He believed that how they moved was an indicator of how they would treat their jobs. The purposeful movers were the energetic types he wanted working in every facet of his company.

When you approach another person, she will be (consciously or unconsciously) doing the same thing Don was with his job candidates. The way you move will show her if you're slow paced, slumped, a foot dragger, or high energy and full of life.

Make each stride about two feet wide. Let your arms swing naturally; don't pump them. Pull back your shoulders and elongate your neck. After you've greeted your *yes* target, match your step to hers.

EYE CONTACT FOR BONDING

You don't want to stalker-stare your new boss, client, or potential date. Pretend the *yes* target has a triangle on his face running from the nose up to each eye. For social bonding, the triangle would point down—from the eyes and nose to the mouth. Eye contact is so important and speaks volumes about your confidence. Sometimes I break up a group I'm working with into pairs and ask them to stare into each other's eyes for three entire minutes. At a distance of three to four feet apart, they cannot speak, laugh, or break eye contact. By the end of this experiment, there is a bizarre bonding that occurs between the two participants, as if they have shared the discomfort and now feel better about each other. At times, I will have them synchronize their breathing as well. When we do this, the breathing helps us to build rapport even quicker and acts as a slight distraction to the intensity of the direct eye contact. Both are powerful experiences, as any one of my participants will tell you. Of course, when making eye contact, individuals need to be culturally cognizant of what is considered polite and what is considered impolite.

SMILE

Regardless of how nervous you are, smile. Smiling lifts the face muscles up so that you appear younger. In addition, it makes you feel and look more confident and happier. An added benefit, of course, is that it causes the other person's mirror neurons to fire up, and she will smile back.

If you have dental problems, do your best to correct them as soon as possible. Growing up, I held my hand over my mouth when I talked. I was ashamed of my smile and my less-than-dazzling-white teeth. Back then, there were no solutions or over-the-counter bleaches, and even if there had been, I grew up without dental insurance. Only after I was an adult did I get the help I needed, and I'm so fanatical about keeping my teeth white that I drink everything—including coffee, tea, and soda—out of a straw. Fortunately, many new products are available to whiten stained teeth and give you the confidence you may have lacked before. Nothing should rob you of your smile.

BLOCK FACE

Our lives aren't consistently perfect, and some of us are better than others at hiding our personal problems. I have worked with people who, regardless of what was happening in their lives, always functioned the same at work. One woman I interacted with on a daily basis showed up with a new name. When I asked what going on, she said, "I was divorced last week." She had kept her emotions guarded the entire time. I'm not going to say I could have done it, but I understood why she did. She kept her private life private and her focus on her performance at work. Furthermore, she avoided breaking down in front of coworkers during a devastating time in her life.

That's where the block face—a neutral look—can serve you well, especially during times of tension. This neutral face is the one that smiles and says: *No worries. Everything is fine.* It blocks your emotions from leaking, and it keeps others from guessing about what is happening in your life. You're putting on a mask, taking your problems out of your outward appearance and falling apart only later at home.

Block face isn't just for when life is handing you lemons. It's the perfect way to cover up any emotion you don't want to reveal, such as great anxiety, great joy, or even knowledge of a friend's surprise birthday party.

FOR WOMEN

Cosmetics

I once had a makeup artist tell me, "Anyone can be beautiful. They just need the right shadows and the right paint." I remember thinking, *Wow, what a perfect attitude for someone with her job.* All women have beauty, and the right cosmetics can bring it out. Unless you're in the entertainment industry, you should avoid heavy foundation.

My favorite color for business is neutral—foundation, blush, and lips. I deplore concealer. As a makeup artist I know says, "It's like telling everyone, 'Look at this spot on my face. I hate it.'" Some cosmetics companies manufacture "revealer," which lights up the area under your eyes and emphasizes the apex of your cheekbones. You can get the same effect with a highlighting cream. Use a very light hand; people want to see your face, not your makeup. In one study, a woman with no discernible makeup was perceived as more qualified for a professional job and was recommended for a higher salary than candidates with visible makeup.

It's not that surprising that more men find red lipstick on a woman sexier than any other. In *The Naked Ape,* Desmond Morris explains that wet, red lips are an unconscious attempt by women to mimic the bright, swollen vulvae of female mammals in heat.

To bald or not to bald? Pulling off the look depends on how well you handle your nonverbal communication.

Hair

Women and men should both groom according to the standards of the industry. In most professional environments, long hair should be worn up.

FOR MEN

A Word About Bald

More and more men with thinning hair are shaving their heads. It's a look I happen to like, and whether or not you can pull it off depends on how you handle the nonverbals. It's amazing how a shaved head and strong, confident, nonverbal communication can improve the appearance of many men. Conversely, with the wrong nonverbal communication, you are just another guy who lost his hair. The difference is in how you carry that baldness.

MANEUVERING

When Alpha Meets Alpha

When two alphas meet each other, there is literally a power struggle. The outcome depends on the situation. Remember, only one is going to come out on top, but that doesn't mean the other has to lose face. If two alphas are getting together to discuss the IT department, and one works in personnel and the other in IT, the personnel alpha can easily defer by recognizing that the IT person knows more; the personnel alpha becomes the "secondary alpha." He knows that the goal is just to look for a solution to a problem, which means not reacting to the small stresses, and he handles the experience in a poised and relaxed manner. The secondary alpha sends out the vibe that the IT alpha will offer the best resolution.

I want to stress here that alpha and beta are just two different behavioral strategies, and both live within us. Sometimes you'll encounter a beta who is a wannabe alpha but either he can't pull it off or it really isn't his nature. This person buys a book, reads a third of it, and thinks, *I'm the chief in charge.* Unconsciously, his insecurity will leak out, especially during a confrontation, and he will lose face.

Beta isn't a negative—it's just different. The goal for this book, however, is to help you achieve the appropriate status for *you.* At times, we're all betas, and there's nothing wrong with that. Can you imagine the unattractive place our world would be if we were all alphas beating on each other all the time? The goal is to be the Alpha You when you need to be—so that others don't take advantage of you, and so you can get to *yes.*

HOW TO SPOT A BULLY

Some bullies are obvious; others are more surreptitious and make you wonder. The obvious people want to get in your face, literally. Some of the signs include a domineering tone and sentences that suffer from *I*-strain: "I think . . ." "I said . . ." "I told her . . ."

Other bullies are not so easy to spot. Once you get that queasy feeling,

check for other signs. Is this person standing over you or invading your personal space? Is she tilting her head down at you, folding her arms, or rolling her eyes?

It's not difficult to rebuff a bully. Just hold your ground in your personal space. Cross you arms as if to say, "That's far enough," or open your arms to show that you are not intimidated but are still open.

There's nothing worse for a bully than someone who won't play the game and back down.

HOW TO GET THE DEAL YOU WANT

As with my friend and the dining-room set salesman, successful negotiations begin with baselining the other person. What is this person's communication style? Is he a faux Mr. Protector, or is he Mr. Glib? Ask a few factual questions about the car, loveseat, or swimming pool you are pricing. That way you'll be able to determine if he's telling the truth later when you ask if he's giving you his best price.

Give away as little personal information as possible. Keep your expression indifferent and your body language closed. Close your lips, cross your arms. Angle your body away from the salesperson and use subtle head shaking when you speak.

If the deal begins to sound sweeter, and you are thinking it might be a possible sale, signal it by opening your body language a little. Keep your expression more neutral and occasionally nod.

Is he biting his lip, flushing, pacing, or covering his mouth with his hand? He's getting desperate and doesn't want you to get away. Give him enough time and enough verbal rope, and you will get the deal you want.

HOW TO CLOSE A SALE

You're dealing with a client and want to close the deal. Of course, you've already baselined him, so you know what signals are "normal" for this person. First, look for *yes* signals. Are his pupils dilated? Is he blushing or nodding? Are his palms open, and/or is he leaning forward? These are all positive gestures.

This man's body language shows that he's still making up his mind.

What about the *maybe* signs? If he takes a drink of water or strokes his chin, he is probably still trying to make up his mind. You haven't convinced him yet.

Look out for hands over the mouth, tapping fingers, bouncing feet, folded arms, or that all-too-revealing head shake—these are signs of a *no.*

The pendulum can be in any one of these three positions: *yes, maybe,* or *no.* Watch for the changes and you'll know the perfect moment to move in.

HOW TO APPROACH A GROUP

In both social and business situations, you'll avoid the cold shoulder if you know how to approach a group. First, check out the body language. A closed group is like a closed door—there's no way you are going to be able to open it. Are their arms crossed? Are their bodies and feet pointed toward each other? Find another group; this one is closed.

Are anyone's feet pointing away from the group? Good. There's your entrance. Pull back your shoulders and take a deep breath. Smile. Then head for the person whose body language is the most open.

Open body language shows a colleague he's safe approaching the group.

HOW TO INSPIRE TRUST

In order to establish rapport, you need to inspire trust. Be sure to smile, but not with the constant faux smile of the desperate salesperson. Study my Psychological Secrets That Sway (Chapter Twenty-one) so that you know what motivates others. Maintain eye contact and use palms-up gestures. Be sure that your gestures match your statements—that you are nodding when making positive statements and shaking your head when making negative ones.

Keep your feet pointed toward your target.

Use the person's name naturally in speech and match her communication style. Be sure to avoid words typically associated with lying, such as *actually*. Not everyone who says that is lying, *actually*, but liars frequently use it, along with words like *honestly*, to emphasize their points. Three is known as the liar's number. Don't fall into the easy "three good reasons" or "I tried to call you three times."

Be on the lookout for any negative emotion. Those good old head shakes or nose scratches may be indications that you're not hitting home with your message. Take a deep breath, slow down, and try again. On the other hand, if your *yes* target begins to mirror your body language, or if she smiles or nods, you are well on your way to building trust—and rapport.

HOW TO MOTIVATE

Although we've discussed motivation elsewhere, here is a down-and-dirty way to be sure you're on track in a supervisory situation.

First of all, don't intimidate. Ask the person if he has a moment to talk to you. Use nonthreatening body language: open palms and posture, steady eye contact, smiles. Vary your pitch and speak a little faster than usual. Mirror the other person's body language.

If you are a woman, stand on the outer edge of the personal zone, at about three feet. Your stance should be face-to-face. If you're a man, also stand approximately three feet away, but at a ninety-degree angle.

Here's a trick. If you are making an intellectual request ("Can you please have this finished by nine a.m. tomorrow? The VP needs to present it at a sales conference."), line up your left eye with the person's left eye. If your request is emotional ("Would you mind working late again tonight?"), line up your right eye with the person's right eye.

Is the other person nodding? Are her pupils dilating? Again, you've probably succeeded. Is she looking down or turning away? Back off. You are probably coming on too strong. You may be the boss, but in order to get the person solidly on your side, you need more than authority. You need rapport.

HOW TO GET THE TEAM TO BUY INTO YOUR PLAN

Team motivation incorporates some of the same tactics as one-on-one motivation. In this setting, more than ever, you need to use open, inclusive gestures. Make eye contact with everyone, and don't exchange private smirks or eye-rolling with another individual.

If at all possible, use a round table so that everyone feels equal. If you must sit at the traditional rectangular table, don't sit at the head. The power will be where you are anyway, but it won't be as blatant if you take a less traditional place. Whenever someone speaks, turn your body toward that person. Keep your gestures small but energetic.

If everyone feels part of the group, you will know it. They will be smiling, probably at the same time. They'll also be nodding, their gestures will be open, and their feet will point toward the people they're talking to. Check it out. If you see someone looking down or avoiding eye contact—or, worse, if most of the team is looking anywhere but at you or each other—you need to backtrack fast.

HOW TO SHOW YOUR FRIENDSHIP

With any target, including someone you're considering for a friend, the first tactic is: Listen! Most people are eager for an audience, and most speakers try to one-up the other person in a conversation. Your target will welcome your attention, especially if you keep an open body posture with open palms and keep your feet pointed toward her. That should be easy if you genuinely like her and want to be her friend. Be sure that you also make eye contact, tilt your head, and lean toward her when you speak.

If you feel her backing off or notice her crossing her arms or using other gestures to shut you out, ease up a little.

I have a friend who works as a newspaper reporter. When we first met, she barraged me with questions. Where was I born? Where did I go to school? What got me interested in communication? The questions ranged from what was my favorite dessert to what was the secret of a long-lasting marriage. Even though I answered the questions, I felt as if I was being grilled, and wove in a few conversational threads of my own in self-defense. She responded happily, and I realized that she had no intention of intimidating me. As a reporter, asking questions is second nature for her. It's what passes as conversation in her life.

When you bond with a new person, you don't want to hog the spotlight by talking only about yourself. Just as important, you shouldn't do what my friend did and mock-interview your new friend. Put the emphasis on her, but also let the conversation assume a natural give-and-take.

RED OR BLUE? DEPENDS ON YOUR JOB

A new study published in *New Scientist* magazine says that while the color red can help you be more accurate in your work, the color blue spurs creativity.

University of British Columbia researchers conducted tests with six hundred people to see how cognitive performance varies when people see red or blue. Participants performed tasks in which words or images were displayed against red, blue, or neutral backgrounds on computer screens. Red groups fared better on tests of recall and attention to detail, and blue groups performed better on tests requiring imagination and creativity.[36]

NINETEEN

ICEBREAKER STORYTELLING

Planned, Not Canned

Now that you know how to dress, speak, and smell, you have to know what to talk about! Most of us love hearing stories; it's probably a vestige from those positive experiences of being a kid and having your parent read to you. You'll find countless opportunities to tell your stories every day. When you exchange small talk on a job interview or have lunch with a new client, the right anecdote based on memories in your life can cement that emotional bond and give the other person a glimpse of who you are. Stories are memories focused to elicit a response from your *yes* target. Understand that I'm talking about *planned* stories, not *canned* stories. You don't just memorize some stock response for all seasons. You *plan* what you will say when the moment and the person are right. Now that you've gotten yourself in the door, it's time to get your conversation spot-on.

If you want to understand the power of a well-told story, listen to politicians trying to persuade voters about their personal merits or the advantages of one of their causes. The tales they tell are rarely about themselves. They are about the ninety-year-old grandmother in Knoxville who is losing her house. Or the police officer in Detroit who is worried about what will happen to his kids if he is injured or killed in the line of duty. They are stories that make us worry, wonder, and, most of all, care.

Your topics can be ironic, embarrassing, awkward, or naïve. They can range from dangerous, such as the time you bungee-jumped; to exciting, such as your parasailing experience; to funny, such as the worst date you have ever had. A key tip is positioning the story as one of personal triumph—for example, how did one of your experiences prepare you for whatever situation you are in now? How did something you strived for or struggled with in your youth impact what you have achieved as an adult? This is the perfect opportunity to discuss an insecurity you once had that you have since overcome. Keep in mind, though, that these aren't the overly revealing stories you share with close friends; they are conversational threads that help you break the ice with people you don't know and perhaps get them sharing some secrets of their own. It's a way to bond.

The goal is natural, spontaneous conversation. So, the other person may say something that triggers your story, or you can steer conversation your way by asking an innocuous question such as, "What did you do last weekend?" Then you can come back with the amazing experience you had last weekend. It doesn't matter if it happened last weekend or last month. It's your story, and if it is appropriate at that moment, use it. Stories are meant to flow out organically like a stream, almost by accident, not surge out like a tidal wave. Remember, telling a story shares a vulnerability or individuality, thereby creating emotional ties. And emotional ties are the foundation for good rapport.

You should always use stories to elevate your status. When a friend of mine worked in the financial industry, he didn't tell people he was a personnel analyst. He told them he worked on Wall Street. Or, suppose I tell you something funny Bob's wife said at the barbecue I attended at their house. Since Bob is the vice president, I'm telling you more about my status and my affiliations than I am about what his wife said.

Some people might wonder, "Tonya, why do I need a story in advance? Why can't I just act spontaneously?" Spontaneity is fine with family and friends. When you are getting to know a new person, your intent is to manipulate the environment to build yourself up and demonstrate where you stand in the social hierarchy. Unless you fall into the very small category of amazing instant-tale weavers, off-the-cuff stories could easily lead to boring, long-winded, unfocused yarns. This is what usually happens to those who don't come prepared. You want to get to the point where you have told each story so many times that you don't even need to think about it, while still keeping it fresh and lively. Have you ever had to sit through a story that bored you to tears—all the while trying to pretend you were interested?

Moving past the critical factor requires you to see eye to eye—or subconscious to subconscious. You do that by using **bonding mechanisms,** some verbal and many nonverbal, many of which have been discussed throughout this book. These are just techniques to engage another and build mutual liking. The goal is to get people in the same mind-set so that they connect emotionally with you.

A media trainer I know teaches clients how to shine in interviews. Keep in mind, just because someone is famous doesn't mean he or she is instantly comfortable in front of a camera. That's where preparation comes in. The media trainer tells her clients to pretend they are in the middle of the ocean. She then helps them come up with three safe islands.

Here's how it works. Pretend you're a client who has just written a book, gotten elected to public office, or been hired to promote a company, product, or cause. Find those three safe islands—the three main points you want to make about yourself, your product, or your philosophy. By giving these answers, you can swim to your islands every time the sharks come near. One island wouldn't be enough; you would look ridiculous giving the same answer to every question, regardless of the topic. Four islands would be too many; you would run the risk of sounding scattered. In order to steer clear of the tough questions and to emphasize your point, you need to prepare.

Stories allow you to tell others about your own values. You're communicating—without explicitly stating—your beliefs, morals, standards, and ideals about specific situations. Telling a story shares a vulnerability with another and creates an emotional tie with that person. Professional writers know to "show, not tell," and in the very *telling* of your story, you are *showing* how you feel without a long speech about "Wonderful Me from A to Z." You're essentially saying, "I am friendly and confident enough to expose my vulnerabilities, my beliefs, and my values." The goal is to keep your *yes* target intrigued as you raise your status.

DECIDE ON AT LEAST TEN TOPICS

Delve into your memory and come up with two stories from your childhood, one from adolescence, two from previous jobs, and at least five adventure stories. It's about captivating your audience. What do you want your *yes* target to know and feel about you? Is it that you're responsible? Spontaneous? Caring? Once you have decided which inference you would like to unfold, manipulate the story to convey that characteristic. In other words, change the variables of the story to fit your intended message. That doesn't mean lying; it means using ideas to tug on the necessary heart and mind strings.

TELL STORIES IN THE FIRST PERSON

Telling stories in the first person gives them an immediacy. (Who wants to hear what your friend did? Tell about what *you* did.) To make the stories even more effective, covertly include details about what others have said about you, such as, "Then John told Sally, 'Mike takes some crazy risks but he is always right in the end!'"

CREATE AN INTRIGUING HOOK THAT TELEGRAPHS THE EMOTIONAL TONE OF YOUR STORY

"I had the most terrifying experience yesterday."

"You would not believe this incredible waterfall that we climbed barefoot, in Jamaica this summer."

"Every time I think about the holidays, I remember a pair of silver skates."

Your first sentence hooks the listener, and it establishes your tone. Is this a rip-roaring funny story; a poignant, sentimental story; a wow-I-did-it story? It's like music: A country ballad doesn't start out the same way as a rock 'n' roll hit.

DON'T FEAR SELF-DEPRECATION

It raises your status. You're not fishing for compliments; you're just making a statement that shows you can laugh at yourself. You verbally take yourself down a notch to show that you're not overly tied to your ego. Use caution, though—you don't want to hurt yourself or appear insincere.

The next step in a story like this should show how you persevered. This will humanize you and keep you grounded in your target's eyes. For example, you're at lunch with a colleague, having a good time. You might tell your coworker how, earlier that morning, you tripped going into the office: "And then, I walked through the door and I tripped." There is a big difference between past and present. If it happens in front of your colleague or if someone sees you trip, your status gets lowered. But if it happened in the past, in telling the story you make yourself appear comfortable in your own skin.

INCLUDE LOTS OF VIVID VISUALS

When you describe people in your story, pick out one element that will help the other person see them. You don't have to go into minute detail, but the visuals should be pretty intense and vivacious so the person actually experiences the moment with you.

The goals are to stimulate the emotions, pique curiosity, and lead the target to experience everything from laughter to tears. Tell your story with passion. Remember, a story is real life in the past—a moment of truth, joy, surprise, happiness, or consequence. In real life, we have an entire range of emotions that we demonstrate both verbally and nonverbally. Make sure you pause to build intrigue, widen your eyes and drop your jaw to demonstrate shock, raise your voice to show strength, lower your voice to express restraint, speed up to demonstrate anticipation, and slow down to convey tranquility.

USE DIALOGUE

When you read a story in a book, your eye will move to the sections of dialogue. People love the immediacy of conversation, so be sure to include that if you can: "So, I said to the officer, 'But everyone was driving over seventy-five miles per hour.' And he said, 'But you were the leader of the pack.'"

CREATE RESOLUTION

A story is not an event; it is a strategic verbal and nonverbal tool to ingeniously encapsulate your message. It has a beginning, a middle, and an end. The end offers some type of resolution. The pertinent piece of this, however, is that a story can be changed in multiple ways for different audiences, as long as the storyline offers your thought-provoking final messages. Did you achieve your goal, or did you fail but learn a greater truth? Did the story change your life in some way?

VARY THE LENGTH

Storytelling is not one-size-fits-all. Adjust the story to the situation, the context, and the *yes* target. Have both a ninety-second version and a four-minute version of each of your stories.

PRACTICE TELLING AND RETELLING

Record yourself telling three stories and then listen to yourself. How did you do? Next, videotape the stories. Wow, I bet you noticed a big difference. Now rate them all for their emotional appeal. Does your pacing work? Is your phrasing on the mark? Is your body language natural? Do you believe you? The idea of the story is to stimulate and intrigue your target. The more stimulated your target is, the more compelling the experience of meeting you becomes.

THE MEDIUM WAS THE MESSAGE

The Nixon/Kennedy debate will forever be a topic of discussion in the world of nonverbal communication. Those who watched the debate on television were sure that Kennedy had outshone Nixon with his polished appearance, sincere look, and calm demeanor. Those who listened on the radio believed that Nixon had won because he sounded more confident and better informed on the issues.

GEAR IT TO YOUR AUDIENCE

Feel-good stories about family work better in a social situation. Overcoming obstacles is a natural topic for business settings.

MESMERIZE, DON'T MONOPOLIZE

Evaluate the other person's reactions so you aren't thought of as boring or overbearing. You want your target to think, *What happened then?* Not, *Will this motormouth ever shut up?*

Tell the story as if it's the first time you've ever told it. Have passion for your topic, and keep your eye on your target's responses. Share a little bit of yourself without telling your whole life story. Start with a genuine emotion and plan out a story that will work every time to bring you closer to strangers.

TELL ME WHY

People like to talk about themselves, and they will if you give them an opportunity. Here are ten quick *why* questions that will make it easy to keep new conversations flowing. Of course, you need to have planned responses because once your target answers the question, he will lob it back to you. These questions should never be posed so that the response can be a one-word answer. Pose it in a "what/why" way that ensures a lengthy response.

Do you like cats or dogs? *Why?*

What do your friends call you? *Why?*

What's the most audacious thing you have ever done? *Why?*

What keeps you up at night? *Why?*

What is your favorite cuisine? *Why?*

Who is your favorite author? *Why?*

What was your best vacation? *Why?*

Who is your favorite group? *Why?*

What is your favorite all-time film? *Why?*

What did you want to be when you were little? *Why?*

ALL THE NEWS

Now you understand the absolute significance of having several perfectly formed stories that demonstrate your values, beliefs, and goals, and that also reveal a little about yourself. You'll be simultaneously charismatic and captivating.

The same goes for having information on hand about the world. If you have nothing else in common with someone, you can always find shared experience in national or world news. Each morning, as essential as that cup of coffee or tea, have a quick study session. Get your news through a few different media outlets, including online newspapers and television. All news is slanted; be sure to get views from all sides so that you get a full scope of what is out there. I'm not saying you must read five newspapers back-to-back; read chunks to gain an overview of various topics, from who is sleeping with whom in Hollywood all the way to what's going on in Middle Eastern politics.

In addition, look for unusual resources. Your local newspaper tells you what's going on in your own backyard, some of the smaller, quirky articles that don't make the front page of the major papers. Sometimes the most captivating information is in one of those tiny articles in the back of the paper, something little known and exciting that you can disseminate. For example, "Did you read that article today about how whispering in someone's right ear is likely to increase the chances of them saying *yes* if you need something? Oh my goodness, it was amazing. It said your right ear is stronger for listening to words because the left brain is better at processing verbal information. Cool, huh? Come here, let me whisper in your ear and see if it works!"

One of books I often give as a gift is filled with useless information and appropriately named: *The Amazing Book of Useless Information.* I can always find plenty of easy conversation openers in this book.

INVISIBLE CONVERSATION THREADS

When you're first meeting people and conversation runs low, it's important to know how to get it back on track. Invisible conversational threads are a perfect fix because you weave them in as you talk in order to give some texture and focus the conversation in a new direction. Here's an example: "I wanted to take my kids to the game this week, but even baseball is so expensive these days." The invisible conversational thread is that everything is getting so expensive. It opens up the possibilities and gives your target any number of potential responses.

"I know," she might say. "It seems like everything is going up in price. It's tough to do anything as a family anymore."

To which you could reply, "That's for sure. It's so expensive just to fill my tank each week. Now is really the time to have a smaller car. Speaking of which, did you see the new electric cars that are coming out?"

Your conversation has gone from baseball games to electric cars in just a few sentences. "Even baseball is expensive" leads to any number of responses and opens up the conversation to a whole bunch of new topics. The thread would be all of the other things out there that are expensive. Instead of using dead-end yes-or-no comments, you weave in comments that intrigue and lead your target to the next stage of the conversation. You can do it with something as innocuous as the weather.

"It's really chilly today, isn't it? Makes me wish I were in California again."

"You were in California? When?"

"San Diego, last month. Have you ever been there?"

"Yes, but not for a long time. I love San Francisco."

"Me too. Where do you stay when you go there?"

Use these techniques and you'll never have to worry about dead air or dead-end conversations.

ASK TONYA

Q: I have a job interview coming up. How can I make the best impression?

A: Make sure you know the company inside and out. Being informed about the company is one way to differentiate yourself from other candidates. Make sure you dress appropriate to the industry. Smile, tilt, and nod to let the interviewer know you are listening. And finally, have your USP ready. Be sure you can answer the question that will surely be posed: "Why should I hire you for this job?" Come up with answers to what makes you better than the other twenty-five people interviewing. You might use some anecdotes or stories—remember, building rapport in this manner while still maintaining professionalism will allow you to form a bond with the interviewer.

Q: I have to give a speech, and I do not enjoy speaking in public. I'll be stammering all over the place for sure. If you could give me some tips, I would appreciate it.

A: The best tip I could offer you is to make your speech memorable. Start off with a powerful story, not an introduction about yourself or about the weather. Give them great content (high energy if appropriate, but don't feel the pressure to be something that you're not) and finish off with another powerful story. People tend to remember the beginning and end of an event, so the opening and closing need to invoke some type of positive reaction.

TWENTY

GENDER DIFFERENCES IN COMMUNICATION

"I feel there are two people inside me—me and my intuition. If I go against her, she'll screw me every time, and if I follow her, we get along quite nicely."

—*Kim Basinger*

On a logical level, you don't need me to tell you that men and women communicate differently, but unfortunately, sometimes we need to be reminded that we are indeed built differently. We are all socially conditioned based on our evolutionary makeup. Men are built and wired for one thing, and women for another. The fundamental issue here is that the two sexes are poles apart—not better or worse; just different. It seems the popular opinion is that women dramatize everything and men are indifferent. But is that really the case? Perhaps we merely need to learn how to pull the right strings to allow the opposite sex to see our frames and help them more easily understand our point of view. Understanding these differences gives you an edge in communication. It may even enhance your personal life. Genetically and socially, we are preprogrammed from birth. Our bodies evolved differently to fit our early job descriptions: men as the hunters and women as the nurturers. There are a few exceptions, but for the most part, we react in specific ways based on that genetic wiring.

A few years ago, a friend of mine had a dog that one day turned up with fleas. I'm not talking one or two; I'm talking infestation. She and her husband were unfamiliar with the nasty little creatures and had no idea what to do about them. All they knew was that fleas were jumping all around the house, including on their beds, on their children, on their dog—and on them. They made the discovery on a Sunday evening, and that Monday, my girlfriend called me in hysterics.

"He left me, he left me. That son of a bitch left me and went to work with all these bugs in the house." She was shocked that her husband would leave the house (to go hunt for the meal) while she stayed back and tended the home. A woman would have instinctively known that you could not leave another woman in that mental state. The husband, however, had missed it. To him, to stay home for something that he considered insignificant was ridiculous and out of the question. She needed him, but he couldn't understand her frustration.

This is different hardwiring at work. Mistakenly, my friend felt abandoned. She thought that her husband didn't care enough to stay by her side. He, of course, cared so much he felt the need to earn money to keep the flea-ridden house. Simply recognizing and accepting these differences between men and women will assist the communication process whether you're discussing fleas on the family dog or your next promotion.

From the time they are babies, children receive sex-appropriate messages and toys. "What a beautiful little girl." "Hey, buster biggums." "How's my precious angel face?" "What a big, strong boy you are." But even without the environmental encouragement, the way you think and act has been influenced and programmed by your hormonal hardwiring since before you were born.

Each of us has forty-six chromosomes. We get twenty-three from each parent. Mom's half is always an X. If Dad's is an X, the result is an XX baby—a girl. If Dad's is Y, the result is XY—a boy. Here's the kicker. We don't find out if we're boy or girl until six to eight weeks after conception. That's when our sexual identity is formed. We all start out as females; our basic blueprint for body and brain is that of a girl. That's right, people—believe it or not, we all start as XX, and this is why males have nipples.

TESTOSTERONE AND ESTROGEN

If you have ever taken part in a weight-loss program, you know that men are able to lose more rapidly than women. They are the hunters; it's how they evolved. Women, on average, have a higher body-fat percentage than men. Their higher percentage of estrogen allows them to bear children and also contributes to their retaining body fat, as it keeps them warmer and is an insulator for the potential babe to come. Male hormones make the body lean and build muscle. Conversely, female hormones fatten us up. These hormonal changes begin during adolescence. As teens, boys have up to 20 percent more testosterone than teenage girls. The boys develop more muscle mass, and the girls get more fat deposits. Unlike the regulated male hormones, women's hormones come in a twenty-eight-day cycle that can create emotional highs and lows. Need proof? Ask any parent of a girl between the ages of eleven and sixteen. And that's only adolescence. The differences are just beginning to reveal themselves!

HIS BRAIN, HER BRAIN

Because men need more neurons to control their larger body size, their brains are frequently 11 to 12 percent larger than women's brains. (I need to add here that this is at least one time that size really doesn't matter. It does not affect intelligence.)

As you could see by our overview earlier in this book, both the right and left sides of a woman's brain are involved in verbal and visual abilities. The right side of a man's brain, however, is almost always used for controlling visual abilities, and the left for verbal. A woman uses both sides of her brain when working with abstract problems, while a man is predisposed to use only the right.

Most women (about 90 percent) have limited spatial ability. Brain scans demonstrate this difference, and studies prove that men have much stronger skills when it comes to spatial ability. It developed to allow them to hunt and determine the speed and distance of their prey, as well as calculate how fast they had to run to catch or escape an enemy. There will always be women who excel at math and men who shine in language; however, we tend to go with the numbers. I'm living proof. Several years ago, when I was seven months pregnant with my third babe, my husband and I drove from New York to the Smoky Mountains in Tennessee with our two young children for a family reunion. Are you getting a visual on this yet? Seventeen hours, a very pregnant woman, a very cranky man, and two very impatient kiddies. Over and over again my husband would ask me where we were on the map, and over and over again I would give him incorrect information. I cannot read maps. They make absolutely no sense to me, and because of that, we wound up taking every back road imaginable. Each time I assumed we were on the correct path, we would end up on a city street with traffic lights. Oh, if only there had been GPS at that time.

We see this difference in young children constantly. Boys excel faster than girls at math, building puzzles, and problem solving. So are guys natural math geeks? It looks like a strong possibility. Scientists at Johns Hopkins University found that there is a region in the brain's cortex, called the inferior parietal lobule, that is significantly larger in men than in women. This same area was abnormally large in the brain of Albert Einstein and in other male physicists and mathematicians.

COMMUNICATION

Estrogen prompts nerve cells to grow more connections within the brain and between the hemispheres. Studies show the more connections you have, the more fluent your speech. Research conducted at the Yale School of Medicine discovered that a woman's brain processes verbal language simultaneously in the two sides of the frontal brain, while a man's brain tends to process it in the left side only. In addition, the two sections of the brain responsible for language are larger in women than in men. This may indicate why women typically excel in language-based subjects.

Men are problem solvers, and women just want them to listen. That's part of what happened with my friend and her husband during the Great Flea Attack. When he came home and realized he was in the doghouse, so to speak, she had moved into vent mode. She didn't expect solutions from him at this point; she just wanted to commiserate. But most men don't get venting for the sake of venting. They hear it and think she's asking for a solution. He left her in mid-vent and headed for the pet-supply store.

Brain scans have shown that when a woman is speaking, her left and right brain centers controlling speech are both operating. Her hearing function operates at the same time. This capability allows a woman to multitask mentally, while speaking and listening simultaneously.

In men, the brain area developed for vocabulary is located at the front and rear parts of the left brain. In women, vocabulary areas are in the front and back of both hemispheres. So how do they understand emotional content? By relying on body language and voice intonation.

In general, a woman's communication style is more emotional than a man's. She focuses on feelings and building relationships, while he focuses on power and status. The same is true with problem solving—while men take a straightforward approach, women tend to establish intimacy and show concern and empathy.

My friend Gina treasures each and every one of her birthdays. As a matter of fact, she treasures everyone's birthday and passionately believes that this one day is their opportunity to be the shining star. So important is this day to her that she makes certain that she reminds everyone about her special day in the weeks prior. That includes her husband. She drops hints for gifts, relates ideas about how she wants to celebrate. She's not being demanding or needy. This is just her thing, and she wants this to be the one day of the year that she gets to celebrate her life.

The problem is, Ralph, her husband, doesn't seem to value the day (her birthday, his birthday, or anyone else's birthday) as much. To him, it is simply another day. "What's the big deal?" he says. "We'll celebrate on the weekend." He doesn't intentionally disregard her feelings, but it seems to happen inevitably. Still, every year she dreams he will morph into a new man and do something big and spectacular for her. And every year she is disappointed. This past year, once again, she told everyone about her day, and as it approached, it was business as usual. The morning started off like any other. Ralph handed her a birthday card in which he had simply signed his name (no love note that she could savor). Then he pecked her on the cheek and said, "Happy birthday," as he headed out the door for work, oblivious to the fact that he had set the tone for the day.

That night he came home to no dinner. When he asked Gina what was wrong, she belted out, "Nothing!" and walked away. Thinking she must have been too busy to cook, he suggested she get started, as it was getting late. As he waited patiently for her to serve dinner, she remained silent, *emotionally* thinking, *He has done it again. He really must not think I'm important enough to either take a day off, or bring me a flower, or offer to pick up dinner, or even take me out.*

Ralph, of course, was *logically* thinking, *Since it's not time to sit down and eat, I might as well go check my e-mail.* So he busily absorbed himself with the computer. Of course, during that time, Gina was predicting the demise of their relationship as she started to brood about the past year's events and how Ralph probably was not happy with her. Now that she was one year older, he probably wanted someone younger.

He always seems to put a lot of significance on appearance, she thought, *and I know that lately I have put on a few pounds. Maybe he's not attracted to me anymore. How many years am I going to waste on a man who no longer cares about me?*

Ralph, meanwhile, read an e-mail from a work colleague who told him about an early meeting the next day. He was now somewhat grumpy as well. The two of them barely spoke the rest of the night (although he still went in for the birthday nookie, which she declined).

The next day, Ralph left for work and it was business as usual. He came home in a good mood and still had no idea that he had put one more nail in their relationship coffin. She allowed her sorrow to dissipate and eventually she filed it away as another birthday down the tubes.

If only we could read each other's minds—but we can't. The best we can do is begin to understand the way we each think.

Women are angered when they feel let down or betrayed by those they trust, or when they feel too much is expected of them. Anger in men is more likely triggered by strangers, societal issues, and objects that don't work correctly. Ralph probably would have been more upset if he had lost his Internet connection than if his wife had forgotten his birthday.

That doesn't mean that Woman A can't be more competitive than Male B, or that Male C can't be more empathetic than Female D. Those are individual cases, but overall, men are wired to be more competitive, and women are wired to be more empathetic. It's not sexist to state facts, and one fact is that women and men are different. And they communicate differently.

STRESS

A 2007 study suggests that men and women vary in their neural responses to psychological stress. Men tend toward the classic fight-or-flight response. Women, however, are more inclined to "tend and befriend."

Thirty-two subjects received functional magnetic resonance imaging (fMRI) scans before, during, and after they were subjected to a challenging arithmetic task under pressure. Researchers frequently prompted participants for a faster performance and asked them to restart the task if they responded incorrectly. The participants were also asked to count backward, without pressure.

The researchers measured heart rate, levels of cortisol (a stress hormone), subjects' perceived stress levels, and regional cerebral blood flow. The cerebral blood flow is the blood supply to the brain at any given time; it denotes where in the brain the most activity is occurring. In men, stress was associated with increased blood flow in the right prefrontal cortex and a reduction of blood flow in the left orbitofrontal cortex. When women were under stress, the limbic system—that part of the brain primarily involved in emotion—was activated. Same stress; different parts of the brain.

The lead author of the study suggested that historically, males might have had to confront a situation or an incident causing stress either by overcoming or fleeing it. Women, on the other hand, may have responded by nurturing offspring and affiliating with social groups that maximize the survival of the species.

Makes sense to me. When we women get wired, instead of reacting with fight-flight responses, we just want to go save the family and the community. We want to take care of everyone. These biological differences stay with us at home, and they follow us to work. They also determine what makes us say yes.

SOUND DIFFERENCES

Women have an advantage when it comes to distinguishing high-pitched sounds, a talent that comes in handy for hearing the baby's cries at night. They are also more sensitive to tone changes in voice and pitch and can translate emotional variances.

While she can better distinguish the sound, he is better able to tell where it is coming from. This ability originates in a group of cells in the auditory region of the brain that maps out the exact location of a sound. As with their superior spatial ability, men needed it in order to hunt.

Women have a range of high- and low-pitched sounds they can hear—a total of five tones. Men have a more restricted pitch range—only three. They have difficulty decoding pitch changes, and their speech tends more to monotone.

TASTE AND TOUCH

Overall, studies tell us that women have a better sense of taste and smell. Humans have thousands of taste receptors that detect the major tastes of sweet, salty, sour, and bitter. We also have a few million skin receptors for pain, and hundreds of thousands for cold, touch, and pressure. A woman's skin is thinner, yet she has an extra layer of fat underneath for more warmth and protection, and she is more sensitive to touch than a man is. Maybe that's why women tend to be more touchy-feely.

In the United States, women are four times as likely to touch another woman in conversation than a man is likely to touch another man. In addition, men tend to touch more in the early stages of a relationship. Later on in a relationship, women tend to touch more. Again, this will not be the case in every single relationship, but it will be the norm more often than not.

Status and touch tend to go hand in hand; as such, men usually initiate a touch via a handshake. Touch is a sign of dominance and is quite often used by men to demonstrate their status. Touch plays one of the most significant roles in any interaction. Typically, the first interaction is a handshake, a touch to the arm, or one person accidentally brushing up against another. Touch between men and women conveys a wide range of messages, from verbal punctuators to love to power. Studies show that most people feel that it is acceptable for men to touch women because men appear to hold higher status in society.

Unless they are well acquainted, men should touch women only on the hand or forearm. Anything else is too personal. Women can touch each other on the hands, forearms, upper arms, and the neck. Because women do touch more, their gestures are sometimes misinterpreted by men.

Did you know that men and women are now participating in cuddle parties? These are interactive (obviously) parties in which people cuddle in groups or cuddle one-on-one. You can play footsie, spoon, or just sit around and rub a perfect stranger. Many of us are so touch deprived that we are willing to pay for an embrace.

ASK TONYA

Q: Is it true that men are more dominant and make decisions easier? I believe this is why we have not yet seen a female president and probably won't live to—no offense to you.

A: There is absolutely no doubt that men and women differ significantly. However, I think your question has more to do with context than with gender. Women might be more hesitant to respond to questions about sports, but ask a man what goes on the eyelashes, eyeliner or mascara, and he might hesitate as well. As for a woman president within your lifetime? Unless you're over eighty-five, buckle your seat belt.

SUSCEPTIBILITY TO PAIN AND ILLNESS

Despite experiencing childbirth, women perceive pain more intensely than men.

In a 2007 study, twenty-five men and twenty-five women were exposed to a harmful agent on their fingers. Following exposure, the subjects were asked to rate their responses based on intensity and level of unpleasantness. After sixteen rounds, researchers found that women reported higher pain levels during and after the agent was administered compared with men. (There was no explanation of how women are able to give birth to seven-pound babies, however.)

Men and women use the two brain hemispheres differently and are susceptible to different disorders. A 2008 *New Scientist* article reported that women's brains typically produce about half as much serotonin, a neurotransmitter that regulates mood, as men's brains. This leaves women more susceptible to depression. So, yes, we can be moody; big surprise.

Boys are more likely to be diagnosed with autism, Tourette's syndrome, dyslexia, stuttering, attention-deficit disorder and early-onset schizophrenia.

APPROACH WITH CAUTION

The Approach

Thanks to women's peripheral vision, it's easier for them to check out a man unnoticed than the other way around. Because men have more tunnel vision, they often use full-body eye movements. Using eye tracking, it has typically been established that both male and female observers primarily gaze at people's faces. Only after this initial face scan do men look significantly sooner and longer at women's breasts, while women look sooner at men's legs.

In Conversation

Men and women both nod, but for different reasons. Women nod more often than men as a means of encouragement and to let the speaker know they are listening—but not always because they agree. Men, however, tend to nod only when they agree with something.

How We Get Along

We may have started as hunters and nurturers, and this may be how we're wired, but in the world of business, we fill all types of roles, and the sex of your *yes* target is another consideration when building rapport. A friend of mine who operates a public-relations firm says a sure way to impress a female client is not necessarily with fancy lunches or expensive gifts; it's giving the client's children tickets to concerts and other events. Her male clients, she said, are usually less interested in the freebies (unless they're tickets to a sporting event) and want to see the bottom line. Does this make her a sexist? She says she's just doing what works. She's going for *yes*.

Keep in mind that we're all individuals, and these are just basic guidelines. But these guidelines are backed by research. If you understand gender differences, you'll be able to build rapport and communicate better with both men and women. Like it or not, we're different animals. And knowing how and why we vary can get you that much closer to *yes*. You'll be ahead of the game once you understand psychological tactics of persuasion.

ASK TONYA

Q: My friend and I go out, and he always seems to get the girl, have sex, and then be done. I never do. I feel like I am doomed the minute I head out to meet him. I am a nice guy, fairly good-looking, and easy to talk to. Why can't I get laid?

A: Your time will come. There is a whole bunch of science behind it, but basically what we know is that women are attracted to dominant, confident men with high levels of testosterone for short-term relationships (especially when the women's estrogen levels are high). For the long-term relationships, however, the nice guy wins out. Figure out your USP and make sure you use it!

HIS SIGNALS/HER SIGNALS

How Hot Are You? Depends on Who's Looking

More than four thousand participants in a 2009 study rated photographs of men and women (ages eighteen to twenty-five) for attractiveness on a ten-point scale ranging from "not at all" to "very." In exchange for their participation, raters were told what characteristics they found attractive compared with the average person. The raters ranged in age from eighteen to over seventy.

The participants judged the photographs for attractiveness, the members of the research team rated the images for how seductive, confident, thin, sensitive, stylish, curvaceous (women), muscular (men), traditional, masculine/feminine, classy, well groomed, or upbeat the people looked.

Men's judgments of women's attractiveness were based primarily around physical features and they rated highly those who looked thin and seductive. Most of the men in the study also rated photographs of women who looked confident as more attractive.

As a group, the women rating men showed some preference for thin, muscular subjects, but disagreed on how attractive many men in the study were. Some women gave high attractiveness ratings to the men other women said were not attractive at all. Bottom line, men consistently judged women by their physical features, and women varied in how they judged men.[37]

TWENTY-ONE

PSYCHOLOGICAL SECRETS THAT SWAY

Now you have the tools that you need, both verbal and nonverbal. The basic psychological tips in this chapter will help you bypass your *yes* target's critical factor and get that much closer to what you want to hear.

Strong persuaders know secrets that make the rest of us say yes. I must admit that the techniques they use are so powerful that even though I recognize what they're doing, I sometimes still just have to buy whatever they're selling.

DEPOSIT IN THE EMOTIONAL BANK

In dealing with people, there are always certain hot buttons you can press to get them to do what you want them to do. For instance, suppose a colleague is crunched for time because he has dinner plans with his wife. You offer to finish up the menial task he is trying to complete. That favor is a deposit in an emotional bank account, and it's waiting for a withdrawal.

You are now in the position of power. It is completely and utterly expected that he will return the favor. When it happens, you can even one-up him and ask for something bigger. You've earned the right because you were the first to demonstrate your good-heartedness. When someone does something for us, our first reaction is to *repay*. It's tit for tat, quid pro quo.

Think back to the last time you received "free" address labels in the mail from a nonprofit. Many of them have a nickel pasted inside them to increase the chances that you will respond. How did you feel when you saw that nickel attached? Kind of creepy? As if not sending a donation would be akin to stealing from the charity? The address labels and the nickel are the nonprofit's way of getting you to give them money. Imagine how much it costs to send out all those nickels. Would they really do that if the return wasn't far greater than the investment?

ENGAGE IN STATUS BUILDING

Status building is demonstrating the significance of your inner circle and the higher value that should be ascribed to you because of your position within it.

People are more likely to respond to status building if they identify with a group and if they feel that group knows more than they do. "Fifty million Frenchmen can't be wrong." That line, taken from an old musical, describes our belief that if everyone else is doing it, so should we. John Dryden was onto this assumption as far back as the early 1680s, when he wrote, "Nor is the people's judgement [*sic*] always true; / The most may err as grossly as the few."

A product's status is elevated when it is in demand, and the same is true of individuals. If you stay in a low-paying job, others will assume no one else wants to hire you—that you are not in demand. If your twin brother runs his own successful company and associates with the rich and famous, he's going to be viewed as superior to you, even if he's a blowhard and you're a nice guy.

Take Hugh Hefner. When he launched *Playboy* magazine, he surrounded himself with beautiful women and built a mansion as a kind of display case for his female trophies. His status was far greater than if he'd had the same amount of success with a newsmagazine and no beauties.

Some theaters plant faux audience members who burst into applause at key moments. The people who rise first when giving a standing ovation are encouraging other members of the audience to stand as well. No one wants to be the only one sitting when the rest of the crowd is on their feet (unless, of course, you are within the walls of Congress). And no one wants to be silent when everyone else is laughing, even when that laughter is canned. Manufactured laugher, irritating as it is, serves the same purpose as those people in the theater audience. And it works.

BENEFIT FROM THE HALO EFFECT

A popular athlete appears in an ad for men's underwear. Or for beer. What made him suddenly credible on any number of topics? The halo effect, that's what. *Top athlete.* That's the *halo.* Its *effect* magnifies the overall impression of him, and the rest of us imagine additional qualities beyond his outstanding one.

An attractive, professional businesswoman walks into a meeting in a crisp suit with neat briefcase, polished shoes and perfectly styled hair. Because of her appearance, those observing her assume that she must also be organized and articulate. Because she is attractive, they also assume a host of other positive attributes such as popularity, kindness, and intellect.

Use this effect to your advantage. Keep your halo fresh and sparkling by keeping your USP handy, recognizing your best attributes, covertly showing others your strengths, and volunteering your time to demonstrate your altruism. Be approachable, and always look your best. Appearance is the halo that tells others you are on the ball and friendly. Last and perhaps most important—avoid criticism of any person, policy, or situation. Your halo shines the brightest when you transmit a positive attitude.

We demonstrate authority by our titles and by the way we dress.

BE THE AUTHORITY

Since childhood, we have all deferred to authority. Mom says make your bed; you make it. Your teacher says take this test; you take it. The doctor tells you to have the surgery, and you have the surgery. The dentist says the wisdom tooth must go, and it's history. Authority is more than power. It's power with credentials.

Here's a crazy—but true!—example. A patient goes to a doctor with an earache. The doctor tells the patient the cause of the earache and writes a prescription. On it he writes, "Place in rear." (Doctors have terrible handwriting!) It was meant to read, "R-ear."

The nurse takes the prescription, reads the label, and says to the patient, "Could you slide down your pants and lie on your stomach, please?" The patient's ear is really bothering him, and while he's a little confused about why the nurse wants him to bare his rear, he does it anyway. The nurse goes ahead and rectally administers the drops the doctor had intended for his right ear! A ridiculous scenario? Yes, but not a fictional one. It was reported in a book on medication errors by two Temple University pharmacology professors. The nurse didn't question what she thought the doctor had instructed her to do, and neither did the patient.

We demonstrate authority by our titles. The more letters that follow our name, the better. We demonstrate it in how we dress. Everything is a uniform, and the one we select communicates how much, if any, authority we possess. So even if you don't have letters after your name, you need to establish your credibility by subtly cueing your competence and authority, from your dress to your body language to the aura of confidence you project.

LIMIT SUPPLY

The exclusive boutique owner brags that she carries only one garment in each size. The art store holds a going-out-of-business sale. If you think you won't be able to get something in the future, you are going to want it now.

It comes down to supply and demand, and if you can make the supply appear scarce, the demand will be greater. Why do people spend huge amounts of money on old cars? Because they aren't being made anymore. Which is more appealing, an entire shelf crowded with boxes of cookies or one with only one or two boxes? Have you ever noticed how much out-of-print books can go for? I have seen them for as much as ten times their initial cost. Why? Because copies of them are scarce.

Several years ago FurReals were launched. FurReal was yet another toy that was under-stocked in stores but over-demanded by children and parents everywhere. It was the holiday season, and I found myself desperately bidding on eBay to buy one to avoid the disappointment my daughter was sure to express if she didn't get the one gift she had asked Santa for. At the time, the toy retailed for about twenty-five dollars, and the opening bid was twenty dollars. I waited patiently to snipe at the last minute in order to get the best possible price. Ninety seconds . . . hit "refresh." Seventy seconds . . . hit "refresh." Forty seconds . . . GO. My high bid went in, and I smiled, thinking I had gotten myself a pretty good deal. I hit "refresh." "You are no longer the high bidder," the machine shouted at me. What? I rebid. Thirty seconds . . . refresh. "You are the high bidder." Whew. Refresh. "You are no longer the high bidder." What?

I rebid in the last six seconds with a price I am ashamed to put out there: $110. I "won" a twenty-five-dollar item for a mere four times its store value.

My brain went berserk, as if there was absolutely not one more FurReal on the planet. Of course, the look on my daughter's face was worth it (almost)—for the two days she played with it. Well, I guess sixty dollars per day isn't bad if you live in Looney Land.

I learned a very important lesson about myself that day. You already know the way this story ends. A few days before Christmas, the stores restocked, and intelligent people got FurReals for twenty-five dollars. Many of you will be able to relate to this story through those of your own from the past few years—everything from Tickle Me Elmo to Lego Star Wars. The lesson: When you want to up the value, continue to limit the supply.

The same is true of you. Don't always be available and your perceived value will go up. Surround yourself with an aura of mystery. Why are you always so busy? You must be very social and very popular. You become more in demand by not always being free to go places or hang out at a moment's notice. I had an acquaintance who would leave her house to walk through the mall and sit at the food court—all day— just to give the impression that she had better things to do than sit home. You know what? It worked. People always talked about how social she was. Of course, I knew she could usually be found either at Nathan's or with Ronald McDonald a town away. At work, you should limit your availability as well. You're an important person, and by limiting your availability, you nonverbally and covertly tell others, *I have commitments.*

More isn't necessarily better. In the same way you limit your availability, you can limit the choices you offer your target. When people have too many choices, you can have a difficult time getting them to *yes* or even *maybe*; they disengage, and the desire to say yes isn't as strong as the desire to rid themselves of choice confusion.

Sheena S. Iyengar of Columbia University and Mark R. Lepper of Stanford University conducted experiments to see how people react to too much of a good thing. One of these experiments showed that shoppers are more likely to buy exotic jams or gourmet chocolates if they can choose from six options rather than twenty-four. When a display in an upscale market offered twenty-four choices, shoppers bought only 3 percent of the time. When offered only six choices, people bought about 30 percent of the time. The only variable was the number of choices. Buyers said they were more satisfied with their purchases when their choices were restricted.

ADD A DECOY

If your client is trying to decide between a jacket and a sweater, she might not purchase either if she can't make up her mind. Introduce a decoy and you'll help her decide what she really wants.

Other research shows that decision making is simplified when a consumer considers a third, less attractive option. Akshay Rao, a marketing professor at the University of Minnesota Carlson School of Management, conducted research that shows that, for example, when a second, less desirable sweater is also considered in the situation above, the shopper could solve her conundrum by choosing the more attractive sweater. The less appealing sweater plays the role of a decoy that makes the other sweater appear more pleasing than before. "In some ways, it is quite straightforward," said Rao. "When a consumer is faced with a choice, the presence of a relatively unattractive option improves the choice share of the most similar, better item."

In fact, volunteers had their brains scanned while they made their choices, and as Rao and his coauthor, William Hedgcock, explained, the presence of the extra, "just okay" possibility systematically increased preference for the better options. The fMRI scans showed that when making a choice between only two equally preferred options, subjects tended to display irritation because of the difficulty of the choice process. The presence of the third option made the choice process easier and relatively more pleasurable. "When considering three options," Rao said, "our 'buyers' displayed a decrease in activation of the amygdala, an area of the brain associated with negative emotions.

"There are several practical implications of this research. Irrelevant alternatives are routinely encountered in a variety of settings, including Web-based travel and vacation markets, cable deals, cell-phone plans, and even newspaper circulars. In these markets, the addition of irrelevant options is a strategy that ought to reduce negative emotion.

RAISE EXPECTATIONS

Suppose you're enjoying an expensive dinner in a restaurant. The wine is a cabernet sauvignon from California. It's delicious and so is the meal. The people at the next table are drinking a cab from North Dakota and don't seem all that happy about it. Your dining experience is certainly far superior to theirs. Actually, you're drinking the same wine they are; your expectations have simply made yours taste better.

That's what happened when Cornell University studied whether changing the label on a wine bottle would change the opinions of diners. It did.

At the Spice Box restaurant in Urbana, Illinois, forty-one diners were given a free glass of cabernet sauvignon with their twenty-four-dollar prix fixe French meal. Half the bottles were labeled from Noah's Winery in California. The labels on the other half were labeled from Noah's Winery in North Dakota. In reality, both groups were drinking an inexpensive Charles Shaw wine. It's known as Two Buck Chuck and retails for about $1.99 a bottle.

Those who thought they were drinking a California wine rated the Two Buck Chuck higher than those who thought they were drinking the North Dakota wine. They also rated their food higher than the other group rated theirs. Furthermore, they ate 11 percent more of their food and were more likely to make return reservations.

What you expect is what you'll get. Expect a wine to taste as if it came from Napa Valley and it won't disappoint you. Expect it to taste bad and it will.

Whether it's designer footwear or a luxury automobile, our expectations soar when we're told we're getting the best.

PRESENT THE BIG TICKET FIRST

I witnessed this dynamic firsthand when I accompanied a friend of mine on a shopping trip. She was buying a suit for her husband, and the salesperson did such a good job of describing the value of the one she had picked out that—just like that—she said, "I'll take it." That shocked both of us, because the suit was going to cost her twice as much as she had budgeted.

The salesperson wasn't done there! (She knew an opportunity when she saw one.) As my friend handed over her credit card, he said, "Your husband is going to need a tie. This one is usually eighty-five dollars, but because you bought the suit, you can get it for sixty-five."

And after already blowing her budget, my friend bit again. What was a mere sixty-five dollars after what she had paid for the suit? The big price tag numbs you to the fact that the second price tag is still more than you would usually spend. In the same way that a person who wants to look thinner stands next to a heavy person, the lower price appears smaller when compared with the humongous price.

If you've ever bought a car, you know how easy it is to be lulled into saying yes to seat and mirror warmers, tire upgrades, and that Bose stereo that's only two thousand dollars. *Only* is the operative word here, and it's *only* two thousand because you just spent in the neighborhood of fifty thousand for the car.

After selling you a pricey laptop, cordless phone, or camera, the salesclerk asks, "Do you need any batteries for that?" Regardless of how much those batteries cost, it's going to sound reasonable after what you just paid.

Even in the world of fast food, you order a cheeseburger and French fries, and the person taking your order asks, "Do you want to biggie those fries? It's only eighteen cents more." The smaller price slips in behind the big price, and the answer is usually yes.

COMPARE TWO EXTREMES

When you do this, your *yes* target will be happy with the middle, which is what you intended all along. Here's how it works.

When my husband and I were looking for our first house, we gave our real-estate agent the full specs of exactly what we had in mind. We wanted a house with nice-size rooms, a pool, central air-conditioning, a fireplace, and a big yard. Peter, our agent, took us out looking. He knew the first house he showed us was twenty-five thousand dollars out of our price range. Mag-friggin-nificent—but he absolutely knew we couldn't afford it. Too bad for us. Perhaps the owner would go down a few thousand.

He then took us to the next house, which fell right into our range. It backed up to a thoroughfare, which we could hear as we pulled up to the front. Inside was even worse. Dirty clothes littered the floors. And while there was indeed a pool, it looked as if it hadn't seen water in a very long time. The rooms were the size of walk-in closets, and the fireplace on our spec list was conspicuously absent.

"Are you kidding?" I asked him. "Is this all that's in our price range?"

"You know," he said, "there is one house that I have not yet seen myself. I think it was just listed yesterday, and I believe it's in your price range. Let's go take a look." We pulled up to a beautifully manicured lawn with two giant fir trees right in the front. The yard was a perfect square that backed a cul-de-sac. The open pool sparkled, and a couple of floats drifted on its surface. The rooms were impeccably clean. In the back, we found a tree with the owners' names carved within a heart: "Bob loves Sue."

"Look at that," our real-estate agent said.

The husband lovingly touched the etching and told us that this was their first home, that they were now moving to Virginia to be closer to the children they had raised in this very house. Well, what do you think happened next? We signed on the dotted line that very day.

I later found out that the first two houses Peter showed us were not his listings, so he would have profited less from them. I also found out that the house we purchased was indeed his very own listing and therefore he earned much more on this sale, and that the house had been on the market for seven months. Peter, it seemed, was a very creative salesperson, and Kenny and I fell for his story. We couldn't wait to say yes. Luckily, we loved the house and moved only after we physically grew out of it.

What tactic did Peter use? Comparison. He showed us a beaut out of our range, showed us a dump in our range, and then showed us *our house,* which was the same price as the dump. It is always best to have a bad, a best, and an out-of-reach option.

MAKE YOUR STATEMENT A QUESTION

"So, you're going to stay late tonight with me and help me finish that report, right?" This is a very powerful verbal tactic to use when trying to get agreement. Just add a question to the end of the statement. It's similar to using the word *because,* because we don't even know why we're responding to it.

In a study to determine if blood-drive attendance could be increased by altering the content of reminder calls, the message was changed to include a question. The caller said, "We'll count on seeing you then, okay?" and then paused for a response. The show-up rate increased from 62 to 81 percent. The simple verbal affirmation brought the level of compliance up by 20 percent.

MAKE THEM THINK IT'S THEIR IDEA

People like it when they think they are coming up with brilliant ideas. Remember *My Big Fat Greek Wedding*? The mother and the aunt get Toula's father to believe that it's his idea for his daughter to work in her aunt's travel agency. In order to help someone make a decision, you will do a great justice to the process if you surreptitiously nudge him into believing the concept was really his own. If a person believes that he either came up with or was the inspiration for an idea, he can easily say yes to it. After all, if he thought it up, it must be a great plan. This significantly ups your chance of getting a *yes.*

PREVENT BUYER'S REMORSE AND EARN TRUST

Remember the advertisement for L'Oréal hair products? "L'Oréal: Because you're worth it." This tactic points out the so-called negative as a way to prevent buyer's remorse once you find out Clairol is cheaper. Of course, it also suggests higher value.

You're going to buy a car, and you've just about made up your mind. "I need to tell you something before we go any further," the salesperson says. "This white is going to pick up dust. You'll need to wash it every week."

He's not trying to talk you out of the sale. He's arguing against his self-interest. This makes him appear more trustworthy. It also keeps you from experiencing buyer's remorse the first time your new car gets dirty. The salesman told you, after all.

The technique works as well in the courtroom as it does in the dealership. When an attorney mentions a weakness in his case before the other attorney gets a chance to point it out, jurors find him more truthful and look upon him more favorably because of his perceived honesty. Mention a flaw up front and gain trust. Mention a small flaw and people will assume that you have no big ones.

GET THEM TO TOUCH IT

What is it about touch that makes us feel so strongly attached? As we have discussed, it is a necessary part of life. If we do not touch or get touched, we perish. A similar theory is apparently just as significant for buying. If you intend to keep your currency, whether it be emotional or physical, you must keep your hands to yourself. The problem is that when we touch, we form an attachment. Studies reported in the *Journal of Consumer Research* validate the idea that if we touch an object, the feelings of ownership increase. Once that happens, individuals are more likely to break into their piggy bank and expend emotional or financial currency.

If the touch is an overly positive one, such as seeing how beautiful that new bracelet looks on your arm or the way that new ring gleams on your finger, chances are you will even be willing to pay more for it. This is why companies so often offer free trials—they recognize that once you have held it in your hands, you'll wind up wanting to keep it. Dressing rooms in stores do more than show you how that little black dress or those tapered jeans will look on your body; they also offer you an opportunity to feel the fabric against your skin.

I'm an insomniac and occasionally tend to watch infomercials while trying to fall asleep. One night a commercial for the Tempur-Pedic mattress came on. It was a full half hour of the spokespeople drilling comfort into my head, drilling the possibility of sleep into an individual who gets too little of it. In addition, there was the added bonus of a ninety-day free in-home trial. I was spellbound. By the end of the commercial, I was running to the phone to order the mattress.

Thankfully, my husband woke up as I frantically dialed. He had to physically take the phone out of my hand and hang it up. Of course, there was more psychological warfare at work there than just the offer of "try it before you buy it." The spokespeople would have snagged me by making me feel what it would be like to sleep on that mattress. Once it had been in my home, it would have stayed there. We seldom return merchandise we have fondled.

In 2003, the Illinois state attorney general's office warned holiday shoppers to be cautious of retailers who encouraged them to hold objects and imagine the objects as their own when shopping. Two authors researched the reasons behind the warning and felt it was valid. They found that merely touching an object increases the feelings of ownership a person has for it. This, in turn, results in a person being willing to pay more for most objects that she touches. When touch is unavailable, such as when someone shops online, having her imagine owning a product increases her perception of ownership and how much she is willing to pay for a product.

This research may help explain the link between touch and impulse purchasing. Encouraging touch in a retail store may increase the feelings of perceived ownership and influence the amount a customer is willing to pay for a product.

POWER WORDS

Words to Use

Accomplished	Discovery	Happiness
Benefit	Don't	Health
Comfort	Easy	High performance
Commanding	Excitement	Investment
Complimentary	Fun	Joy
Deserve	Guarantee	Love

Luxury	Prove	Titillating
Money	Provocative	Triumphant
Now	Results	Trust
Paradise	Save	Value
Please	Soothing	Vital
Powerful	Sorry	You
Profit	Spicy	
Proud	Thank you	

Words to Avoid

Bored	Impossible	Sad
Can't	Limiting	Sick
Depressed	Lonely	Stupid
Difficult	Lose	Temper
Empower	Mad	Try
Fat	Restrictive	Won't
Hate	Ridiculous	

GUILT: THE GREAT MOTIVATOR

We are naturally good at being guilters. Ask anyone about the power a mother has to guilt a child for just about anything. My mother is great at it, her mother was great at it, and I presume it runs up the whole family line. How do great guilters do it? They manipulate you by negatively working on your emotions.

When an individual takes a situation and moves it from rational to emotional, you are headed for trouble. Emotions are powerful manipulators and when an individual recognizes he might not be able to score points logically, he will quickly move to emotions, because he knows there are numerous strings he has the ability to pull. People tend to work off of fear and intimidation or our desire to be needed, wanted, and loved.

Almost every choice we make is emotion based. We act on feeling and then try to back it up with logic. In order to influence someone, you must get her to a state of emotional stimulation. Whenever possible, maintain composure within yourself while evoking emotions in others.

"Mom, do you need anything before I go out?" my daughter will ask.

"No." Sigh. "I'm fine. You go ahead."

That motivates her to think of what task she might do in order to lessen my burden, and I'm thrilled that I didn't have to come out and ask her.

It works in the office as well. The vice president says, "We're all going to the Blarney Stone for lunch. Meet us there."

"Sorry, I can't. I have lots of stuff to do to catch up."

The vice president thinks, *She's not going. If I get somebody else to help her out, she'll be finished quicker.* I'm not suggesting I need help. I'm just explaining why I can't go to lunch, and that makes the other person feel responsible for helping me out.

BE WILLING TO WALK

Reading people and determining if they are being sincere puts you in charge. One easy way to do this is to put yourself in the other person's position. For example, I recently went to buy a car. I knew I wanted a car but I also knew that there were several other places I could go to get one. In other words, I was in a good place because I wasn't desperate. I knew I could easily walk away if I didn't get the deal I wanted.

The salesman gave me his exciting presentation and then the "I can't go below it" rock-bottom price. I instantly knew I didn't like him (that's a chapter for another book), so being slightly disappointed that I had wasted time there, I said, "Okay, thanks again. I'll think about it." That was it. The tables turned. I gave no indication that I was interested, and he came running after me.

"Well, you know, this sale is going on all day, and I bet if I spoke to my manager, we could get you some extra money taken off." (Wink, wink, wink.) "If you give me your number, I can call you later to see blah blah blah. You're really not going to find another dealership that will offer you blah blah blah. Today is the last day I can offer you blah blah blah."

What happened here? He was insincere, and I was willing to walk away. That's what a person does when she is not interested. She walks away. Needy and apprehensive individuals pretend that you're not an essential piece of the puzzle. Where does that leave you? The next time you are going into a negotiation, talk the talk but then be willing to walk the walk—right out the door if need be.

ASK TONYA

Q: I know advertising is powerful, but is it really possible to make me unknowingly buy one brand of coffee over another?

A: I'll give you the quick and dirty on this. Yes! So often we see the name of a brand but it goes under the radar of our conscious mind because we are so bombarded with advertisements. You're in the city on a hot summer day, and a bus drives by with a picture of Fiji water. A few minutes later, you find yourself buying a bottle of water and, hey, that bottle of Fiji looks inviting. Do you consciously know why? No way. Do you even remember seeing the bus? No way. But you took a mental shortcut and made a decision on autopilot. Substitute coffee for the water and you're there. Luckily, it's not only advertisers who can tap into the techniques of subconscious persuasion—you can too!

HIS SIGNALS/HER SIGNALS

Losing It for Beauty

A study in the *Journal of Experimental Social Psychology* measured brain function in forty heterosexual student volunteers. The idea for the study came from one of the scientists, who had been so impressed by a beautiful woman he had met that when she asked where he lived, he forgot his own address! He had temporarily lost his mind.

The subjects were asked to perform a standard memory test in which they were shown a stream of letters and had to quickly say if each was the same as the previous letter. They then spent several minutes talking to either a man or an attractive woman and then repeated the test. Researchers found that even a few minutes with the attractive woman was enough to make the students slower and less accurate on the test. The more attracted they were, the worse their results.

They then asked female students to perform the same test and then talk to handsome men. The women's test scores were unaffected. Psychologists theorized that evolutionary processes have programmed men to regard women first as potential mates. They temporarily concentrate on trying to impress a woman and are subsequently unable to concentrate on their tasks.

TWENTY-TWO

MAGNETISM

What It Is and How to Get It

"You can stroke people with words."

—*F. Scott Fitzgerald*

At its heart, magnetism *is* the *Yes* Factor. Some people are born with it, but most people, including many who seem naturally charismatic, develop it. Magnetism makes you the person others first notice, then admire, then trust. You develop it by using the 21-Day Plan. The goal is to create new neural pathways in both yourself and your *yes* target, through the techniques we've discussed throughout this book. These techniques will soon be second nature to you.

D × V × F > R = CHANGE

Richard Beckhard and David Gleicher developed the Formula for Change (D x V x F > R) as a model for organizational change in business. They said that three factors must be present in order to create change. They are **Dissatisfaction** with the current situation, **Vision** of what is possible, and **First** concrete steps for reaching the vision. If the product of these factors is greater than the **Resistance,** change is possible.

The same is true of changing yourself. First you must want more than your current situation. Next, you need to see what is possible for you; you must visualize the kind of life you want. Finally, you take your first concrete steps toward your vision, step after step, throughout your implementation of the 21-Day Plan and beyond. In doing so, so long as the product of these actions is greater than any internal or external resistance, you will be able to change. I'm not offering you instant solutions here; I'm offering you permanent solutions.

THE FOUR STAGES OF COMPETENCE: FROM *GROW* TO *KNOW*

The concept of the four stages of learning is believed to have originated in the 1970s, and its development is attributed to Noel Burch of Gordon Training International. I find it helpful to remember these stages whenever I work on a new goal. Realizing that learning new things is part of a process keeps me focused and dedicated.

At the first stage, **unconscious incompetence,** the individual neither understands nor knows how to do something. He does not recognize the deficit and therefore has no desire to address it. At the second stage, **conscious incompetence,** the individual recognizes the deficit, hasn't yet addressed it, and does not understand how to overcome it.

This is where this program, and the individual's active participation in it, comes in. At the third stage, **conscious competence,** a person understands or knows how to do something. However, demonstrating the skill or knowledge still requires a great deal of awareness or concentration. Eventually, the individual arrives at the fourth stage, **unconscious**

competence, in which he has had so much practice with a skill that it has become second nature and can be performed easily, often without his concentrating too deeply. Depending upon how and when it was learned, he may also be able to teach the skill to others.

Again, discovering and communicating your Alpha You is a process of growing into knowing. You are going to move through the steps and become more competent, until one day, techniques in this book become second nature to you. Think about the first time you ever used a computer. Were you very young? Older? Were your fingers uncertain on the keyboard? But you formed those neural pathways; you learned a new skill. And somewhere along the way, you developed unconscious competence. You don't have to fumble with the mouse or think about where the "shift" key is. *You just know.*

So as you work on implementing the skills you've learned here, you should remember that they're part of the end goal of establishing one of those naturally charismatic and magnetic personalities—the hard work is in the service of making you a better you!

I do think it's important to be specific about one thing, however—what I call **goal-focused planning,** or **GFP.** Some people read a book or take a course and rush out and start practicing their newfound attitude and techniques just because they can. Without GFP you may get that *yes,* but are you sure it's for something you really want? Is getting that *yes* going to get you where you're looking to go? Or are you just going through the motions, getting *yes*es for a job you don't really want or a relationship you don't need? You need to decide on the results you want first. What do you want from your *yes* target? How will that help you get to your next goal? Desired results first. Then, work backward to get there.

ASSESSING

Some call this calibration, a way of getting in tune with the other person. Assessing takes place in three stages, and only after you have gone through GFP. The first step is making a **mental determination** of who your *yes* target is. This is a type of emotional baselining. For example, is he like the furniture salesman I mentioned earlier in the book, who was condescending and dominant? The second step is **frame assessment.**

Our frames change all the time. What's this person's frame right this minute, in this interaction? In the case of the salesman, it was making his female client feel that he was taking care of her when indeed he was giving her nothing (until she turned it around on him, that is). The third step is **resolution.** Based on what you know about this person and his frame, you resolve to take a next step. You've deduced what you need to portray to him in order to reach your goal.

The more you practice your game plan, the stronger those neural paths will become, and even when you doubt yourself, the tools to *yes* will be easier and easier to draw on.

LISTEN

Too many conversations suffer from *I*-strain. We tend to think that we can one-up everyone. There's a reason we have two ears and one mouth, and that's so we can listen more than we talk.

People love it when you find them fascinating. Most are wonderfully self-absorbed and love to rattle on about themselves and be the center of attention. Therefore, the fastest way to another's heart is to express interest in that person. You could spend hour upon hour trying to convince someone how wonderful you are, and she couldn't care less. But demonstrate how interesting she is, and now you're getting warm.

Most people will feel rapport with you if you make them feel good in your presence. That's why it is so important to exude happiness and confidence, because when you do, the stardust sprinkles on them, as well. Your charm becomes contagious.

DEMONSTRATE SELF-CONTROL

One of the components of magnetism is demonstrating a degree of self-control. Should you put that big bonus in your savings account or splurge for a cruise? Do you skip dessert so that you don't have to do double duty in the gym? Chances are, if you can delay that satisfaction and control your impulse, you may be more successful in all areas of your life.

In a study with children at Stanford University Bing Nursery School in the late 1960s, Professor Walter Mischel headed an experiment dealing with delayed gratification. Children were told that they could ring a bell and have one marshmallow while Mischel was out of the room for approximately fifteen minutes, or they could wait until he returned and have two marshmallows.

In 1981, Mischel began analyzing the results of those early studies and continued to do so, following the children into adulthood. He noticed that the "low delayers," the children who rang the bell quickly or ate the marshmallow without ringing the bell at all, seemed more likely to have behavior problems. They received lower SAT scores, averaging 210 points below those who had waited it out. They found it difficult to maintain friendships and were more troubled, more indecisive, and less confident. This lack of impulse control followed them throughout their lives and resulted in less rewarding marriages and low job satisfaction.

Those who were able to delay gratification and resist the marshmallows tended toward healthier friendships as adults. They were more positive and successful. They tended to have higher incomes and were self-motivated.[38] Regardless of how you feel about marshmallows, be sure you're demonstrating self-control in your life.

GET OUT OF YOUR COMFORT ZONE

You can't effectively mirror someone else until you understand and respect yourself. Remember this; write it down: The comfort zone is your nemesis. It limits you and keeps you from growth. That's the truth. Where you are right now, the way you currently interact with everyone in your world, is your comfort zone. In order to change your life and the way you interact, you have to be willing to go outside of your box.

"Do I *have* to?" you ask. I know what you mean. Your comfort zone is what you're used to. It's what you do. I can remember countless company meetings, and you can too, with all of these little betas who went along for the ride and then did what the alphas told them to do.

Taking the initiative is your first step. If you aren't going out of your comfort zone, you're not growing. Focus on these little tactics to make yourself feel better:

Stand up straighter. It works.

Try to look upon yourself as someone who is good. Even if you don't feel genuinely happy right now, you have to smile inwardly. You must if you are going to feel better about yourself. Be the Alpha You.

Review all of your positive traits. Successful people, those who attract others, don't get that way by focusing on what's wrong with them. They make a mistake, acknowledge it (perhaps chastise themselves for a fleeting moment, but next they forgive themselves), and then they move on, realizing that even mistakes are opportunities for growth.

Remember that you have to move forward constantly. Come out of what you know in order to grow.

For some, breaking out of that comfort zone could be as simple as refusing to give in to shyness. If this describes you, walk right up to someone and initiate a conversation. At work, stop being the quiet one. Abandon your comfortable beta role. Form an opinion about something, and then state it in front of your group. Convey that opinion with both your words and your gestures. Then you will be ready to mirror and to lead others.

You know why? Because the first step to getting anyone else to say yes is saying yes to yourself.

In March 2008, I appeared on the Fox News show *America's Newsroom.* Cohost Bill Hemmer asked me to comment on a film clip of Hillary Clinton drinking a beer on the campaign plane.

He asked if it was "an honest moment, a moment of levity."

I didn't think there was anything to the gesture, as sometimes a beer is just a beer, and the way you hold it is just that. I did my best to show how insignificant the gesture was. "You know, the only thing that struck me as odd is, she's holding the beer with her left hand and she's a righty," I said. "And if you think about how you would normally take a sip, it's a little bit awkward to drink with your nondominant hand, unless you have a reason to be doing that."

Hillary Clinton campaigns in Ohio ahead of the primary.

"Well, what would that reason be, then?" Hemmer asked.

"It could be anything," I said. "Maybe she's really just holding that cup to hold that cup, you know. Maybe she wants to give the appearance of being light and easy."

Apparently, that innocuous statement was considered a harsh criticism, and I was viewed as picking on Mrs. Clinton. A couple days later, a producer from another show called.

"Congratulations," she said, very excited. "I saw you last night. You made it!"

"Made what?" I asked. "I wasn't on last night."

"Oh my god, you don't know yet?"

"Don't know what?"

"You were on MSNBC last night."

"No, I wasn't," I insisted. "You're confusing me with somebody else."

"Tonya," she said. "Keith Olbermann named you one of the worst persons in the world last night."

I'm familiar with that segment of his show, and so my first thought was, *My kids! What are my kids going to think? Their mother was just named one of the worst persons in the world.* My stomach plunged, and I nearly drove off the road.

That required having a little talk with myself. When you put yourself out there, you have to take the bad with the good. It was a tough talk, but I agreed with me that since I was offering my opinions about others, I couldn't fold just because I didn't like what someone said about me.

Looking back at the experience now, I'm tempted to say you win some and you lose some, but even then, embarrassed at having been picked apart, worried about my children, and humbled at the experience, I gained. True, I was the "Worrrrst Person in the Worrrrld," but instead of running from it, I embraced it as you would a gift. It put me in the same shoes I had so often invited others to wear, though not of their own accord. I learned a lot about myself as I ruminated. It was an enlightening experience, and I am a stronger person because of it. It made me more determined than ever to continue my path of discovery—my journey of finding the Alpha Me. *Yes.*

TONYA'S TINY TIDBITS

1. Learn bite-size chunks of information and retain them. Try using words as triggers for full memories.
2. We all have stumbling blocks on our path to success. Keep in mind that what some call failure should be thought of as experience.
3. Take responsibility for your actions. Blaming others both professionally and personally is a major turnoff.
4. Visualize positivity. Mentally see yourself getting the job, winning the girl, finishing the marathon, seizing the day.
5. Appreciate the automatic triggers in the brain and learn to use them to your advantage.
6. Understand fully that your comfort zone is your nemesis. Be open to new experiences.
7. Family is wonderful but don't go to them for strength. You might just hear, "I told you so."
8. Surround yourself with people who make you feel good, not those who drag you down.
9. Remember to finish negative thoughts with the phrase "but it doesn't matter," because it doesn't unless you believe it does.
10. Finish what you start.

NOW WHAT?

Frequently when I consult with someone regarding verbal and nonverbal communication, the question is, "Tonya, how am I ever going to remember all that?" The answer is by having a game plan, and that's what you're going to get next. This doesn't happen overnight. It doesn't happen in one week or two weeks. I could certainly help you cram for a job interview in a week—you would do great on that interview, but you would not have structured a new neural pathway, and you wouldn't succeed in your next interview. If you cram you get exactly what you deserve: temporary knowledge, and then it's gone.

Suppose you stop smoking. After three weeks, you have formed a new habit; you are no longer a smoker. At the five- to six-week mark, you start climbing the walls; the craving is there. As any recovering addict can attest, you never lose that old pathway. Your goal is to make the new neural pathway stronger.

The mental muscle can't grow if you don't do the exercise. That's what you're going to do next.

Opportunity awaits all of us who possess determination. Sometimes we need a little help, and that's okay. What's important is that you seize the moment. So take this 21-Day Plan. Map your success. Don't let your moment go by.

THE 21-DAY PLAN

This is it! Twenty-one days to a persuasive, creative new Alpha You. This plan develops both your verbal and nonverbal skills. Follow every single step of the plan—no time-outs and no days off. You are building habits here. This plan is cumulative, and each day builds on the prior day's work. Every morning you will wake up and do the assignment for that day. Although each day you will be asked to perform a new task, the ultimate goal is to keep practicing the prior days' skills to ensure they will form long-lasting habits. The next twenty-one days are going to pass regardless. Using this plan will bring you closer to your end goal, whatever it may be (a raise, a date, a sale, a new client).

Sure, you could read this book and stack it on your shelf or desk next to all the others you've bought over the years, but I don't want you to do that. Now that you know that success, although not instant, is attainable, use this book and this plan to create real change in your life—possibly for the very first time.

Tempting as it may be to read the plan first, don't do it. These actions will make sense to you only after you've read the book and you understand the power of verbal and nonverbal techniques. Merely performing the actions isn't enough—the book and the plan work together. You *have* read the book, right? Now, here's the plan.

WEEK ONE

day one

In order to induce change, you need to believe that you are making change. The best way to begin each day is with a session of self-hypnosis. This simple three-minute process will help you start your day off right, every single day. Here's how.

Record the hypnosis session shown in the text box on the next page and then play it and listen to your own words. While listening you'll want to do the following: Sit or lie down in a comfortable position. Take a deep breath, inhaling through your nostrils while you fill and expand your abdomen. While you exhale, close your eyes and begin relaxing your face; feel the tension leave your forehead. Relax your eyelids, your cheeks, and your lips. Now let this comfortable state go down your neck and spread right to your chest and back. Imagine a warm, content feeling crossing into your stomach. Relax your arms and hands now. Feel your legs, ankles, and toes becoming deeply relaxed and comfortable. Perhaps you'll notice some tingling in your hands and toes. That's just your body telling you that it's listening to you. Now, count backward from ten; you'll be completely relaxed as you listen to your own recorded voice.

YOUR PERSONAL HYPNOSIS SESSION

Ten . . . nine. I begin to relax. Eight . . . seven . . . six . . . five . . . I feel good, strong, calm, and focused. I accept every suggestion for change. Four . . . three . . . two . . . one . . . I now recognize that everything I set my mind to, I can really do. I focus and become confident and secure. As each day passes, I become more in control and stronger. I feel myself becoming positive and the feeling starts NOW. These changes are becoming more powerful with every passing day. Each day they are cemented into my daily life. I am positive and confident in each and every way. I am healthier and more energetic. I feel the strength pulsing within my body as I begin to come back to the room—counting one, two, three, four, five. My mind is clear, and I am at peace with myself. Six, seven, eight. I have an inner core of strength. Nine, ten. Every day in every way, I get better and better.

day two

Smile

That's all you have to do today—just make eye contact and smile at everyone you see. Will they all smile back? Amazingly, most will. Practice in the mirror by making your smile as wide as possible and seeing how that looks. Then work smaller until you find a smile size that feels comfortable and is not strained. When you can literally feel the smile in your eyes and ears, you'll be on your way to perfect. Make sure you smile broadly enough to mimic some characteristics of the genuine smile, such as a crinkle around your eyes and a slight lift in your cheeks, but not so broadly that you expose your gums. Now that you know what it should look like, practice—in the shower, in the car, at strangers. Do it every one of these twenty-one days, and it will soon become a habit.

The more genuine your smile, the more favorably it will be received. Psychologist Paul Ekman had subjects rate personality characteristics of people on video. The subjects had much more positive feelings for those whose smiles were genuine than those whose smiles were posed. Without knowing why, they judged those with the genuine smiles as more pleasant, relaxed, and natural. *We* know why, though. It's because the true smiles were triggering the mirror neurons in the participants' brains, and they were also feeling genuinely happy.

day three

Explore Space

This is Spatial Awareness Day. Spend your third day studying spaces and your relation to them. Continue to smile and make eye contact, but now it's time to get your body involved. Before just automatically taking a seat in the restaurant or office, decide what kind of statement you want to make and sit in the position that will bring you the most personal power. In addition, practice taking up more room than you normally would. Use some expansive gestures to get comfortable with the idea of power and confidence. Notice how close to other people you stand and sit; take note of their reactions. Are you too close or not close enough?

day four

Focus on the Eyes

You're still smiling and still aware of spaces. Today I want you to notice how many times people blink. You don't have to match them; you need only observe.

Here's an exercise to get you out of your *dis*comfort zone. Sit across from a friend or mate and gaze into each other's eyes, without looking away, for three minutes. Intimate, isn't it? In fact, eye gazes are so powerful that at least two university studies found that after looking into each other's eyes, strangers of the opposite sex felt a surge of romantic feelings for each other. I'm not suggesting you fall for strangers—just witness firsthand how simply looking at someone else can connect you. This is something you should practice regularly. At first, because it makes you uncomfortable, you might try to disregard this step. Don't. It is as imperative as putting on your business suit or uniform. Making eye contact forges bonds. That's what this book is all about.

day five

Perfect Your Posture

Symmetry is beautiful, and this seemingly effortless neutral posture position will convey confidence to everyone who sees you. Place your feet apart and let your arms rest at your sides, with your elbows slightly bent. You probably aren't used to standing like this—most of us don't stand this way. If it's awkward at first, begin by holding a pen or a notebook. Soon, you'll be able to automatically assume this stance and instantly appear comfortable and in charge.

Carry yourself with confidence. Involve the head, neck, shoulders, and spine. If you suffer from poor posture, today you become aware of how you are standing. Although having excellent posture is a key indicator of status when others are forming their first impression of you, it is also key to your own confidence. Our posture greatly determines our own sense of worth. According to a 2009 study, when we stand up straight we are more confident about our own thoughts and convictions.

Inner confidence stems from the strength of our inner core, but in addition to that, we need to acknowledge that how we stand affects how we think. Note your head position—is it forward or neutral? What about your shoulders—are they rounded or straight? Is your neck elongated or tucked? Finally, how is your pelvis lined up? Do you tuck your backside in or thrust forward with your chest and backward with your butt? Stand with your head, back, and shoulders against the wall and your feet a few inches away. There should be some room between your mid-back and the wall. Now pull your shoulders and head ever so slightly off the wall. Practice daily because it is going to be a significant change from what you are used to. Good posture is imperative to looking prepared and confident.

day six

Dust Off Your USP

Remember back when you came up with a unique description of who and what you are? Now it's time to adapt it. Memorize your elevator pitch, then repeat it into a recorder. Pretend you're just meeting a new person. Also memorize and repeat conversational openers and threads.

Play back your words and rate both your message and your delivery. A USP often sounds different spoken than it looks written, so this is the time to be tough on yourself. What about your voice? Is it as you intended? Would you want to listen to yourself on your recorder? Would you want to get to know this person (you) better? In order to persuade, you first have to believe in you; developing your USP will remind you of why you deserve every single *yes*, and help you hone in on precisely how to transmit your best self to others.

day seven

Approach with Ease

Practice everything you are learning thus far, only today add an exercise that will help you conquer approach anxiety. "What's approach anxiety?" you might ask. "Are you just coming up with another fancy term, Tonya?"

Well, how do you feel when you walk into a room of strangers? How clammy do your hands get when you're meeting someone for the first time? Approaching and talking to people we don't know makes us anxious, but exposing ourselves to the source of the anxiety will neutralize fear.

Here's how to do it. Make small talk with five people, from the grocery-store clerk to your hairstylist. Ask for directions, offer a compliment, find out if the shrimp at the deli counter is fresh or frozen and what type of wine would go best with it. If you are feeling bold, and time permits, you can even start a full conversation with multiple threads that can expand the direction of the discussion. Engage anyone you can by simply starting small talk.

Jaidan: "Did you see the XYZ movie?"

Kimberly: "Yeah, I saw it last week."

Jaidan: "What did you think?"

Kimberly: "It was good."

Jaidan: "I love [insert actor]. Did you know that he also does a lot for animal rights?"

Kimberly: "No, I didn't know that. I'm a big supporter of animal rights."

Blah blah blah.

Anything can be a conversation opener. "Did you watch the game last night? I couldn't believe in the last quarter they scored twenty-one points." Pretty soon, you will be desensitized to the fear of engaging strangers in conversation. You'll know from experience that people won't go running down the street screaming just because you talked to them.

WEEK ONE WRAP-UP

self-check: did you actually go through all of these steps this week?

By now you should have created your hypnosis session, smiled at and made eye contact with many people, noticed spatial significance, practiced excellent posture and keeping your hands in the neutral position. You have also learned how to approach and engage others. If you haven't, *do not* continue—your twenty-one days haven't started until you do every single step, day by day. I'm not being a stickler here—lasting change takes repeated effort; you cannot improve outcomes and create new habits if you don't do the exercises. If you did go through the steps, you should be finding that it's easier to smile spontaneously and talk to strangers. Congratulations! You're developing a stronger sense of self. And you are ready to move into week two.

WEEK TWO

day eight

Create Icebreakers

Think of memories in your life that you can turn into anecdotes for icebreaking stories. Make a list of ten headings: Life's Little Ironies, Big-time Embarrassed, Adventure of a Lifetime, Exciting, Sexy, Awkward, Naïve, Touching, Heroic, Romantic. What stories bubble up when you look at these headings? Think about your childhood, family life, work, travel, recreation, and dating experiences. How do they fit into your categories?

Get out your recorder again and tell a good story. It should have a strong beginning that builds to an intriguing middle and a dramatic ending. Include vivid detail and add humor. Test these out on a loved one, and then identify appropriate potential listeners. Keep in mind that some stories are appropriate for cocktail parties and not job interviews. If you are struggling with this, refer back to Chapter Nineteen.

day nine

Baseline

Continue to build upon and practice everything you have learned thus far. Baselining (norming) is next.

Today, when you are out among people, you need to tune in to everything from personality types to handshakes to specific word usage (particularly the language people use when relaxed). Pay close attention to handshake, posture, trunk, and torso—be on the lookout for the nonverbal clues disclosed in body positioning, gestures, facial expressions, and eyes. Refer back to the chapter on body language for some specific pointers.

Next, while doing banal activities—everything from speaking to people to listening to the radio—try to identify various representational systems. Can you distinguish Visual, Auditory, and Kinesthetic types? Memorize key words from each system. Now, the fun part. Tell one of your new stories to the recorder. Once you've finished, analyze it to see which representational system you are using.

day ten

Tell an Icebreaker Story

It's time to use one of your stories today. Tell it spontaneously to someone whose reaction will not change (or ruin) your life. Did you feel as confident as you did when you spoke it into the recorder? How did your *yes* target respond? How would you edit or rewrite the story for future use? Do that right now. Rerecord and practice again.

day eleven

Reach Out and Touch

Eleven is Touch Day. Practice that perfect handshake, remembering that the goal is to apply just the right amount of pressure to convey warmth and professionalism—you don't want your *yes* target to feel like he's grabbing onto a jellyfish, but you also don't need to break any bones. Now go out and shake hands with at least five people.

You're not finished yet, though. Now pick out another five unsuspecting people, and generically and nonsexually touch them. Keep in mind, touch equals status. Touch is a strong indicator of a dominant individual, and I cannot stress enough the significance of initiating that touch. Laying a hand upon an individual, whether it be through a handshake, an arm pat, a light touch on the hand, a pat on the back, or a high five or ten (if appropriate), sends strong signals of control and authority. Experiment with the power of touch.

day twelve

Practice with Space and Gestures

Today you're going to experiment with personal space. Pick a target, then slowly but purposefully step into this person's space. In addition, practice angling toward and away from people.

When you meet someone and step into his space, notice if he holds his ground or takes a step back from you. If he holds his ground, you have a challenge ahead of you, because he has proven that he is not willing to give up his power and is not likely to concede on any interactions. What you want to see, ultimately, is him step back, even slightly, to intimate that he is apprehensive of your space invasion and you now have control. Monitor the reaction and see how you can learn to use this tactic for power when necessary.

Finally, find opportunities to use gestures of confidence. Use the palm-open gesture, eye contact, steepled fingers, and the other power gestures you learned about in Chapters Eleven and Twelve. Be both emphatic and empathetic.

day thirteen

Negotiate

Welcome to Don't Be a Verbal Victim Day. Find something you want to buy, anything with a negotiable price (and most prices are). It is imperative that you learn how to read and maneuver each interaction to gain the upper hand. Every time you communicate with an individual, you have entered into a negotiation. The goal is always to ensure that you control the direction of the exchange.

You don't have to rush out and purchase a new Beemer or Jag for this experiment. Your item could be a treadmill at a yard sale, a bunch of basil at a farmers market, or a small piece of jewelry. Step one is to baseline the seller. (We practiced that a few days ago.) Then—and only then—decide how to tackle the negotiation. You want to be dominant without being overbearing. Be aware of the message you are sending. Use verbal and nonverbal tactics to negotiate the deal: the confident gestures you practiced on day twelve combined with your use of power words, such as your target's name, *now, because, thank you,* and so on.

Going into any negotiation, if you are to be a master communicator, you need to recognize that you are in complete control. The only way to practice this is to be willing to walk away if you aren't getting the deal you want. The goal is to recognize the psychological tactics that others may try to use on you. Keep in mind that you want to leave the salesperson thinking and feeling that he got a good deal as well. Two happy parties are better than one! Once you're comfortable with the technique, you'll be more comfortable when shooting for higher stakes such as landing a new job or a new client.

day fourteen

Focus on the Ears

Are you still repeating all of the other steps you've learned thus far? Good. I'm going to reward you today with a little ear-otica. Focus on talking in someone's right or left ear. Switch back and forth with your significant other and notice if there is a difference. As with eye alignment, ear alignment is significant. The right ear, which connects to the left brain, is typically dominant in verbal processing. Studies find that compliance goes up when you make a request speaking toward or into a person's right ear. The left ear, connected to the right brain, prevails in emotion processing, and would therefore be better at picking up the subtle nuances of pitch, timbre, melody, and volume.

So what does it boil down to? Practice requests in the right ear and whispers of sentiment in the left. If you are looking for a response that does not require feelings, the right ear is the way to go. If you are trying to ignite some emotion, speak softly into that left ear.

WEEK TWO WRAP-UP

self-check: what did you learn this week?

This is the end of your second week. Just think, by practicing each and every day, these new habits will be second nature. Which skills were most helpful to you this week? Was it practicing baselining, telling a story, touching, or shaking hands? Maybe it was negotiating for the right deal. You've been busy, but have you also added a new component every single day? If not, you are going to rob this plan and yourself of energy. You need twenty-one days—consecutively. Stay on track and you will reap the benefits.

WEEK THREE

day fifteen

Check Your Delivery

Today I'm sending you back to the recorder with a new assignment. We're going to work on pronunciation. Sounding professional and trustworthy—I'm talking actual sound, not content—is one way you can control how people perceive you.

Have you started reading a daily newspaper? (If you've gotten this far through the plan, I know you have been following directions!) Today, I'd like you to take ten to fifteen minutes and read from the newspaper into your recorder. Play it back to check your pronunciation—no mush-mouths allowed. Now say the days of the week. Are they Monday, Tuesday, Wednesday? Not Mundee, Tuesdee, Wensdee?

Make a list of words you use most frequently and speak them into the recorder. I once knew a brilliant, wealthy man who never could say *reimburse*. He pronounced it "reinverse." But as is the case with the rich and powerful, everyone pretended they didn't notice. One day that could be you, but for now people *will* notice, and probably comment on (or at least judge) your glitches. Avoid looking foolish by making lists of your trouble words and reciting them until you have them spot-on.

day sixteen

Practice Framing

Take five negative situations from your life, past or present. Ideally, pick a range—a story from childhood, one about family, another about school, one from your career, and one about your love life. Write them down. Now, how can you reframe each one? Here's an example:

Johnny was raised in an environment that was physically and mentally abusive. He was exposed at a young age to the addictions of drugs and alcohol through his parents, and he rarely had supervision.

Frame: Poor Johnny—he must have had a terrible childhood.

Reframe: Johnny learned a lot of important lessons early in life that helped him succeed as an adult.

Reframe: Johnny grew up learning early about the dangers of drug and alcohol addiction. He recognized that inner strength and courage are important. He also realized the impact of being a loving and responsible parent.

Something a little simpler, perhaps? How about reframing a specific thought, such as one that many parents can relate to:

Frame: My son Ralph is terrible at coloring—he never stays in the lines.

Reframe: My son Ralph is becoming so creative that he makes his own lines.

Frame: You just blurt out whatever is on your mind—don't you ever think of anyone else's feelings?

Reframe: I appreciate your honesty.

Frame: I am climbing the walls since I stopped smoking.

Reframe: I think I will take the money I saved by stopping smoking and go get a massage to help me relax.

Frame: Your beliefs are just wrong.

Reframe: Everyone is entitled to their opinion.

Frame: A father who is a sixty-hour-a-week laborer fell and broke his leg; he is out of work and money is tight.

Reframe: The father has an opportunity to reconnect with his family.

Frame: I have no work experience.

Reframe: Luckily I can learn excellent work ethics by training under your (potential employer's) tutelage.

If you are struggling with this concept, refer back to the chapter on framing.

Now think of five feelings you want to evoke in five different people. (Five feelings in a single person would be too much of a challenge, even for me!) It might be nostalgia in an old friend, passion in a lover, excitement in a client. How can you frame these imaginary encounters to get positive results? Once you've worked out your strategy in your head, pick at least one of these people and actually go through the steps of framing. For example:

Frame: Hi, I'm from XYZ Home Alert System, and I would like to sell you a security system.

Reframe: Can you really put a price on peace of mind?

Frame: I am going to get married and have sex with the same man for the rest of my life.

Reframe: I will know everything about my husband and what pleases him most.

Frame: My supervisor gives me far too much work.

Reframe: My day flies by, and I am never bored.

How did it turn out? Did you study the other person's body language as well as what he or she said? Remember, someone can say yes, but her body can say no. Before moving on, you should confirm that you were able to evoke the desired response in your *yes* target. If you received a positive response, move on to the other four people on your list.

day seventeen

Build Unity

Practice finding a common enemy and a common goal. Remember, these two things should go together—you can use a negative and a positive to establish a strong bond with a colleague, friend, or family member; there's no need to connect with someone exclusively over something negative. Who is the common enemy in your family tree? In your place of business? In the political sphere or culture at large? Perhaps it's the crazy ex-wife, the obnoxious coworker, the IRS. Once you've identified the enemy, find one person who either shares your feelings about this person or institution or who might be swayed to see your perspective. This isn't about using force; it's about establishing a relationship based on a shared outlook.

Now go for the common goal. What's a goal you share with a family member? What's a common goal in your place of business? What about in society? Is it your emphasis on going green? Is it support of a nonprofit charity that everyone in your neighborhood or office contributes to?

Today is about linking ideas and finding common ground. Work on putting together conversational threads that pick up on your shared interests or dislikes, and then spin the positive. Forging bonds over common enemies and shared causes makes it all the more likely that your *yes* target will sway in your favor in the future.

day eighteen

Play Around with Yes *Sets*

If you recall, *yes* sets are the way you lead someone into positive responses and nodding of heads. Here's an example:

It's been fun working with this twenty-one-day plan, hasn't it? *Yes, Tonya.*

You've made remarkable changes, haven't you? *Sure have, Tonya.*

You're feeling a little bit adventurous today, aren't you? *Yes, Tonya.*

I just know you're going to be able to turn your life around and use verbal and nonverbal tactics to get the right responses every time, don't you agree? *Yes. It's happening.*

Believe it or not, you can even use something on which your target doesn't agree with you in order to continue the *yes* set. For example:

Considering that we don't see eye to eye on this subject, I guess we can agree to disagree, right? *Yes, Tonya.*

Now that you have the person getting into the established pattern of answering yes, make sure you slip in the question for which you really want the *yes* answer. Watch how the question slides under the radar. Practice coming up with potential *yes* sets and then try them out on at least two different people today.

day nineteen

Prime for the Alpha You

This is Priming Day. Remember, when you prime someone you are really just offering subtle suggestions to your target's subconscious mind, which can then influence subsequent behavior; what you say—the actual words you use—can change the way someone else feels. In turn, what that someone says about you influences how others react to you.

So let's get started. Find a partner. Practice priming introductions for each other. In a perfect world, how would you like an invisible audience to be primed for you? Go back to your USP. What are five words that best describe you? Make a mental list right now. Your USP discusses your best attributes, and those attributes are what you want to prime your audience with. Which of the five is the most important word? Now list five ways you can prime another person to see that important quality in you.

day twenty

Practice Your Mask

Use your block face a few times today to make sure you can use it on cue when you need it. There are times when people do not need to know what you're feeling; therefore, a block face can serve you well, especially during times of tension. It is your emotional disguise, preventing your true feelings from escaping. You become the chameleon when you wear your block face, blending in and remaining ambiguous.

It's important to recognize when a block face is appropriate; you'll want to be sure you can fall right into that tell-nothing expression. Learn the signals—what sets you off, what overexcites you—and be sure you're prepared to hide your emotions as necessary.

day twenty-one

Celebrate

Congratulate yourself on becoming your own Alpha You. You are on the path to growing and progressing on your own terms; I want you to make a promise to stay on track. Look at what you have achieved in just twenty-one days. You've learned how to read and build rapport with people instantly. You've gained confidence. You're building skills that are in the process of becoming habits.

Now, imagine what you can do when you have mastered these skills and can execute each with unconscious competence. Find a physical anchor—something that costs nothing but means everything—that will serve to remind you of your success. Mine are small, soft, smooth rocks from my children. I carry them everywhere, and this way, I get to take a small piece of them with me. Your alpha anchor needs to be special to you, and will function as a reminder of the confidence you've built and the skills you now have at the ready. Keep it in your wallet and touch it daily.

A friend of mine once told me that being successful means bringing happiness to others. I hope this book has achieved that goal. More important, I trust that with all you've learned and all you are becoming, you can make the lives of others a little happier as well.

NOTES

1. Janine Willis and Alexander Todorov, "Making Up Your Mind After a 100-Ms Exposure to a Face," *Psychological Science* 17, no. 7 (2006): 592–98.

2. Paul Ekman, *Emotions Revealed,* 2nd ed. (New York: Holt Paperbacks, 2007).

3. Malcolm Gladwell, *Blink* (New York: Back Bay Books, 2007).

4. Dave Elman, *Hypnotherapy* (Glendale, CA: Westwood Publishing Co., 1984).

5. Ellen Langer, Arthur Blank, and Benzion Chanowitz, "The Mindlessness of Ostensibly Thoughtful Action: The Role of 'Placebic' Information in Interpersonal Interaction," *Journal of Personality and Social Psychology* 36, no. 6 (1978): 635–42.

6. Alia J. Crum and Ellen J. Langer, "Mind-set Matters: Exercise and

the Placebo Effect," *Psychological Science*, vol. 18, no. 2 (February 2007): 165–171.

7. Virginia Satir et al., *The Satir Model: Family Therapy and Beyond* (Palo Alto, CA: Science and Behavior Books, 1991).

8. Milton H. Erickson, *Life Reframing in Hypnosis* (London: Free Association Books, 1998).

9. Richard Bandler and John Grinder, *Reframing: Neuro-Linguistic Programming and the Transformation of Meaning*, 5th ed. (Boulder, CO: Real People Press, 1982).

10. George Lakoff, Howard Dean, and Don Hazen, *Don't Think of an Elephant!: Know Your Values and Frame the Debate: The Essential Guide for Progressives* (White River Junction, VT: Chelsea Green Publishing, 2004).

11. Frank Luntz, *Words That Work: It's Not What You Say, It's What People Hear* (New York: Hyperion, 2006).

12. Louann Brizendine, *The Female Brain* (New York: Broadway Books, 2006).

13. John Bargh, Mark Chen, and Lara Burrows, "Automaticity of Social Behavior: Direct Effects of Trait Construct and Stereotype Activation on Action," *Journal of Personality and Social Psychology* 71, no. 2 (1996): 230–44.

14. Elizabeth F. Loftus and John C. Palmer, "Reconstruction of Automobile Destruction: An Example of the Interaction Between Language and Memory," *Journal of Verbal Learning and Verbal Behaviour* 13, no. 5 (1974): 585–89.

15. Kimberley A. Wade, Sarah L. Green, and Robert A. Nash, "Can Fabricated Evidence Induce False Eyewitness Testimony?" *Applied Cognitive Psychology*, August 20, 2009, http://dx.doi.org/10.1002/acp.1607.

16. Ingrid R. Olson and Christy Marshuetz, "Facial Attractiveness Is Appraised in a Glance," *Emotion* 5, no. 4 (2005): 498–502.

17. David Grande et al., "Effect of Exposure to Small Pharmaceutical Promotional Items on Treatment Preferences," *Arch Intern Medicine* 169, no. 9 (2009): 887–93.

18. John T. Jones et al., "How Do I Love Thee? Let Me Count The Js: Implicit Egotism and Interpersonal Attraction," *Journal of Personality and Social Psychology* 87, no. 5 (2009): 665–83.

19. Clive Thompson, "The Eyes of Honesty," *New York Times,* December 10, 2006.

20. V. S. Ramachandran, "Mirror Neurons and Imitation Learning As the Driving Force Behind 'The Great Leap Forward' in Human Evolution," Edge, http://www.edge.org/3rd_culture/ramachandran/ramachandran_p1.html (2009).

21. Robert B. Cialdini and Noah J. Goldstein, "The Science and Practice of Persuasion," *Cornell Hotel and Restaurant Administration Quarterly Report* 43, no. 2 (2002): 40–50.

22. Joseph A. Devito and Michael L. Hecht, *The Nonverbal Communication Reader* (Long Grove, IL: Waveland Press, 1989).

23. Carie Forden, "The Influence of Sex-Role Expectations on the Perception of Touch," *Sex Roles* 7, no. 9 (1981): 889–94.

24. N. T. Alves, J. A. Aznar-Casanova, and S. S. Fukusima, "Patterns of Brain Asymmetry in the Perception of Positive and Negative Facial Expressions," *Laterality: Asymmetries of Body, Brain and Cognition* 14, no. 3 (2009): 256–72.

25. Joe Navarro and Marvin Karlins, *What Every Body Is Saying* (New York: Harper Paperbacks, 2008).

26. Marie Helweg-Larsen et al., "To Nod or Not to Nod: An Observational Study of Nonverbal Communication and Status in Female and Male College Students," *Psychology of Women Quarterly* 28, no. 4 (2004): 358–61.

27. F. J. Tolkmitt and K. R. Scherer, "Effect of Experimentally Induced Stress on Vocal Parameters," *Journal of Experimental Psychology: Human Perception and Performance* 12, no. 3 (1986): 302–13.

28. Laura K. Guerrero and Kory Floyd, *Nonverbal Communication in Close Relationships* (Philadelphia: Lawrence Erlbaum Associates, 2005).

29. Wen Zhou and Denise Chen, "Fear-Related Chemosignals Modulate Recognition of Fear in Ambiguous Facial Expressions," *Psychological Science* 20, no. 2 (2009): 177–83.

30. Claire Wyart et al., "Smelling a Single Component of Male Sweat Alters Levels of Cortisol in Women," *Journal of Neuroscience* 27, no. 6 (2007): 1261–65.

31. F. Bryant Furlow, "The Smell of Love," *Psychology Today,* March 1, 1996, http://www.psychologytoday.com/articles/200910/the-smell-love.

32. C. Wedekind and D. Penn, "MHC Genes, Body Odours, and Odour Preferences," *Nephrology Dialysis Transplantation* 15, no. 9 (2000): 1269–71.

33. Mark McClish, *I Know You Are Lying* (Winterville, NC: the Marpa Group, 2001).

34. Arianne Cohen, *The Tall Book* (New York: Bloomsbury USA, 2009).

35. D. Singh, "Adaptive Significance of Female Physical Attractiveness: Role of Waist-to-Hip Ratio," *Journal of Personality and Social Psychology* 65, no. 2 (1993): 293–307.

36. J. Zhu, "Colour Your World Blue," *New Scientist,* May 6, 2009, http://www.newscientist.com/article/mg20227072.800-colour-your-world-blue.html.

37. Dustin Wood and Claudia Brumbaugh, "Using Revealed Mate Preferences to Evaluate Market Force and Differential Preference Explanations for Mate Selection," *Journal of Personality and Social Psychology* 96, no. 6 (2009): 1226–44.

38. Jonah Lehrer, "Don't! The Secret of Self-control," *New Yorker,* May 18, 2009, http://www.newyorker.com/reporting/2009/05/18/090518fa_fact_lehrer.

REFERENCES

Alves, N. T., et al. "Patterns of Brain Asymmetry in the Perception of Positive and Negative Facial Expressions," *Laterality: Asymmetries of Body, Brain and Cognition* 14, no. 3 (2009): 256–72.

Bandler, R., and J. Grinder. *Reframing: Neuro-Linguistic Programming and the Transformation of Meaning*, 5th ed. Boulder, CO: Real People Press, 1982.

Bargh, J., et al. "Automaticity of Social Behavior: Direct Effects of Trait Construct and Stereotype Activation on Action," *Journal of Personality and Social Psychology* 71, no. 2 (1996): 230–44.

Baron, R., and D. Byrne. *Social Psychology: Understanding Human Interaction.* Boston: Allyn & Bacon, 1987.

Bear, M., B. Connors, and M. Paradiso. *Neuroscience: Exploring the Brain*, 3rd ed. Lippincott Williams & Wilkens, 2006.

Bloom, F., and A. Lazerson. *Brain, Mind and Behavior*, 2nd ed. W. H. Freeman & Co., 1988.

Blum, D. *Sex on the Brain.* New York: Penguin, 1998.

Braiker, H. *Who's Pulling Your Strings?: How to Break the Cycle of Manipulation and Regain Control of Your Life.* New York: McGraw-Hill, 2004.

Brizendine, L. *The Female Brain.* New York: Broadway Books, 2006.

Bruckert, L., et al. "Women Use Voice Parameters to Assess Men's Characteristics," *Proceedings of the Royal Society B: Biological Sciences,* 273:1582 (February 2006).

Burgoon, J., et al. *Nonverbal Communications: The Unspoken Dialogue.* McGraw-Hill College, 1995.

Cialdini, R. *Influence: The Psychology of Persuasion.* New York: Collins Business, 1984.

Cialdini, R. B., and N. J. Goldstein. "The Science and Practice of Persuasion," *Cornell Hotel and Restaurant Administration Quarterly Report* 43, no. 2 (2002): 40–50.

Cohen, A. *The Tall Book.* New York: Bloomsbury USA, 2009.

Crum, A., and E. Langer. "Mind-Set Matters: Exercise and the Placebo Effect," *Psychological Science* 18 no. 2 (2007): 165–71.

Damasio, A. *Descartes' Error: Emotion, Reason, and the Human Brain.* New York: Penguin, 2005.

Darwin, C. *The Expression of the Emotions in Man and Animals.* Edited by Paul Ekman. 3rd ed. New York: Oxford University Press, 1998.

Devito, J. A., and M. L. Hecht. *The Nonverbal Communication Reader.* Long Grove, IL: Waveland Press, 1939.

De Waal, F. *Our Inner Ape: A Leading Primatologist Explains Why We Are Who We Are.* New York: Riverhead Trade, 2006.

De Waal, F. *Primates and Philosophers: How Morality Evolved.* Princeton, NJ: Princeton University Press, 2009.

Ekman, P. *Emotions Revealed.* 2nd ed. New York: Henry Holt, 2007.

Ekman, P., and W. Friesen. *Unmasking the Face: A Guide to Recognizing Emotions from Facial Expressions.* Cambridge: Malor Books, 2003.

Ekman, P., and M. O'Sullivan. "Who Can Catch a Liar?" *American Psychologist* 46, no. 9 (1991).

Elman, D. *Hypnotherapy.* Westwood Publishing, 1984.

Erickson, M. H., E. Rossi, and F. Sharp, eds. *Life Reframing in Hypnosis.* Free Association Books, 1998.

Etcoff, N. *Survival of the Prettiest: The Science of Beauty.* Reprint edition. New York: Anchor, 2000.

Fast, J. *Body Language in the Workplace.* New York: Penguin, 1994.

Fisher, H. *Anatomy of Love: A Natural History of Mating, Marriage, and Why We Stray.* New York: Ballantine Books, 1994.

Flett, C. V. *What Men Don't Tell Women About Business: Opening Up the Heavily Guarded Alpha Male Playbook.* Hoboken, NJ: Wiley, 2007.

Forden, C. "The Influence of Sex-Role Expectations on the Perception of Touch," *Sex Roles*, 7, no. 9 (1981).

Foreman, J. "A Conversation with Paul Ekman: The 43 Facial Muscles that Reveal Even the Most Fleeting Emotions," *New York Times*, August 5, 2003.

Furlow, F. Bryant "The Smell of Love," *Psychology Today*, March 1, 1996 (http://www.psychologytoday.com/articles/200910/the-smell-love).

Givens, D. *The Nonverbal Dictionary of Gestures, Signs, and Body Language Cues.* Spokane, WA: Center for Nonverbal Studies Press, 2006.

Givens, D. *Love Signals: A Practical Field Guide to the Body Language of Courtship.* New York: St. Martin's Griffin, 2005.

Givens, D. *Crime Signals: How to Spot a Criminal Before You Become a Victim.* New York: St. Martin's Griffin, 2008.

Gladwell, M. *Blink.* New York: Back Bay Books, Little, Brown and Company, 2007.

Goldstein, N. B., et al. *Yes!: 50 Scientifically Proven Ways to Be Persuasive.* New York: Free Press, 2008.

Goleman, D. *Emotional Intelligence: Why It Can Matter More Than IQ.* New York: Bantam, 1997.

Grande, D., et al. "Effect of Exposure to Small Pharmaceutical Promotional Items on Treatment Preferences." *Arch Intern Medicine* 169, no. 9 (2009): 887–893.

Greene, R. *The Art of Seduction.* New York: Penguin, 2003.

Guerro, L. K. and K. Floyd. *Nonverbal Communication in Close Relationships.* Philadelphia: Lawrence Erlbaum Associates, 2005.

Helweg-Larsen, M., et al. "To Nod or Not to Nod: An Observational Study of Nonverbal Communication and Status in Female and Male College Students," *Psychology of Women Quarterly* 28, no. 4 (2004), 358–61.

Hogan, K. *The Psychology of Persuasion: How to Persuade Others to Your Way of Thinking.* New York: Pelican Publishing Company, 1996.

Jones, J. T., et al. "How Do I Love Thee? Let Me Count the Js: Implicit Egotism and Interpersonal Attraction." *Journal of Personality and Social Psychology*, 87, no. 5 (2009): 665–83.

Lakoff, G., et al. *Don't Think of an Elephant!: Know Your Values and Frame the Debate: The Essential Guide for Progressives.* Chelsea Green Publishing, 2004.

Langer E., A. Blank, and B. Chanowitz, "The Mindlessness of Ostensibly Thoughtful Action: The Role of Placebic Information in Interpersonal Interaction," *Journal of Personality and Social Psychology,* 36 no. 6 (1978): 635-42.

LeVay, S. *The Sexual Brain.* Cambridge, MA: MIT Press, 1994.

Loftus, E. F., and J. C. Palmer. "Reconstruction of Automobile Destruction? An Example of the Interaction Between Language and Memory." *Journal of Verbal Learning and Verbal Behaviour* 13, no. 5 (1974): 585–89.

Lehrer, J. "Don't! The Secret of Self-control." *New Yorker*, May 18, 2009 (http://www.newyorker.com/reporting/2009/05/18/090518fa_fact_lehrer).

Lewis, T., et al. *A General Theory of Love.* New York: Vintage, 2001.

Lindstrom, M. *Buyology: Truth and Lies About Why We Buy.* New York: Broadway Business, 2008.

Luntz, F. *Words That Work: It's Not What You Say, It's What People Hear.* New York: Hyperion, 2006.

Luria, A. R. *The Working Brain: An Introduction to Neuropsychology.* New York: Penguin Books, 1973.

Moir, A., and D. Jessel. *Brain Sex: The Real Difference Between Men & Women.* New York: Delta, 1989.

Montague, A. *Touching; The Human Significance of the Skin.* New York: Columbia University Press, 1971.

Morris, D. *The Naked Woman: A Study of the Female Body.* New York: St. Martin's Griffin, 2007.

Morris, D. *The Naked Man: A Study of the Male Body.* New York: Thomas Dunne Books, 2009.

Navarro, J. and M. Karlins *What Every Body Is Saying.* New York: HarperCollins, 2008.

Nevin, J. A. "The Momentum of Compliance," *Journal of Applied Behavior Analysis*, 29 (1996), 534–47.

Olson, I., and C. Marshuetz. "Facial Attractiveness Is Appraised in a Glance," *Emotion* 5, no. 4 (2005), 498–502.

Overstreet, H. A. *Influencing Human Behavior*. New York: W. W. Norton & Company, 1925.

Pease, B., and A. Pease. *Why Men Don't Listen and Women Can't Read Maps*. New York: Broadway Books, 2000.

Peck, J., et al. "The Effect of Mere Touch on Perceived Ownership." *Journal of Consumer Research* (2009).

Pincott, J. *Do Gentlemen Really Prefer Blondes? Bodies, Behavior, and Brains—The Science Behind Sex, Love & Attraction*. New York: Delacorte Press, 2008.

Ramachandran, V. S. "Mirror Neurons and Imitation Learning as the Driving Force Behind 'The Great Leap Forward' in Human Evolution," *Edge*, 2009 (http://www.edge.org).

Ridley, M. *The Red Queen: Sex and the Evolution of Human Nature*. New York: Harper Perennial, 2003.

Satir, V., et al. *The Satir Model: Family Therapy and Beyond*. Palo Alto, CA: Science and Behavior Books, 1991.

Singh, D. "Adaptive Significance of Female Physical Attractiveness: Role of Waist-to-Hip Ratio," *Journal of Personality and Social Psychology* 65, no. 2 (1993): 283–88.

Spiegel, A. "Hotel Maids Challenge the Placebo Effect." National Public Radio (2008).

Tecce, J. J. "Body Language in 2004 Presidential Debates." Boston College. (http://www.bc.edu/schools/cas/metaelements/html/teece_analysis_2004.htm)

Thompson, C. "The Eyes of Honesty," *New York Times*, December 10, 2006.

Tolkmitt, F. J., and K. R. Scherer. "Effect of Experimentally Induced Stress on Vocal Parameters," *Journal of Experimental Psychology* 12, no. 3 (1986): 302–13.

Vrij, A. *Detecting Lies and Deceit: The Psychology of Lying and the Implications for Professional Practice*. Chichester, UK: John Wiley and Sons, 2003.

Wade, K. "Can Fabricated Evidence Induce False Eyewitness Testimony?" *Applied Cognitive Psychology* (2009).

Wedekind, C., and D. Penn. "MHC Genes, Body Odours, and Odour Preferences," *Nephrology Dialysis Transplantation*, 15, no. 9 (2000): 1269–71.

Willis, J., and A. Todorov. "Making Up Your Mind After a 100-Ms Exposure to a Face," *Psychological Science* 17, no. 7 (2006).

Wood, D., and C. Brumbaugh. "Using Revealed Mate Preferences to Evaluate Market Force and Differential Preference Explanations for Mate Selection," *Journal of Personality and Social Psychology* 96, no. 6 (2009): 1226–44.

Wyart, C., et al. "Smelling a Single Component of Male Sweat Alters Levels of Cortisol in Women," *Journal of Neuroscience* 27, no. 6 (2007): 1261–65.

Zhow, W., and D. Chen. "Fear-Related Chemosignals Modulate Recognition of Fear in Ambiguous Facial Expressions," *Psychological Science* 20, no. 2 (2009): 177–83.

Zhu, J. "Colour Your World Blue." *New Scientist*, May 6, 2009 (http://www.newscientist.com/article/mg20227072.800-colour-your-world-blue.html).

Zillmer, E., and M. Spiers. *Principles of Neuropsychology.* Florence, KY: Wadsworth Publishing, 2000.

Zillmer, E., et al. *Principles of Neuropsychology.* Florence, KY: Wadsworth Publishing, 2007.

ACKNOWLEDGMENTS

To Laura Dail, my literary agent who I now call my friend—thank you for always going to the mat for me, yet still being tough when I need tough; you have been a constant source of encouragement, motivation, and inspiration. To Bonnie Hearn Hill, for your endless hours of patience, creativity, integrity, and excellent sense of humor. Thank you for working tirelessly to ensure our voices were one.

Thanks to the wonderful folks at Penguin who have been such a pleasure to work with: Elizabeth Keenan, Alexandra Ramstrum, Cristi Hall, Lavina Lee, and Eve Kirch. I am especially grateful to Anna Sternoff for her vital contributions and thoughtful editorial attention. Those suggestions and ideas have served to make this book extraordinary.

To Bill O'Reilly, thank you for helping to spread the power of communication to the public—thanks to you, *body language* is a household term. To Kevin Hogan, for helping me find my path, knowing when I needed support, and for giving it in the most bighearted way possible; you are the definition of Christmas spirit. To Todd Bramson, for your kindness. And, to Sammy—for always being there.

And of course, to my mother, Denise, stepfather, Joe, mother and father-in-law, Carol and Ken, I am so grateful for your unconditional love and encouragement; you have been there at every crucial moment. Your support has allowed my ambitions to come to fruition.

INDEX